# Radical
# Education
# Reforms

The Series on Contemporary Educational Issues
Kenneth J. Rehage, Series Editor

*The 1994 Titles*

*Radical Education Reforms,* edited by Chester E. Finn, Jr., and
Herbert J. Walberg
*Rethinking Policy for At-Risk Students,* edited by Kenneth K.
Wong and Margaret C. Wang

The Ninety–third Yearbook of the National Society for the
Study of Education, published in 1994, contains two volumes:

*Teacher Research and Educational Reform,* edited by
Sandra Hollingsworth and Hugh Sockett
*Bloom's Taxonomy: A Forty-year Retrospective,* edited by
Lorin W. Anderson and Lauren A. Sosniak

All members of the Society receive its two-volume Yearbook.
Members who take the Comprehensive Membership also
receive the two current volumes in the Series on
Contemporary Educational Issues.

Membership in the Society is open to any who desire to
receive its publications. Inquiries regarding membership,
including current dues, may be addressed to the Secretary-
Treasurer, NSSE, 5835 Kimbark Ave., Chicago, IL 60637.

# Radical Education Reforms

Edited by:

**Chester E. Finn, Jr.**
The Edison Project
and on leave from
Vanderbilt University

**Herbert J. Walberg**
University of Illinois
at Chicago

**McCutchan Publishing Corporation**
P.O. Box 774, 2940 San Pablo Ave., Berkeley, CA 94702

ISBN 0-8211-0509-4
Library of Congress Catalog Card Number 94-75318

Printed in the United States of America

# Contents

# Contributors

**Francie Alexander,** Edison Project, Washington, D.C. Formerly Associate Superintendent for Curriculum, Instruction, and Assessment, California State Department of Education

**Joseph L. Bast,** President and Chief Executive Officer, Heartland Institute, Chicago

**John Cairns,** Partner in the law firm of Briggs and Morgan, Minneapolis

**Saul Cooperman,** Chair of the Education Advisory Panel of the New American Schools Development Corporation, and President, Education Programs, Amelior Foundation. Formerly Commissioner of Education, New Jersey

**Fenwick W. English,** Professor of Education, University of Kentucky

**Edgar G. Epps,** Marshall Field Professor of Education, University of Chicago

**Chester E. Finn, Jr.,** Founding Partner and Senior Scholar, Edison Project. Currently on leave from Vanderbilt University. Former Assistant Secretary, U.S. Department of Education

**Nancy Hechinger,** Deputy Director of Curriculum, Edison Project

**Michael Heise,** Research Fellow, Hudson Institute, Indianapolis

**Dustin H. Heuston,** Chairman, Waterford Institute, Provo, Utah

**John A. Murphy,** Superintendent of Schools, Charlotte-Mecklenburg, North Carolina

**Thomas W. Payzant,** Assistant Secretary, U.S. Department of Education, formerly Superintendent, San Diego City Schools

**Albert Shanker,** President, American Federation of Teachers

**Betty Steffy,** Associate Professor of Education, University of Kentucky

**Herbert J. Walberg,** Research Professor of Education, University of Illinois at Chicago

# Preface

## Chester E. Finn, Jr.
## and
## Herbert J. Walberg

April 1993 marked the tenth anniversary of the epochal report entitled *A Nation at Risk*. That means it has been a full decade since we were warned that the United States is menaced by a "rising tide of mediocrity" in our schools and education system, and that we had best make every effort to set matters right or we will be in serious trouble.

The nation has spent much of the ensuing time in conscientious efforts to do precisely that. Some of these efforts are recounted in the pages that follow. Yet by most indicators, the problems pointed out by the National Commission on Excellence in Education remain essentially unsolved. For example, despite the report's recommendation that the school year be lengthened, and a mound of research in support of this proposal, the American school year remains at 175–180 days, the shortest among industrialized countries. Achievement surveys of industrialized countries, moreover, still rank U.S. students near the bottom, even on American-made tests. Those scores remain low despite steadily increased spending on public schools. During the half century between 1940 and 1990, inflation-adjusted per-student costs rose more than five times: from $878 to $5,292 (National Center for

Education Statistics, 1991, p. 155). Current school spending figures place the United States first in the world among major industrialized countries (National Center for Education Statistics, 1992, p. 132).

In retrospect, it is clear that the incrementalist approach we took to educational reform in most of the country in the 1980s, while well-meaning, sincere, often imaginative, and usually costly, has not worked nearly as well as we had hoped. When fed, tugged, cajoled, and occasionally whipped, the old horse can pull the education buggy a bit faster. But it remains a horse, it remains a buggy, and their combined speed is constrained by the inherent limitations of the mechanisms.

That is not to say that every education reform undertaken in the United States during the 1980s is fairly dismissed as "incrementalism." In some schools, communities, and states, bolder and more sweeping changes were made. Certain of the most imaginative and far-reaching of these are chronicled in this volume. By decade's end, the country as a whole was even embracing something long deemed heretical—the setting of *national* goals and standards for our heretofore decentralized education system.

Yet it does the education reforms of the past decade no gross injustice to say that their essential nature was the making of change within the framework of traditional rules, familiar power relationships, and hoary assumptions of the public school system and its customary appendages—teachers colleges, textbook publishers, university-based research centers, and so forth.

Will the remainder of this millennium see more of the same? That is certainly possible. But we see some reason to predict that more radical strains of education change may predominate in the coming years. And we see ample reason to conclude that this would be desirable, perhaps even necessary, if the results of American education are to improve significantly.

One reason is that the rest of the world is not sitting still. Though education is not the only cause of diminished U.S. competitiveness—and international competition surely is not the sole rationale for better education—we are persuaded that this imbalance is one of the more potent reasons for intensifying and perhaps "radicalizing" the U.S. effort to shape up its education system.

Nobody should be surprised, in education any more than in other fields, that where incremental efforts at reform are perceived to be not working very well, more revolutionary changes will be tried by those discontented with the status quo. (Indeed, the history of politics is replete with radicals who sought to *discourage* evolutionary and incremental change lest people be satisfied—or mollified—by it and thus lose their zest for a complete overthrow of the old regime.)

What is "radical"? One dictionary definition says it is "marked by a considerable departure from the usual or traditional; . . . tending or disposed to make extreme changes in existing views, habits, conditions, or institutions."

But it also needs to be said that "radical," like "beautiful," is to a considerable extent in the eye of the beholder. One person's idea of a dramatic change may be another's notion of the natural and obvious way to proceed, and vice versa. Time also tends to blunt the edge of radicalism; some of the changes depicted in this book have already been underway long enough or have occurred gradually enough so that they no longer appear all that stunning. We must cast our minds back a distance to recall how startling they were when first propounded.

Radical is also relative—and sometimes transitory. What seems revolutionary today may appear quite moderate tomorrow if something even more drastic has by then been proposed. The sagas of school choice and standards, recounted in part in this volume, are excellent examples of this phenomenon. Observe how the formerly startling idea of public school choice has, in just a few years, been widely embraced, either out of authentic conviction or as a tactical maneuver to fend off the more upsetting notion of private school choice.

Though it is usually reasonable to expect "radical" changes— by definition—to alarm traditional interests and upset the defenders of the status quo, we observe that sometimes this is not so. Some sweeping measures presented in this volume are championed by individuals and organizations not unfairly characterized as pillars of the establishment. Much the same could be said of the authors of these essays. Their number includes veteran school superintendents, state and federal officials, professors and union leaders, scholars and practitioners who have spent many years working within the enterprise of American education. If they have been "radicalized" by that experience, surely this must be seen as a commentary on the enterprise itself.

As we scan the U.S. education landscape, we see "radicalism" assuming seven major forms that are illustrated in the ensuing chapters:

1. *A fundamental shift in basic beliefs, values, and ways of thinking* about education itself. The most portentous instance of this shift has been the change from an emphasis on "inputs" to a preoccupation with "outcomes." As Chester Finn wrote in 1990:

> Under the *old* conception, . . . education was thought of as process and system, effort and intention, investment and hope. To improve education meant to try harder, to engage in more activity, to magnify one's plans, to give people more services, and to become more efficient in delivering them.
>
> Under the *new* definition, now struggling to be born, education is the result achieved, the learning that takes root when the process has been effective. *Only* if the process succeeds and learning occurs will we say that *education* happened. Absent evidence of such a result, there is no education—however many attempts have been made, resources deployed, or energies expended.
>
> This new conception of education goes far deeper than what has sometimes been described . . . as a change in emphasis from educational inputs to outcomes. Such a shift has indeed been evident, but it represents barely the warning tremors of the policy earthquake to come. . . .
>
> To define education in terms of ends rather than means is to invite substantial changes in the means themselves. So long as processes are the focus of discussion and the locus of consensus, one can be pretty sure that tomorrow won't be very different from yesterday. If all stakeholders need to agree about plans, regulations, and the flow of resources and if these are the "indicators" on which accountability systems are based, we are apt to be cautious, incrementalist, and moderate. But when the focus shifts to strategies, radically different tactics become thinkable. The ways we are accustomed to operating the education system are far more likely to be dramatically altered, even jettisoned, once we assert that these are not what really matter. [Finn, 1990, pp. 586, 591]

Though this view still encounters resistance in some quarters of the education profession, it has won important allies. In this volume, Albert Shanker, for example, shows how outcomes-based education might best be employed within a national system of goals and a national assessment of progress. Francie Alexander describes how such an approach has been working statewide in California.

2. *The transfer of political power*, for example, from producers to consumers (the "choice" movement) or from central controllers to decentralized decision makers, as Edgar Epps describes in his account of Chicago school reform. John Cairns introduces an increasingly popular variation on this theme with his discus-

sion of the "charter school" idea in Minnesota, already authorized by law in six states (including Minnesota) and heading
toward adoption in at least as many more.

Of course, power can also be transferred in the other direction; the press for national standards, discussed by Shanker, is
one example of this. Kentucky school reform would seem to move
power in both directions at once, as described in the essay by
Betty Steffy and Fenwick English.

3. *A change in what may be termed the "ownership" or "auspices"
of the education enterprise,* notably the growing emphasis on privatization of what has heretofore been deemed a "public" system.
The essential transformation here is from the proposition that
"public education" means an empire of government-built, gov-
ernment-owned, and government-managed institutions staffed by
government employees, to the recognition that "educating the
public" can be done—perhaps even more efficiently—through
diverse means and instrumentalities.

This idea is bigger than education, to be sure. It is part of
"reinventing government," an idea popularized by David Osborne
and reportedly finding favor with the Clinton administration and
in a number of states. (The Bush administration's version was
sometimes characterized as a "new paradigm.") In pursuit of these
ideas, diverse "public" services are coming to be provided through
arrangements such as contracts with private vendors and service
providers, transfers of resources and authority from providers to
consumers (who are then free to obtain their goods and services
from suppliers of their own choosing), and the emergence of
wholly private alternatives—and supplements—to traditional public
services. Thus recently enacted federal day-care legislation includes a "voucher" element (as federal aid for college students
has long done). Thus the city of Chelsea, Massachusetts, has
arranged for Boston University, a private institution, to manage
its public schools; Baltimore has contracted with a for-profit firm
named Education Alternatives, Inc., to manage some of its public
schools, Christopher Whittle's "Edison Project," described in part
in Nancy Hechinger's essay, is devising a wholly private system
of "break the mold" schools—and is conversing with state and
local officials about managing public schools as well.

Joseph Bast and Herbert Walberg's chapter on public and
private school choice reviews the rationale and research on empowering education consumers. Michael Heise analyzes choice
programs currently being tried in Indiana and elsewhere in the

United States. John Cairns describes Minnesota's new legislation that allows public school teachers to start new schools and get them "chartered" by their school district, an idea whose rapidly increasing popularity around the nation carries with it the prospect that an array of dramatically different schools may sprout in the meadows of public education, affording students and families (and teachers) many more educational alternatives than have historically been available in the public sector.

4. *A thoroughgoing overhaul of the goals, standards, and norms by which the system operates,* particularly where these standards are tightly coupled to actual operations and practices. Examples here include national standards and statewide reforms, as illustrated by Shanker and Alexander. In addition, John Murphy describes how a new superintendent and leadership team undertook a comprehensive rethinking of the goals, standards, and organization of a medium-sized urban school system, availing themselves of strategic advice from a panel of nationally known experts. The result was a communitywide strategy for radically boosting student performance without foregoing the community's history of successful desegregation.

5. *Big changes in the technology that the enterprise uses.* Dustin Heuston describes an ambitious experimental program of computer-assisted instruction in the elementary schools of New York City, designed to demonstrate that children learn more and faster when their education program includes these supplements to the regular classroom experience. Nancy Hechinger's account of technology's role in the forthcoming schools of the Edison Project conveys an even more ambitious vision of this potential.

6. *Setting aside, even jettisoning, old institutions, in order to start all over again.* Saul Cooperman describes the $200 million initiative by corporations to fund "break-the-mold" proposals for schools to raise students' achievement. Charter schools and the Chicago and Kentucky reforms also pioneer in this respect, as does Whittle's Edison Project.

7. *Restating the scope, mission, or mandate of the enterprise itself.* The San Diego saga, recounted by former long-time superintendent Thomas Payzant, entails making the school a far more comprehensive participant in the lives of children and communities. He argues that the needs of children, especially poor children, are so great that schools must dispense, coordinate, or provide referrals for child care, medical, dental, psychological, and other

services. In Payzant's view, schools must radically extend their purposes and their operations rather than concentrating solely on their traditional goal of cognitive learning.

We acknowledge that radical is not always good—certainly is not good in and of itself—and that something does not necessarily work just because it can be termed radical. Usually we cannot tell in advance whether and how well it will work, because it is radical precisely by virtue of not having been done before. That weakness is often exploited by opponents who argue—with seeming reasonableness—that we should not make a change until we can be certain that it will "work." But how can we be certain of this until the change is tried? A favorite tactic of opponents of school choice, for example, is to announce that the policy should not be adopted until it has proven itself. Of course, it can never do that if it is not tried!

Radical change is usually harder to implement than incrementalism, because it nearly always elicits stronger resistance. Occasionally that is not so; the Kentucky example is a remarkable tale of change made more possible by its very suddenness and comprehensivess. But bear in mind that getting a change "enacted" can be a far different thing than seeing it put into successful practice. Often it is fraught with unanticipated consequences and surprise implementation problems. Aggrieved vested interests dig in their heels; newly empowered decision makers turn out not to have many interesting ideas about doing things differently; the permanent bureaucracy swallows the innovation and spits it out in unrecognizable shape.

Where does radicalism come from? Sometimes it comes from exasperation with the status quo and frustration that one's efforts to make incremental change in it have been so often and thoroughly stymied. Sometimes it comes from visionaries capable of imagining something completely different from that which surrounds them, that which they grew up with. But like other sorts of prophets, explorers, and inventors, they are often pooh-poohed by those who lack their vision. (And a dearth of such vision—or imagination—is an intractable problem with U.S. education.)

It is difficult to be radical in a democracy. Since majority consent is usually necessary before a change can be made, at least in a "public" enterprise such as education, and since at any given moment the odds are good that most people will be reasonably content with—at least accustomed to—the version they have always known, actually making a radical change usually depends on extraordinary leadership. It is seldom a bottom-up or grassroots phenomenon.

Radical change in education creates curious problems for traditional political labels; what is "conservative" if what is being proposed by people described as such would knock established practice and institutions on their head? What means "liberal" if those so labeled are disposed to keep things pretty much as they are?

We cannot guarantee that the changes described in this volume will yield better-educated children. Indeed, it is important to note that the authors do not necessarily agree with one another—nor do the co-editors embrace with equal ardor all the suggestions that follow. We are mindful that some of these proposals do not co-exist comfortably with others, but we did not see it as our place to attempt here to reconcile those differences. Yet nearly all the measures advocated in these pages are underway somewhere today. One need not endorse all of them in principle to be eager for evidence as to how they actually work in practice. And it seems to us acceptable to take some risks, if only because the nation *is* still gravely at risk. The present condition of our education system remains unsatisfactory notwithstanding a decade of incremental reform. It seems to us likely to improve only if and when we are prepared to adopt a different strategy.

## REFERENCES

Finn, Chester E., Jr. "The Biggest Reform of All," *Phi Delta Kappan* 71 (April 1990): 584–592.

National Center for Education Statistics. *Digest of Education Statistics 1991.* Washington, D.C.: National Center for Education Statistics, U.S. Department of Education, 1991.

National Center for Education Statistics. *The Condition of Education 1992.* Washington, D.C.: National Center for Education Statistics, U.S. Department of Education, 1992.

# I
# NATIONAL AND STATE STRATEGIES

# 1

# National Standards

## *Albert Shanker*

The biggest problem facing American education is massive under-achievement, and we are confronting it throughout our education system—at all levels and with all students. At one end of the scale, a huge number of students leave school, either as drop-outs or as graduates, with such poor levels of achievement that they are unprepared for any but low-paying, dead-end jobs. At the other end of the scale, the percentage of our graduates who achieve at the highest level is pitifully small. For example, the 1990 results of the National Assessment of Educational Progress (NAEP) examination in mathematics tell us that only 5 percent of seventeen-year-olds score at or above the top achievement level of 350, which means that they know some algebra and geometry and are prepared to do college-level mathematics (National Center for Education Statistics, 1991, p. 90). The poor showing is not limited to this exam or this group of students: results of past NAEP exams in mathematics, reading, and writing have been as bad—or worse.

The average achievers among seventeen-year-olds are also doing very poorly. According to the 1990 NAEP mathematics test, these students were working at what NAEP considered to be about a seventh-grade level. Moreover, despite all the talk about achievement in private schools, average students from private and parochial schools did very little better than those in public school (Shanker and Rosenberg, 1992). (See Table 1–1.) In other words, this is a problem of *all* American K–12 education, not just public education.

Its seriousness is compounded by the fact that our youngsters are achieving much less well than students from most other industrialized nations. International examinations, where U.S. students consistently score at or near the bottom, offer one piece of proof (National Center for Education Statistics, 1992, Table III.1, p. 26). Some people object that these tests are unreliable and their results worthless, but we get further confirmation of the vastly superior achievement levels of youngsters in our competitor nations when we look at the examinations that they must

Table 1-1

**Average Proficiency and Percentage of Students at or above Four Anchor Levels on the NAEP Mathematics Scale by Type of School**

| | Percentage of students | Average proficiency | Percentage of students at or above | | | |
|---|---|---|---|---|---|---|
| | | | level 200 | level 250 | level 300 | level 350 |
| Grade 12 | | | | | | |
| Public schools | 90(1.3) | 295(1.1) | 100(0.1) | 90(0.7) | 45(1.4) | 5(0.6) |
| Catholic schools | 6(1.1) | 302(3.0) | 100(0.0) | 96(1.2) | 54(4.5) | 4(1.0) |
| Other private schools | 4(0.8) | 301(3.1) | 100(0.0) | 97(1.1) | 51(4.8) | 4(1.8) |

Description of NAEP Levels:

Level 200: Simple additive reasoning and problem solving with whole numbers; content typically covered by third grade.

Level 250: Simple multiplicative reasoning and two-step problem solving; content typically covered by fifth grade.

Level 300: Reasoning and problem solving involving fractions, decimals, percents, elementary geometry, and simple algebra; content introduced by seventh grade.

Level 350: Reasoning and problem solving involving geometry, algebra, and beginning statistics and probability; content generally covered in high school mathematics courses in preparation for the study of advanced mathematics.

*Note:* Numbers in parentheses are standard errors of the estimated percentages and proficiencies.

*Source: The State of Mathematics Achievement: NAEP's 1990 Assessment of the Nation and the Trial Assessment of the States.* U.S. Department of Education, National Center for Education Statistics, June 1991, Table 2.6 and *Executive Summary,* pp. 6–7.

pass in order to get into college (Shanker, 1991). For example, only 2 or 3 percent of our students perform as well as the 30 percent of all German students who pass the *Abitur*, which consists of difficult written exams in four subjects. Another explanation of the poor performance of our students—that other countries educate only a percentage of their youngsters whereas we educate them all—is also without foundation. Other industrial democracies, with the exception of other English-speaking countries, do as well as we do or better.

This is not simply an issue of national pride—of wanting to be the best. We live in a world economy. If we are to compete successfully, our students must achieve at the same high levels as students in other countries. Our students, though, are failing badly. It is urgent that we figure out what the problem is and what we can do about it.

## A COMMON THREAD

What are successful school systems in other industrialized nations doing? Of course, they differ greatly from one another. However, in spite of their differences, these high-achieving educational systems all share certain characteristics:

- Each has national education standards based on a clear and agreed-on picture of what youngsters leaving secondary school should know and be able to do. In other words, they agree on the content of their curriculum. That is not the case in the United States. Here, states and communities and, to a large extent, individual teachers are free to decide what the curriculum is.
- In addition to content standards, these countries have performance standards that answer the question, "How good is good enough?" There are common standards for all students in the earlier grades and, at some point, differentiated standards depending on whether students hope to go to a university, to attend a technical school, or to obtain an apprenticeship. With the exception of the English-speaking countries, these nations provide challenging standards for every group. In the United States, a single set of standards for all means that standards are low and fail to challenge most students.

- In these countries, the standards drive the entire educational system. Content standards determine what students will learn and when they will learn it. Textbooks are focused on the standards and on helping students to master them—in sharp contrast to the superficiality and fuzziness of our textbooks. And assessment systems find out how successful students have been in meeting the standards, whereas our assessments merely compare student achievement without applying any standards for what is a good, adequate, or poor performance. We report only the percentage of students above and below average without questioning whether our average is high enough.

  The standards also shape teacher education. Coursework and requirements for students preparing to enter teaching ensures that these future teachers have a firm command of the subject matter and skills prescribed by the national standards as well as the pedagogical skills necessary to help youngsters attain these standards.

- But standards alone are not enough to produce high-achieving students. Teachers do what they can to make their students passionately interested in learning for its own sake. But learning is hard work and most students, like most adults, are willing to exert themselves only enough to get something they want. In these other countries, students work because they know that getting into college or getting the job they want depends on how successful they have been in meeting the education standards. Our system offers no clear incentives of this kind because there is no apparent connection between what goes on in school and life after graduation.

## FIFTEEN THOUSAND SETS OF STANDARDS

In the successful education systems of other industrialized nations, external standards, curricula, assessments, textbooks, teacher training, and incentives are all connected, and they push in the same direction—that is, toward getting students to master certain skills and a certain body of material that the society deems important.

In the United States, we have not formally developed a consensus about what students should know and be able to do except in the most general terms. We generally agree, for example, that students in high school should study English, mathematics, and science, but we have not tried to come to any agreement about what those courses should include or what a student who has taken them should know and be able to do. State curriculum guidelines are usually broad recommendations rather than specific curricula. In principle, this leaves the decision about exactly what our students will be taught to our 15,000 school districts. In practice, the decision is often left to individual teachers, who are encouraged to select on the basis of their own interests or the interests of their students.

We are accustomed to this relaxed, take-your-pick attitude toward curriculum and standards, but we pay heavily for it. It means we have no way of making sure that all our students have the advantages of a first-rate curriculum and high standards. Students in one school or class might be following a rigorous program, while those in ten or twenty or one hundred other schools doze their way through a lot of soft courses.

We cannot even ensure that our students are learning enough of the common culture to make them competent at communicating and understanding what they hear and read. Reading is not just a matter of decoding sounds and understanding some basic vocabulary. It is a well-established fact in cognitive science that one of the essential elements in reading, writing, and speaking is common background knowledge. Without this knowledge, you cannot decipher what is being said to you and you cannot send messages. That is why Americans who know nothing of British politics or sports or scandal would not be likely to understand a British newspaper very well, even though it is written in English. And that is why our elementary school children, who are still reading stories about Dick and Jane, score pretty well on reading exams, whereas high school students, who are reading material that demands background information, score very poorly.

Successful learning to some extent depends on continuity, and our ad hoc standards and curriculum mean that there can be enormous variations, even within a school. Teachers can never be sure of what students entering their class in September have already covered. A child who has moved to a new school—or is merely joining a different class—could spend the rest of the year just trying to figure out what is going on.

Because there is no common curriculum, the work students do is determined by the teacher's expectations or by negotiations between the teacher and the students. Teachers often adjust standards according to their estimate of what students in a given class can do. They sometimes tailor the curriculum to ask less of certain students than of others because of their socioeconomic or racial or ethnic background. This watered-down curriculum shortchanges the youngsters who could do real work if, as happens in an education system with external standards, teachers were required to give students certain required material and help them to master it.

Sometimes, when teachers demand higher standards, students and their parents put pressure on the teacher to let up. They accuse the teacher of being unfair because, they say, other teachers or schools do not expect that much work. However, where there are external standards and incentives for meeting them, the situation is very different. The teacher can point out that the work he is demanding is exactly what other students at this level are doing. So youngsters see the teacher as a coach, someone who is helping them succeed, rather than as a nasty person making arbitrary demands. And the parents, bolstered by the external standards (and the consequences of not meeting them), are more likely to support teachers in their efforts to get youngsters to work hard. The external standards provide legitimacy for the demands that both teachers and parents make of students (Bishop, 1989).

In countries that have national standards, examinations are an important part of the system. German or French school-leaving exams, for example, show to what extent students have succeeded in meeting the standards. And for students who have worked hard and done well, these examinations lead to entering a university or a technical school or to finding a good job. The standardized tests that pass for an assessment system in the United States are curriculum-neutral and provide no useful information about what students know and can do. They compare students, schools, districts, and states with each other, but they do not tell us what scores are good enough—they merely reflect the percentage of students above and below average. In a land of pygmies, you can be above average in height and still be pretty short. Also, these standardized tests have no immediate or visible consequences for the students. From their point of view, these tests do not count. So they do little to try to get good scores.

However, our standardized tests often exercise a powerful and negative influence on teaching. The yearly publication of the test scores by the local newspaper is a big event in many communities, and a few points gained or lost can make a tremendous difference in the public image of schools and teachers. So teachers are often under pressure to prepare students for the tests. This means emphasizing test-taking techniques and the recognition of lots of meaningless bits of information deemed likely to be on tests. As a result, the curriculum, which may already be pitifully thin, is further impoverished.

Our lack of agreed-on standards also handicaps us in the training of teachers. In countries with national standards, teachers can be trained in the body of knowledge and the skills that they will be teaching their students no matter where in the country they work. Our colleges and universities have no such guidance about how to train prospective teachers. Their students will end up teaching many different curriculums in different school districts and probably in different states. Even though the most important and powerful skills are embedded in content, schools for teachers have to fall back on courses that teach generic skills. It is no wonder that most teachers say their education courses were a waste of time.

## QUESTIONS AND ROADBLOCKS

When *A Nation at Risk* appeared ten years ago, it was deemed old-fashioned because it emphasized proficiency in subject matter disciplines. But adopting the National Education Goals, which were unveiled in 1990, has led to a greater acceptance of that approach to reforming U.S. schools. A number of the goals require us to deal with issues of content and standards. Goal number three calls for our students to "demonstrate competency in challenging subject matter, including English, mathematics, science, history, and geography." But what must students know and be able to do in order to be "competent" in English or science or history, and how can we measure this competence? Goal number four calls for "American students [to] be first in the world in mathematics and science by the year 2000." But what does being first in the world in mathematics and science mean in terms of achievement? And how will we be able to tell whether we have gotten there? The only way to answer these questions is to decide on standards for content and performance that are comparable to those we find in the successful school systems of other industrialized nations, and then to design assessments to determine whether students meet these standards. The content and performance standards created by the National Council of Teachers of Mathematics (NCTM) have been widely accepted, and they are a promising start. However, there are serious and strenuous objections to standards that could derail the process. And the four following issues that affect the development of standards must be considered.

## National versus Local Control

In the United States, except for a few special and relatively recent programs like Chapter 1, education has always been the province of the states rather than the federal government, and there is a long tradition of states delegating their authority to local school boards. So, many people find the possibility of federal involvement in education standards alarming.

They wonder who would create the national standards—a central bureaucracy? Private professional groups? Would the standards be mandatory or voluntary? And even if private professional groups created them, would they be administered and disseminated (or enforced) by a central bureaucracy? Do these standards mean that the federal government would dictate the entire curriculum?

The only national standards that have been developed thus far are those of the National Council of Teachers of Mathematics (NCTM), a private professional group, so it is clearly possible—and I think desirable—for professional groups like this to take charge of developing standards for their own subject areas. While the federal government has made no attempt to impose the NCTM standards, a number of states, finding them superior to their existing standards for mathematics, have adopted them, and several states are developing standards of their own based on the NCTM model.

As for national standards determining every detail of the local curriculum—and exactly how teachers teach it— it would be possible to have content standards on which a profession agrees without having that content occupy the entire curriculum. Moreover, agreement on content and performance standards would still leave open how the standards would be realized—through technology, traditional lectures, cooperative learning, team teaching, or other methods.

*Accountability*

The system of accountability used in the United States is very different from that used in other countries. In the United States, only the professionals in the schools are viewed as accountable. If students do well, it is because the professionals have taught well; if students fail to achieve, it is because the system—and the adults in it—have failed. Even so, there are few consequences for teachers and schools in which students consistently do very well or very poorly. However, this idea of accountability teaches young people the bad lesson that they are not responsible for their success or failure. Parents and students in other countries believe that success is based on the youngsters' hard work, whereas in the United States, we tend to attribute success to the brains children were born with or to teachers.

No successful education system operates on this assumption. Typically, youngsters in other systems face two high-stakes assessments. The first, which takes place somewhere between grade 4 and grade 9, determines the track youngsters will be in. The second assessment, which takes place at the end of secondary school and is differentiated according to track, determines whether or not a youngster will get into a university or a technical school or what kind of job opportunity he or she will get. Students, their teachers, and their parents understand this system, and students work very hard to do well on the assessments.

People who oppose such a system in the United States offer various objections. They say that tests are unreliable and that such a system would put too much pressure on students and destroy the self-esteem of those who are not successful. It is hard to believe that our privileged, middle-class youth would be unable to handle demands similar to those handled by youngsters elsewhere in the world. Learning to take pressure, dealing with failure, and gaining a sense of self-esteem from one's own achievements are important parts of growing up; they are things we should be helping students learn in school. We cannot expect to raise students' achievement to the levels we need unless our students are compelled to accept a large measure of responsibility for their education.

However, the question of whether stakes like these would impose an undue hardship on poor minority youngsters needs to be taken seriously. Higher standards and accountability might be a very good thing for middle-class students, but will making

new and tougher demands on poor minority children simply
exacerbate existing inequities and put those who are already
performing poorly at a further disadvantage? Under our current
system, very little is demanded of these students, and their achievement is correspondingly low. In countries with standards-driven
educational systems, poor minority children fare much better.
And our experience in the United States with minimum-competency exams also suggests that standards and accountability will
help these youngsters instead of further disadvantaging them.

Minimum-competency examinations, which were introduced
in over twenty states during the late 1970s and early 1980s, required that students be able to read simple material and perform simple calculations before they could get high school
diplomas. The exams were denounced by people who said they
would result in increased dropout rates, thus denying minority
youngsters high school diplomas and a chance for further education and decent jobs.

However, as Barbara Lerner (1991) points out, instead of leading to an increased dropout rate, these exams raised the achievement of minority students. She cites the case of Florida where,
on the first few tries, 80 to 90 percent of the state's high school
minority students failed the test. But they did not drop out, as
had been predicted, and by the fifth year, over 90 percent passed.

Minimum competency worked, according to Lerner, because
it provided a clearly understood standard that students and their
teachers could work toward (Can you read and do arithmetic at
this level?), and because there was an important incentive involved—students did not get their high school diplomas until
they passed the test. They knew what they were supposed to do
and they knew what was at stake.

Some people who do not oppose accountability for poor and
minority children believe that it should come into force only
when these youngsters have been able to get a good early start
with health care and early childhood education and have the
same school resources and opportunities to learn as do middle-
class children. But waiting until every poor child gets these advantages is the same thing as putting off making changes for
years or perhaps forever. While we cannot wait until all schools
are equal, we can move quickly to get rid of the worst problems
and establish strong minimum standards. Even without the same
opportunities to learn, if these poor and minority children were
presented with a more demanding curriculum and shown the

consequences of doing well, they would do much better than they do now and would be much more qualified for employment.

## Incentives

There is no point in talking about stiffer standards and accountability unless there are powerful incentives for youngsters to meet those standards. Every country with a successful school system has also worked out the question of incentives by connecting successful performance in school with further schooling or a job, and we too need to do that.

Getting into college needs to be connected with meeting world-class college-entry standards. But can we introduce such a system without generating serious adverse consequences? If we raise standards and require that students meet them in order to get into college, many fewer students will be able to attend. And a number of colleges might have to go out of business.

To avoid or minimize the shock for students and colleges, we should gradually raise our low college-entry standards over a period of twelve to fifteen years—the time it takes for a kindergarten class to reach college—until they correspond with standards in other industrialized countries. Experience in other countries shows that higher standards would not lead to fewer college graduates. Though more of our students enter college than do students in other industrialized countries, their four-year college graduation rates are comparable to ours.

High standards for four-year institutions should not deny students who cannot meet these standards the chance for further education. They should be encouraged to take advantage of community college, technical school, and other continuing-education opportunities. And of course, students who do not meet entrance requirements for college when they graduate from high school must have an opportunity to meet them later on. Our system is based on giving people a second chance to succeed, and we do not want to change that now.

We need similar incentives to do well in school for those who plan to go to work rather than attend college. Nearly half of our high school graduates fall into this category. They are sometimes called the "forgotten half" because our current system pays so little attention to what they need.

Like our college-bound students, those who are not college bound do not work very hard because it does not seem to make any difference. Top U.S. companies seldom employ recent high school graduates; they prefer to hire workers in their twenties who already have experience and a work record (Bishop, 1989). Employers who hire students right out of school do not ask for transcripts to find out the courses youngsters took or the grades they made; they are interested only in whether their prospective employees have a diploma. As a result, a student who took tough courses and worked hard could end up with the same poor job as a youngster who took a collection of soft courses that he barely passed.

Making these connections could involve some major changes by schools and businesses and government. Schools might offer a credential, recognized by business, that shows youngsters have gained certain skills. There is an increasing interest in a youth apprenticeship system, adapted from the German model, that would involve paid internships while youngsters continue in school. But even some simple changes could make a difference. Just think what would happen if McDonald's, Pizza Hut, and Roy Rogers were to say to high school students applying for part-time employment, "Bring us a copy of your last report card and a letter from your teacher saying that your school performance is strong enough to warrant your taking an after-school job." That would send an immediate message that the quality of school-work counts.

### Litigiousness

A major problem for any system of standards and assessments that involves real stakes is the litigiousness of American society. No one in Germany or France would go to court because of failing the *Abitur* or the *baccalauréat*. People in these countries accept the idea of professional judgment on assessments—and even the possibility that the professionals might make a mistake. But in the United States any high-stakes exam would probably face numerous court challenges as to its fairness and validity. Knowing this might so constrain the people preparing the new standards and assessments that they would be unable to create a system that was rigorous enough to be worthwhile.

A draft of a bill that seeks to establish national standards, the "Goals 2000: Educate America Act," which was introduced in the Congress in April 1993, gives a good indication of the thicket that people writing assessments would have to negotiate.

As they try to devise questions that fairly represent the subject matter studied in school, assessment writers would also need to be aware of and sensitive to the concerns of "disadvantaged students, students with diverse racial, ethnic, and cultural backgrounds (including American Indians and Alaskan Natives), students with disabilities, students with limited English proficiency, and academically talented students." Any question on any exam that was construed as insensitive or unfair by one of those groups could lead to a legal challenge (Goals 2000: Educate America Act, 1993).

No assessment used anywhere else in the world has to stand up to this kind of scrutiny. Neither do the bar or medical exams that people take in this country. Given legal constraints like these, we are unlikely to create a system at all. Or if we do manage, we might find it destroyed by a whole series of successful lawsuits.

However, the situation is not entirely hopeless. When minimum-competency exams were first established, they were challenged in court as being discriminatory. Instead of caving in, those who believed that the exams would, in fact, help poor minority children stood up for the exams and won. We cannot make our society less litigious, but we can make a strong fight in court based on the importance and validity of a standards-driven system and assessments that have real stakes.

## WHAT KINDS OF SCHOOLS?

Because of the atrocious performance of our schools, many people—and I am one of them—have advocated creating totally new types of schools. It is now clear, given the effectiveness of "traditional" schools in other countries, that the problem with our schools is not that they are traditional but that they have no standards and no stakes. It would be criminal to continue experimenting with new and untried methods—especially since such efforts take time—instead of instituting what is known to work much better than our current system. The right thing to do is to improve U.S. schools by putting in a system with standards and consequences. This does not mean that we should not continue experimenting with new ideas so that we can create different kinds of schools and better ones. However, when we come up with some successful nontraditional schools, we will find that being part of a system with standards and stakes will make nontraditional schools too work better.

In *The Learning Gap: Why Our Schools Are Failing and What We Can Learn from Japanese and Chinese Education* (1992), Harold Stevenson and James Stigler describe how the standards-driven system in Japanese, Taiwanese, and Chinese elementary schools leads to superior performance by Asian youngsters. One striking passage lays out the way Japanese teachers, in what we would call a traditional school, successfully use whole-group instruction in heterogeneous classes—a technique that is often a failure in U.S. schools.

This technique is very common here. The problem is that when American teachers pitch the discussion to one part of the class—perhaps the middle third—the other two-thirds tune out. Students at the bottom tune out because they have been left behind and are bored and those at the top, because they catch on quickly, also are bored. So a majority of the students miss what the teacher is saying every day. This difficulty with conducting heterogeneous classes so that they are profitable for every student is one reason why so many people consider some kind of tracking a practical necessity.

The Asian teachers Stevenson and Stigler observed avoided this problem, even though they taught classes that typically had forty or more students—considerably more than we consider optimum. How did they do it? To begin with, they did not try to cover a lot of material. A mathematics class, for example, might be organized around solving a single problem. As a result, teachers had time to engage the entire group of forty or so students in finding a satisfactory answer.

In the course of this search, each student described to the class how he or she had obtained the answer, whether it was correct or not. Students were able to see where those with incorrect answers went wrong. They could also see that there are many different ways of solving a problem—some of them quicker or more elegant than others but all productive. Teachers made sure that the slower students had a chance to catch on, but at the same time they kept the attention of the brighter ones by challenging them to come up with elegant solutions. By the end of a lesson, teachers could be reasonably sure that everybody in their mixed-ability class understood the solution—and the various ways of getting to it—well enough to build on it in future lessons.

What Stevenson and Stigler observed Japanese teachers doing is not inconsistent with the kind of classroom practice that many U.S. educators favor, though few have figured out how to achieve it in a heterogeneous classroom. The answer seems to lie in the radical notion of teachers working together on the same lesson, something that seldom if ever happens here. Stevenson and Stigler tell us that Asian teachers collaborate to develop or revise an approach to a topic and to craft questions and examples. By pooling their expertise and knowledge, they create common lessons that are of consistently high quality, and they go back to these lessons year after year to improve and polish them.

A cultural difference is one reason that American teachers do not collaborate in this way or work over time to perfect lessons. Many American teachers consider preparing a lesson analogous to standing in front of a canvas on which they paint. Working on the same lesson year after year would probably sound like turning teaching into a rote exercise. Stevenson compared the Asian teachers' approach to the way a number of different pianists would approach a concerto: though they might have different interpretations and different styles, they are all playing the same notes. And unlike U.S. teachers, they are not writing the music while they play.

However, even if we could sell teachers on the collaborative method, it would require major changes in U.S. schools. This is true partly because our school day is not set up to allow teachers to meet and share ideas. Most elementary school teachers are with their classes throughout the day, except, perhaps, for a preparation period and a brief lunch break. This is not the case in the Asian schools Stevenson and Stigler observed. Japanese teachers, for example, spend more time in school every day than do American teachers, and they are in charge of classes during only 60 percent of the time they are in school; class hours are similar for teachers in other Asian schools (Stevenson, 1992).

Standards are an essential piece of this whole picture. They give Asian teachers a strong incentive to collaborate that U.S. teachers lack. All fourth-grade teachers in Japan or Taiwan know that their students are going to have to meet certain standards, and this common goal encourages them to work together to prepare the most effective lessons possible. The fact that there are stakes for the youngsters also encourages teachers to push students to do their best, to insist on their working hard and getting as much as possible out of every lesson. Teachers here are less likely to do that because it does not seem that anything of real consequence rides on whether or not their students learn as much mathematics as they are capable of learning.

Perhaps it is not surprising that traditional classroom arrangements, such as the Asian ones Stevenson and Stigler describe, fit into and benefit from a standards-driven system. But this kind of system can accommodate experimental schools as well. The Köln-Holweide school, which overturns all the assumptions behind the traditional model of schooling, flourishes within the highly structured German system. It shows that even new ways of organizing schools can work better in the context of standards and stakes ("Creating a School Community," 1988).

Holweide is a comprehensive school of over 2,000 students that runs from the equivalent of our grade 5 through grade 10. Its student body includes the children of Turks, Moroccans, and other foreign "guest workers," as well as many native German children from poor or single-parent families. Students at Holweide are not tracked—a rarity in Germany where tracking generally begins in grade 5—but most of them have already been identified as not being "college material."

At Holweide, teachers work in teams of six to eight and make all the decisions that are made for teachers in the United States. In the United States, a bell schedule tells mathematics teachers that they have fifty minutes or English teachers that they have forty-five minutes. At Holweide, the team decides how long to spend on a subject and which team member is going to teach it. We assign students to a teacher for a semester or a year. There, the team groups the 120 students for whom it will be responsible the entire time they stay at Holweide. And the team decides when and if the groupings should be changed.

Having students stay with the same group of teachers throughout their time at Holweide helps make the school a learning community instead of a factory or a bureaucratic institution. Students do not feel as though they are on a conveyor belt being moved from one teacher to another—the way youngsters here often do. On the other hand, if school is not going well, they cannot decide to write this year off because they are going to get a new teacher next year. They have to face their problem. The arrangement gives teachers a chance to know their students and a feeling of responsibility about what happens to them. Most of all, it has the effect of lengthening the school year. Teachers do not need to spend time organizing a new class with new students in September or doing the June paperwork needed to hand their students on to the next teacher.

The student groups are designed to encourage the idea that

students are workers who are responsible for their own education. There is a minimum of teacher talk, and questions predominate over answers. Pupils sit together at tables in mixed-ability groups of five or six, working together on problems. Peer influence promotes learning, and children are not continually humiliated by being called on before the whole class to give answers they do not know.

It is no surprise that this intimate and responsible atmosphere means that most of the discipline problems that plague urban schools are reduced. The fact that students are drawn to members of their peer group is an asset rather than a liability. Since teams suffer when individuals suffer (academically or socially), students take more responsibility for each other. Since students and teachers work together over a five-year period, each student can also form a close relationship with at least one teacher, something that is very difficult to do in our schools.

The results are impressive. Most students come to Holweide already written off as lacking academic potential. Despite this, a disproportionate number end up meeting Germany's high academic standard: They take the demanding school-leaving exam, the *Abitur*, pass it, and go to a university. Their untraditional school is able to help them meet the demanding standards of the German education system.

Holweide is not successful despite the standards-driven system of which it is a part; it is successful because of the system. The strict standards tell teachers what their students must know and be able to do but leave them free to decide how to achieve these outcomes. That is why Holweide succeeds where most of our progressive schools have failed. People in our schools did not know what they were supposed to produce. They had lots of creativity and enthusiasm, but they lacked the direction that external standards would have given them.

Adopting a standards-driven system does not mean putting an end to school reform; and revolutionary schools are by no means limited to the Holweide model. We know far more about the human intelligence and the way youngsters learn than we used to. Moreover, modern technology is presenting us with new tools for teaching and learning that will transform education beyond anything we now imagine. We might see a twenty-first century version of a one-room school, an ungraded school where students work by themselves or in small groups under the supervision and the teacher or other adults and where work is organized according to the plan of Boy Scout merit badges. We might see "schools without walls" that use the resources of the community or apprenticeship schools where students spend summers and after-school time working in jobs that can turn into real entry-level positions when they are ready to take them. We need to continue trying to create new schools that make use of our new knowledge, but whatever form these schools take, they will gain direction and coherence from being anchored in external standards and assessments and high stakes for results.

The schools cannot solve all the problems students bring to school with them. But youngsters who have a feeling that they are succeeding and who can see a connection between what they are doing all day in school and the rest of their lives will have fewer problems. They will be less likely to take drugs, become pregnant, drop out of school, or give up on their future. The schools in a standards-driven system will give all our children a better education. As they do so they will also help to make our society a better place in which to live.

## REFERENCES

Bishop, John H. "Why the Apathy in American High Schools?" *Educational Researcher* 18 (January–February 1989): 6–10, 42.

"Creating a School Community: One Model of How It Can Be Done. An Interview with Anne Ratzki." *American Educator* 12 (Spring 1988): 10–17, 38–43.

Goals 2000: Educate America Act. Draft bill of the U.S. Senate and House of Representatives, April 16, 1993, pp. 2, 27.

Lerner, Barbara. "Good News about American Education," *Commentary* 91 (March 1991): 19–25.

National Center for Education Statistics. *The State of Mathematics Achievement: NAEP's 1990 Assessment of the Nation and the Trial Assessment of the States*, Report No. 21–ST–04. Washington, D.C.: U.S. Government Printing Office, 1991.

National Center for Education Statistics. *International Mathematics and Science Assessments: What Have We Learned?* NCES Report No. 91–011. Washington, D.C.: Office of Educational Research and Improvement, U.S. Department of Education, January 1992.

Shanker, Albert. "Flunked," *New Republic*, 16 December 1991, pp. 20–22.

Shanker, Albert, and Rosenberg, Bella. "Do Private Schools Outperform Public Schools?" In *The Choice Controversy*, edited by Peter W. Cookson, Jr., pp. 128–145. Newbury Park, Calif.: Corwin Press, 1992.

Stevenson, Harold W. "Learning from Asian Schools," *Scientific American* 276 (December 1992): 70–76.

Stevenson, Harold W., and Stigler, James W. *The Learning Gap: Why Our Schools Are Failing and What We Can Learn from Japanese and Chinese Education*. New York: Summit Books, 1992.

# 2

# The New American Schools Development Corporation

## Saul Cooperman

DeTocqueville once described the United States as a "land of wonders" in which "what is not yet done is only what we have not attempted to do." In that spirit, business executives from across the country agreed in the summer of 1991 to join with the Board of Directors of the New American Schools Development Corporation (NASDC) in a new effort to reform education. This corporation (a private, nonprofit, nonpartisan group) committed itself to the mission of succeeding where so many other reform efforts had failed—by providing a nationwide systemic approach to changing our schools. But why business leaders, and why now?

To get people interested in change, one must be convinced there is a problem. Otherwise, why change? The problem was forcefully stated in the publication *A Nation at Risk* (National Commission on Excellence in Education, 1983). This publication raised awareness in fields unrelated to education that our students were leaving our public schools ill-prepared for the world as citizens and as workers. Occasionally, a newspaper article or a television spot would point out that students in other countries scored better on tests. Until *A Nation at Risk*, however, the full impact of a weakening educational system was not felt outside the education community.

Many reasons are offered to explain why the education system is in trouble. Some have to do with problems of the family unit. As that institution weakens, schools find their mission to be as much social as academic. Some of the problems are inherent in a school's inability to renew itself. Even though some schools have bucked the pressure to maintain the status quo, there are those who believe that the lack of self-renewal is inherent in the culture of our schools. There are, of course, accounts of situations in which individuals and groups within a school have achieved success. But many times these successes have been in an individual class, in a particular discipline in the school program, or within a grade in the school. And even when a school is outstanding in almost every respect, it appears difficult and almost impossible for the successful school to be replicated or its program adopted in other schools.

The very nature of school organization argues against adopting or adapting a successful accomplishment in another school. Each school or each school district is a virtual monopoly, and there is no need to be competitive with other schools in the state or to strive to meet agreed-on national criteria. There is simply a general lack of high expectations and high standards for accomplishment.

The problem of bringing about meaningful change, of adapting or adopting a successful practice, is made even more difficult because of an inherent "educational gridlock" arising out of territorial battles between employee organizations within a school. At times when educational scrutiny and change is needed most, the education agenda becomes trivialized. Conversations often revolve around issues such as the number of class periods, the number of minutes in a period, employee benefits and compensation, work rules, and so on. Little time is spent by the teachers and administrators discussing what should be taught, whether the teaching is effective, and whether the children are actually learning.

I recently visited the high school I attended forty years ago. Except for some computers in the classroom, there was little change. Teachers' desks were in front of the classroom, twenty-five desks were arranged in straight rows, the teacher taught primarily by lectures that were interspersed with questions to students. In that school, 1992 was very much like 1952.

But 1992 was unlike 1952 in one very important way. In 1952 we did not have national goals. In 1992 we did. For the first time in the history of this nation, the President of the United States met in 1989 with participants in an education summit in Charlottesville, Virginia. They agreed on six national goals for the education of all students:

1. By the year 2000, all children in America will start school ready to learn.
2. By the year 2000, we will increase the percentage of students graduating from high school to at least 90 percent.
3. By the year 2000, American students will leave grades 4, 8, and 12 having demonstrated competency over challenging subject matter, including English, mathematics, science, history, and geography, and every school in America will ensure that all students learn to use their minds well, so that they may be prepared for responsible citizenship, further learning, and productive employment in our modern economy.
4. By the year 2000, U.S. students will be first in the world in mathematics and science achievement.
5. By the year 2000, every adult American will be literate and will possess the knowledge and skills necessary to compete in a global economy and exercise the rights and responsibilities of citizenship.
6. By the year 2000, every school in America will be free of drugs and violence and will offer a disciplined environment conducive to learning.

This conference provided the impetus for action, and for many people this was just the encouragement they needed to get involved in education. If the President and the governors were serious about education, then why not others?

Why not others indeed? Twenty business executives agreed in 1991 to support systemic comprehensive education reform by forming the NASDC Board of Directors, and a plan began to take shape. The challenge was (1) to underwrite and monitor the effective development of designs for schools that will restore American education to world preeminence; (2) to demonstrate that schools using these designs can help all students perform at high levels; and (3) to assist communities across the country in adapting and using these designs.

But how is systemic and comprehensive education reform to be defined? NASDC speaks about "systemic" in two ways. The first is reform throughout the system—at local, county, state, and federal levels. The other way to think about "systemic" is to consider the human body, which is composed of many interdependent systems (such as the respiratory, cardiovascular, and digestive systems) that are parts of an entire functioning unit. So also does education involve many systems—systems, for example, for governance and organization, for curriculum development, for staff development, and for assessment. Without change in each of these systems, fundamental change in the school system as a whole is not likely to occur.

To accomplish fundamental change in institutions, four conditions are required:

1. *Dissatisfaction with the status quo.* The institutional culture in an organization cannot be uprooted if most people are satisfied with the familiar and the comfortable.
2. *A new shared vision.* Of critical importance is the need to create a new shared vision of where to go and strategies to get there. Without both, frustration triumphs.
3. *The capacity for change.* Visions and strategies are fragile. The capacity of organizations to change is critical, particularly the capacity of people in the organization to reshape what they do and how they do it.
4. *Concrete practical first steps.* Revolutions begin in fits and starts. The important thing is that they begin. Practical, measurable first steps are essential to overcoming institutional inertia. They build a sense that fundamental change is in the wind.

The NASDC effort encouraged citizens around the country—the dreamers and doers in our society—to pull together to design an education program for schools and systems of schools. They were encouraged to cast aside commonly held ideas about how schools should operate and to take a "clean-sheet-of-paper" approach to thinking about education. They were held to only four requirements: (1) their designs must be for all children; (2) their designs must address students' achievement of world-class standards in at least the five core subjects (English, mathematics, science, history, geography); (3) the costs of the designs must be comparable to the costs of schools of today; (4) their

designs must address a whole school, not just a particular subject area or a single grade.

In the summer of 1991, NASDC decided to seek such designs for new schools. It sought input from people across the
country on how designs should be structured. Over 1,500 people
attended a series of design conferences where participants were
asked to react to a draft of a Request for Proposals (RFP). Had
NASDC missed something in preparing the draft? Was the emphasis clear throughout? What questions had NASDC not thought
about that might impact the work of those preparing proposals?

In October 1991, over 30,000 copies of the Request for Proposals were distributed. Proposals were to be submitted by February 14, 1992. No one had any idea of the number of responses
to expect, but it soon became clear that the response would be
huge. NASDC received 686 proposals from respondents in forty-
seven states. All proposals were read and evaluated by a group
of volunteer readers coming from all walks of life. They were
selected because they represented "break-the-mold" thinking in
either education or business and because they had demonstrated
a firm commitment to education and children. Each proposal
was read by at least three people. After weeks of reading, 119
proposals were selected for further evaluation. Sixteen proposals
were submitted to the Board of Directors by the NASDC management and an Education Advisory Panel. This eighteen-mem-
ber panel included notable educators from public and private
schools (kindergarten through grade 12) and from higher education institutions.

The Board of Directors then directed the NASDC staff to
hold interviews with all sixteen design teams and to make recommendations to the Board regarding proposals to be funded
during the first phase of the project. Eleven proposals were accepted by the NASDC Board of Directors for such funding.

Each of the eleven design teams is made up of parents, teachers, community leaders, business leaders—a whole family of people
who have chosen to make education their issue. The NASDC
plan calls for the work of the design teams to be carried on in
three phases. In Phase I, the 1992–1993 school year was to be
devoted to planning, refining, and testing the designs, and the
eleven projects selected by the Board were funded for this phase.
The two-year Phase II, to begin in the fall of 1993, was to be
used for implementation of the designs in at least two sites, and
in some cases in as many as twenty-five sites. Continued funding

of the eleven proposals in Phase II was to depend on an assessment of progress in Phase I as well as on the extent of the resources available from NASDC. Phase III calls for widespread national dissemination of the designs that will have been tested during Phase II.

Performance-based contracts were negotiated with each of the eleven design teams selected by the NASDC Board for funding through Phase I. Brief descriptions of the proposals submitted by these eleven teams are provided by Mecklenburger (1992). In June 1993, NASDC announced that it would continue funding nine of these teams. Summaries of the nine projects to be funded may be found in *Education Week* (1993).

Among the features of many but not necessarily all the design proposals are (1) child-centered schools, (2) grouping of students by developmental level rather than by age, (3) individual educational plans for all students, (4) multiyear contracts between students and teachers, (5) promotion only when students have mastered material, (6) project-centered or thematic instruction, (7) use of technology to individualize instruction and provide access to advanced materials, (8) team teaching and differentiated staff functions, (9) high standards for both students and teachers, and (10) substantial autonomy for the school.

We know that there will be barriers to progress, for change of any kind runs into resistance. As part of its proposal to NASDC, each design team was required to present a plan for overcoming common barriers to change, among which are (1) federal and state regulations, including court orders, (2) state regulations on curriculum, teacher certification, testing, and school attendance, (3) school boards and administrators who may be hostile to changes in practice, (4) collective bargaining agreements, (5) school funding issues, (6) the absence of agreement on and support for high standards, (7) the inability of communities to integrate educational, health, and social service resources to serve their youth, and (8) a lack of willingness on the part of communities to support schools that have a vision of what is possible through education.

NASDC established criteria for the assessment of the work of the teams during Phase I. The work of the eleven teams as they moved through Phase I was monitored by a review team consisting of representatives from the Education Advisory Panel, the NASDC staff, and the Advisory Council. Specific milestones were agreed to during the negotiation of the contract between NASDC and each design team. The design teams were allowed to set their own schedules, so that each contract is different. Requests for funding and support differed, depending on where and how the teams planned to implement their ideas. Each team was eligible for up to $3 million for Phase I of their work. They were responsible for submitting monthly expense and budget reports to NASDC.

NASDC teams visited and otherwise communicated with the design teams periodically during Phase I to provide oversight of the work. Were the milestones being met? Was the quality of the implementation acceptable? Were funds being spent properly? Each visiting team reported to the chief executive officer of NASDC, who then made a recommendation to the NASDC Board of Directors regarding the continuance of each design team's contract. In June 1993, the Board voted to continue funding nine of the eleven design teams.

NASDC believes that anything is possible when communities work together, and that includes transforming schools for their children. The design teams are essentially working laboratories where ideas are tested and refined and where conclusions are drawn about how to create schools in which all students can learn and achieve world-class standards. The hope is that communities around the country will watch and learn from the work of the design teams in their initial sites, and that those communities will then support the adoption or adaptation of the work of the design teams in their own schools.

## REFERENCES

Mecklenburger, James A. "The Braking of the 'Break-the-Mold' Express," *Phi Delta Kappan* 74 (December 1992): 283–288.

"NASDC Project Summaries," *Education Week* (4 August 1993): 8, 10–11.

National Commission on Excellence in Education. *A Nation at Risk*. Washington, D.C.: U.S. Department of Education, 1983.

# 3

# What I Saw at the California Education Revolution

## *Francie Alexander*

With gratitude and credit to Peggy Noonan, former presidential speech writer, I have paraphrased her book title. "Revolution" accurately describes the state of education in California over the past decade—and I had the opportunity to be on hand for much of it. The revolution has transformed education in California and the nation and is still underway.

The state curriculum framework for English-language arts, which is the mechanism for communicating policy recommendations on curriculum design and content to be covered to local school districts, calls for a "quiet intellectual revolution." It is only a slight exaggeration to assert that this kind of movement in the curriculum takes on the significance of other major shifts in thought, as described by Thomas Kuhn (1962) in *The Structure of Scientific Revolutions*. Once the Copernican theory was established, for example, the world's political and social order changed. And recently, for example, new health information has led to major lifestyle changes, including altered smoking and drinking habits, increased seat belt usage, greater nutrition awareness, and increased exercise. In similar manner, the state's commitment to high educational expectations for all its students and a comprehensive strategy for improving its schools has already affected what is taught and learned in California classrooms and has catalyzed the national standards and systemic reform movements.

It was unlikely that a move toward statewide standards would have happened in California, long a state that promoted local control of education policy and practice. In 1982, I surveyed graduation requirements in a cross section of central California school districts to determine the impact of not having statewide graduation requirements for more than a decade. The discrepancies among school districts were alarming, with some school districts graduating students with a hundred fewer credits than students in other districts had. Some students managed to get through high school without taking a single real course in mathematics or science. Bill Honig, who was running for State Superintendent of Public Instruction at the time, decried the fact that students could take a course in whale watching in Baja California and thereby satisfy their high school science requirement. My survey merely scratched the surface of the problem, looking at quantity issues (such as the number of courses taken) but not at the quality of the course content. Included in the survey was a recommendation that graduation requirements be reestablished and, more important, that their course content be described. The report did not have a big impact on the Department of Education at the time, but some of the State Board of Education members were enthusiastic about it. During the process of developing strategies for raising standards, Bill Honig was elected and the project became a higher priority. The board moved aggressively to adopt model graduation requirements and accompanying course outlines and set forth its recommendations in the report *Raising Expectations* (California Department of Education, 1983).

Honig had campaigned for higher standards for students and deftly turned around the argument that such standards were elitist by accusing his critics of elitism for believing that all students could not read and enjoy good literature, conduct scientific activities, value the arts, and otherwise participate in a rich core curriculum. Using the Board's document to foreshadow what was to come, he made it clear that on his watch there would be an unprecedented effort to define what California students should know and be able to do.

The first of many task forces was called together. The new superintendent understood that new education standards would need widespread consensus in order to be successfully implemented at the district and classroom levels. One indicator of the intellectual nature of the revolution that was to take place was Honig's letter encouraging all school personnel to read a few books that he felt would help inform the statewide debate and discussion on student standards. He recommended *The Troubled Crusade* (1984) by historian and Assistant Secretary of Education Diane Ravitch, so that there would be a historical perspective on the problems facing schools and a shared sense of urgency about the mission to improve the achievement of California's diverse student population. He also recommended E. D. Hirsch's *Cultural Literacy* (1988) to lay the groundwork for developing student standards that were content specific. Ernest Boyer's *High School* (1982) was suggested, since it provided support for Honig's case that the high school curriculum had become vapid and was not adequately preparing students for the future. Calling together various committees and task forces, drawing on the best resources available, and stimulating a statewide discussion were hallmarks of the California effort to rethink education.

To bring focus to the discussion, Honig got the debate going on how to develop education goals for California's students. Broad agreement was reached on three goals: (1) to prepare today's students for tomorrow's jobs, (2) to assist students in becoming active participants in the democratic process, and (3) to encourage students to realize fulfillment and develop sound ethical values.

Honig had managed to persuade the legislature that his version of school reform must be implemented if California's deteriorating schools were to regain their former luster. The deterioration was evidenced by declining test scores and increasing dropouts. With so many students voting with their feet, radical change was required to get them back and to restore public confidence, which had eroded as test scores fell. The radical changes undertaken represent shifts from an undemanding course of study for most students to a rich core curriculum for all students; from fragmented, piecemeal attempts at school reform to a comprehensive plan; from texts and tests that contradicted the curriculum to engaging instructional materials and tests worth teaching to; and from an emphasis on inputs to an emphasis on results and accountability.

By mobilizing the public, Honig was able to get the governor to sign an omnibus school reform bill in 1983 that linked the new reforms with increased funding for education. More important,

Honig was authorized to head up the development of model curriculum standards that would define what the substance of schooling for high school students should be.

In a kind of Manhattan Project for curriculum, the standards were pulled together in a remarkably short period of time. The committees that did this were representative of the state's diversity, and their products were closely scrutinized.

It is important to note that the legislation did not require local school districts to implement the standards, only to review their course content against the standards every three years. For this reason, critics charged that model standards would not make much difference. Seeing this effort as "the-field-of-dreams" approach, they compared those who supported standards to the man who (in the book and movie entitled *A Field of Dreams*) builds a baseball field in the middle of Iowa so that his dead father would come back. But despite such criticism, educators, representatives of the business community, policymakers, and the general public believed that standards would catalyze the revitalization of the schools—and that if they were done well they would change the landscape of California education.

The California approach to statewide school reform has been defined by James R. Smith, former deputy superintendent in the California Department of Education, as reform by leadership rather than by control (Smith, 1992). The approach worked, however, and the model standards and curriculum documents that evolved now represent a new conventional wisdom for California education. However, it did not happen overnight and it was a complex undertaking. This chapter describes the curriculum documents that served as centerpieces of the reform effort, illustrates the principle of curriculum alignment among the various elements of the education system, looks at student achievement, and offers recommendations for others pursuing similarly ambitious agendas for radical educational change.

## A NEW CONVENTIONAL WISDOM ABOUT WHAT CALIFORNIA STUDENTS SHOULD KNOW AND BE ABLE TO DO

While the model curriculum standards were designed for high schools only, they were meant to be a starting point for revamping the entire curriculum, kindergarten through grade 12. These documents set forth expectations for what students would learn at each grade level and in each course taken at the high school level. The state's curriculum frameworks were selected as the primary means to communicate a new curriculum design and recommend content to be covered.

Frameworks were a relic of legislation passed in the late 1960s. To say that these early documents were unremarked on and unremarkable is an understatement. It is reported that a department of education official, when pressed by a state legislator at a hearing, allowed that frameworks made good doorstops. However, during the Honig administration the rewritten frameworks came to be acknowledged as landmark documents in the state and attained national recognition as well. Engaging in authorized activity did provide a certain legitimacy to the new effort, especially since the frameworks had to be approved by the State Board of Education. Since the superintendent is elected and Board members are selected by the governor, this also provided an opportunity for nonpartisan cooperation and collaboration. That is exactly what happened for the first seven years of the Honig administration; unfortunately, the breakdown in cooperation that characterized the next three years sapped energy from necessary reforms.

Frameworks are approved cyclically, with a framework developed each year and updated approximately every eight years. It took the better part of the decade to develop publications for mathematics, science, history/social science, the visual and performing arts, English-language arts, foreign languages, and health and physical education. (See references at the end of this chapter for key California curriculum documents published by the California Department of Education.) The process of developing the frameworks brought teachers, other educators, business representatives, policymakers, and the public into a discussion of what California students should know and be able to do. All participants were encouraged to draw on the best from practice and research. Experts from outside California were consulted in the process, as were practitioners in each of the disciplines, such as scientists and historians. There was not total agreement but there was surprisingly widespread consensus. While the frameworks emphasized what is unique about each subject, several common themes emerged:

- *All students can achieve at high levels.* Each framework described a rich, challenging core curriculum for all students.

For example, the English-language arts framework found unacceptable the old notion of two-tiered literacy where some students were exposed to literature and engaged in meaningful communication activities while others barely read at all and were consigned to low-level skill work. The framework advocated instead that all students be engaged in a literature-based program and be able to read, write, speak, and listen effectively.

- *There is a body of knowledge that should be acquired by all students.* The frameworks were content specific and called for students to know more about mathematics, science, history, geography, literature, the arts, health, and foreign languages. The frameworks identified themes and concepts in science, significant ideas and ideals in history/social science, and examples of high-quality literary works to be read in the English-language arts program. In the arts, each student was to be exposed to the vocabulary of the disciplines of visual art, music, dance, and drama. This rich body of knowledge is designed to help students better understand the physical, ethical, political, and social worlds.

- *Less is more.* The frameworks promised both richness and depth. The old curriculum was a mile wide and an inch deep. Science was taught like a foreign language, with thousands of superficial definitions covered in one year. The new framework for science lays out carefully selected concepts to be learned in depth. The history/social science curriculum had been so shallow that teachers lamented, "Drop your pen in this class and you miss the French Revolution." The new framework recommended instead that deeper study of history and geography be achieved by more years of study and a new multiyear course organization. It was suggested that American and world history and geography be taught for six years in connected courses.

- *Thinking is emphasized.* According to the frameworks, students were to be actively engaged in a "thinking curriculum" that affords them the opportunity to build understanding and to apply what they learn in real world situations. In mathematics, students are engaged in problem-solving activities so that they are able to use reasoning skills and can communicate mathematically.

The content of the California frameworks exemplified the intellectual revolution that was taking place in the state's education system. As in the Copernican revolution, when the world view changed so did everything else. As a new conventional wisdom about what students should know and be able to do evolved, it became clear that radical changes were required in other parts of the education enterprise.

## NOW COMES THE HARD PART

Early in the process of creating standards "curriculum alignment" was the focus. This meant that curriculum, professional development, instructional resources, and assessments would be coordinated and made complementary. As Associate Superintendent of the Curriculum, Instruction and Assessment Division, I felt like a curriculum chiropractor—it was under Honig that these activities were connected at the state level for the first time in the office I administered.

While it was not easy getting agreement on high standards for students and communicating those standards through curriculum frameworks and other publications, Bill Honig steadfastly maintained that the hard part would be getting the system to work in support of the standards. The California strategy was detailed and comprehensive. It was the inspiration for what researchers now call systemic reform. The attention he brought to the substance of schooling and the invention of a coordinated approach to education reform may be Bill Honig's greatest accomplishments. For these reasons, some education historians and pundits have called him the Horace Mann of this generation. Also like Mann, critics used his wife's involvement in an education venture to attack him. Despite the legal action taken against him, Honig's place in the history of education reform is secure.

The coordinated effort he envisioned included developing accountability and assessment programs; upgrading instructional materials; providing professional development opportunities; using new technologies in all facets of running the schools; involving parents; involving the business community in new ways; and organizing the schools in ways that supported the new agenda for California schools. These activities were considered a package and work on them proceeded simultaneously. The intellectual revolution did not put the department of education at the center of the education universe. However, the department was in a unique position to, as Honig frequently said, "pull all the levers" and impact what others in the system do. The areas that were addressed in the comprehensive strategic plan had the highest payoff in terms of making radical change. The assessment program is a good example of what Honig called "strategic investments." Assessment is an expensive, big-ticket item and it yields a high payoff because tests can reinforce the vision in the curriculum frameworks. Some recommend a linear approach that proceeds accordingly: first, identify the curriculum; then decide on how to deliver the curriculum, engage in professional development, and obtain the necessary instructional resources; then change the tests or assessments. The California approach was to do everything at once. For example, work on a new assessment program began immediately so that assessments embodying the new student standards would be in place as soon as possible.

### Assessment

The assessment program in California is still evolving, but the changes to date have had a considerable impact and they send a powerful message about the seriousness of the reform. When major school reform legislation was passed in 1983, it included an expansion of the California Assessment Program (CAP). Additions and improvements to CAP that have been made in support of the curriculum reform effort include development of a grade 8 test that accurately reflects the state's new curriculum guidelines; revision of the grade 12 test to achieve coherence with the curriculum; creation of content tests in history/social science and science; direct writing assessment for students in grades 8 and 12; development of high school end-of-course Golden State examinations; and development of performance-based items to illustrate the requirements of a "thinking curriculum" that demands more problem solving and applications of learning to various situations (Alexander, 1992). The assessment program used a matrix design so that each student took a small part of a larger test. The whole test may be envisioned as a pizza with each student getting a slice. That approach allows for more of the curriculum to be examined and yields results for schools, although it cannot provide individual student scores. Assessment legislation passed in 1991 modified the levels examined in grades 4, 5, 8, and 10, called for individual scores as well as program evaluation, and continued the push for a more performance-based system.

The importance of assessment in trying to achieve radical change should not be underestimated. The state adopted a British scholar's acronym WYTIWYG—what you test is what you get. Many teachers indicated that the current tests were influencing what was taught and learned in their classrooms in ways that were contradictory to the curriculum frameworks. This is consistent with a study conducted under the auspices of the National Science Foundation that revealed that on the six commercial mathematics tests most widely administered to students, 97 percent of the questions tested only low-level conceptual knowledge and 95 percent of the questions tested only low-level thinking (Center for the Study of Testing, Evaluation and Educational Policy, 1992).

Teachers were key players in the development and administration of the new assessments. They were pleased that they knew what would be tested and felt that the new assessments were worth teaching to. The new direct writing assessment included prompts for eight types of writing, such as an "autobiographical incident," and demonstrated the positive impact that assessment can have on the instructional program. A study by the Center for the Study of Writing at Berkeley found that most teachers surveyed (78 percent) indicated that they now assign more writing than they did two years earlier (California Department of Education, 1988a). They also indicated overwhelmingly that they assigned more types of writing.

### Accountability

Assessments were no longer an obstacle to reform. Instead they came to function as incentives for teachers to use the curriculum frameworks and as cornerstones of the state's accountability system. This system is joined to the overall reform effort, and its components reflect a consensus just as curriculum frameworks do. Its aim is to provide the right information to the right audience at the right time.

In 1983, California became the first state in the nation to begin developing quality indicators. Figure 3-1 is an example of how quality indicators are reported in annual school performance reports.

**California Department of Education**
**School Performance Report Summary, 1989–90**

**School:** Sunny Valley High School
**District:** Sunny Valley Unified
**County:** Norcal
**CDS:** 12–12345–1234567

| | 1989–90 Target Percentage Met* | 1-Year Growth[1] from 1988–89 | Growth[1] from Base[2] 1987–88 | 1989–90 Relative Rank[3] |
|---|---|---|---|---|
| **Percentage of students reaching the following performance levels** | | | | |
| CAP Achievement | | | | |
| Reading—Adept and above | 37.1 | * 0.0 | −0.9 | 92 |
| Reading—Adequate and above | 80.2 | * 3.1 | 4.1 | 93 |
| Mathematics—Adept and above | 32.5 | * 1.1 | 2.1 | 53 |
| Mathematics—Adequate and above | 75.0 | * 3.4 | 2.1 | 59 |
| Direct Writing— | | | | |
| Commendable and exceptional | 32.1 | 1.0 | 1.8 | 91 |
| Adequate and better | 75.2 | * 0.0 | 1.2 | 98 |
| Curriculum | | | | |
| Geometry completion | 70.1 | * 1.2 | 2.6 | 82 |
| Four or more years of English | 95.4 | * 4.6 | 5.3 | 85 |
| A-f course enrollments | 52.0 | 0.1 | 1.7 | 72 |
| Dropout Complement (100 minus % dropping out) Three-year derived rate, weighted by four to calculate averages | 89.3 | * 1.4 | 2.3 | 70 |
| College Bound | | | | |
| A-f course completions | 48.2 | * 2.2 | 2.0 | 86 |
| Four-year college attendance | 30.1 | * 1.6 | 0.8 | 91 |
| SAT Verbal—at least 450 | 17.3 | −1.4 | 1.2 | 68 |
| SAT Mathematics—at least 500 | 25.1 | * 0.7 | 1.7 | 81 |
| Advanced placement—3 or better | 11.4 | 1.1 | 1.4 | 51 |
| AVERAGES Divide sum by 18 | 57.7 | * 1.4 | 2.0 | n/a |

| | 1990 Average Percentage | Percent Change from 1988–89 | Percent Change from Base | Relative Rank |
|---|---|---|---|---|
| School values | 57.7* | 2.5 | 3.6 | 76 |
| District values | 60.0* | 2.0 | 2.5 | 78 |
| State values | 49.3 | 1.6 | 1.9 | n/a |

*Percent change is the increase in the pool of students who met performance levels.*

*continued*

Figure 3-1
**School Performance Report Summary, 1989–90**

* Targets Met: Asterisks (*) indicate performance or growth targets were met for the quality indicators and the 1990 average percent value. Refer to the interpretive guide for details.

[1] Growth indicates the average change in the percentage of students meeting performance levels. Each positive percentage point indicates that 1 percent more students met performance levels than in the past.

[2] The base year for all indicators is 1987–88 except CAP direct writing, which is 1988–89.

[3] The relative rank is the rank a school achieved when compared to other schools with similar background factors.

Figure 3-1
**continued**

Each report also informs a community of how it compares to other schools with similar student bodies and to the performance of all schools in the state. Report content is under continuous review and new indicators are added when necessary. The state is also working on a mechanism for providing a single score that would take all the indicators into consideration and provide the equivalent of a Dow Jones average.

The accountability system also includes report cards for each school. Proposition 98, an initiative approved by California voters in 1988, requires these annual report cards, which contain data on student achievement, use of substitute teachers, dropout rates, expenditures, class size, teacher placement and evaluation, instructional materials, counseling, discipline, and quality of instruction.

Other features of the system are recognition of high achievement and identification of areas where improvement is needed. All information provided by the program informs the process of making radical changes in support of the curriculum frameworks. It affects both day-to-day and long-term planning activities at the school, district, and state levels and provides coherence and direction to other systemic reform activities.

### Instructional Materials

Like tests, the texts used by teachers greatly influence what is taught and how it is taught. The old texts were widely perceived as an impediment to implementing the recommendations contained in the curriculum frameworks. The market-sensitive nature of the textbook industry resulted in books that were dull and poorly written. By responding to the competing demands of fifty states and numerous localities, the books lacked a point of view or crisp narrative. The twenty-two textbook adoption states (in which schools may use only those books that are adopted at the state level) are thought to have a larger voice in this market than do other states. The state superintendent and State Board of Education, which has the constitutional authority to adopt K-8 materials, determined that if textbook adoption was part of the problem, the same procedure could also be used as part of the solution.

Since California textbook adoptions represent almost 12 percent of the national market, educators sought to use this clout to get better books. Toward that end, the more explicit frameworks were designed to send a clear message to publishers. In subjects where a new framework would not be ready to provide publishers sufficient preparation time, "instructional materials criteria" were prepared in advance. The state updated its legal compliance criteria in such areas as representation of men and women, ethnic groups, and the aged. The new criteria made it clear that historical accuracy and literary quality were to be taken into account when applying the criteria. In the past, the criteria list had become so expansive that publishers even worried about what foods they could mention, thinking that junk food was banned. (Actually, the criteria called for only an emphasis on nutritious foods, and this was made clear to the publishers.) Readability formulas were no longer to be used in determining appropriateness of text, as they have often been misused by publishers attempting to assure the users of textbooks that the materials could be read at a certain grade level. These formulas inhibited authors on word choice and sentence length. What California educators *did* want were materials that were linked to the frameworks and that demonstrated respect for both learners and teachers. There was a demand for books and other materials that reflected the integrity of each discipline and care about the quality of writing. Down-written, dumbed-down, and "teacher-proof" materials were on their way out. The guidelines for adoption were also designed to encourage the inclusion of new technologies. It took some time for publishers to get the message, and junior high science books were returned for rewriting in 1985 and all K-8 mathematics texts were turned down in 1986. The publishers had the opportunity to provide rewrites in mathematics, so it was a learning experience for all involved.

Real progress has been made, as evidenced by the science materials adopted in 1992. An emphasis on technology is an outstanding feature of the new materials. One of the multimedia sets of instructional materials adopted, the product of a developmental grant by the California Department of Education, uses state-of-the art technologies to teach 150 interactive lessons. In mathematics, a publisher is preparing a new high school text with lessons developed by California teachers. The battle for better instructional materials has resulted in improved classroom resources that are congruent with the state's curriculum frameworks and has provided new collaboration between educators and publishers.

## Professional Development

The most important resources are not texts and tests, but people—teachers and principals. Their professional development was and continues to be the most important investment in school reform. In California in 1983, staff development was a hodgepodge of programs and activities. Most teachers' professional-growth opportunities were limited to afterschool meetings and weekend workshops. In response to the need for dramatically different development opportunities, subject matter projects that were designed to help teachers upgrade their skills were established in each area for which there is a curriculum framework. All projects provided in-depth sessions while teachers were on breaks or vacations and support for teachers when they were back in school experimenting with the new technologies they had learned. In some subjects, teachers had the opportunity to work for a summer month in residential settings. The California Literature Project is an excellent example of how the projects work. The project followed a three-part model: first, teachers as readers, which provided teachers with the opportunity to study literature as students do; second, teachers as teachers, where teachers practiced techniques for helping a diverse student population understand what they read; and third, teachers as leaders, where teachers were encouraged to work with other teachers in order to improve instruction along the lines of the recommendations in the framework. While administered by the department and representatives of the college and university system, each project has a board with a majority of teachers who set the direction and policy for the activities.

Work is also underway to align teacher education and credentialling with curriculum frameworks. There is much to be done in this area and it seems to be taking more time, partly because teacher licensing is not a function of the California Department of Education. The goals, however, are clear: to have preservice and in-service activities seamlessly linked, to create new assessment devices to approve qualifications for teaching, and to develop new ways of assisting teachers into the profession that are like the internships and residencies for medical professionals.

Principals are key to providing the instructional leadership and support that is needed for teachers to implement the curriculum frameworks in their classrooms. Thus, a statewide system of administrator training and leadership institutes was designed to inform the work of principals and future school leaders.

## Technology

New technologies are being used to increase learning, improve administration, and enhance efforts in other areas. California now has a master plan for technology that includes its uses as a management tool and as an instructional resource. Because the focus is on helping students achieve high standards, the emphasis in the plan has been on instructional applications. Since 1984, $176 million has been invested in educational technology. All schools now have a VCR, computers are more accessible in laboratories and classrooms, and improved software that reflects the content of the frameworks is available. The last point is particularly important and illustrative of the California experience. Much early software was inadequate to help students and teachers handle the new "thinking curriculum." As well as reviewing software produced by others, the state entered into a partnership with the National Geographic Society, Lucas films, and Apple Computer to produce the highly acclaimed "GTV" (geographic television), an innovative multimedia program that teaches geographic skills in creative ways (such as "Map Rap"), and supports the state's history/social science framework.

## Parent Involvement

Parents have been involved as important partners in their childrens' education and in the statewide campaign for better schools. Curriculum frameworks were rewritten in brief booklets that explained what changes were taking place and provided suggestions for how parents could help their own children. Parents and the general public were vocal in the statewide discussion of student standards.

## Business Partnerships

New ways of working with business also brought representatives of industry to the table to set priorities for California schools and to participate in setting standards. School-business partnerships have gone far beyond the adopt-a-school approach, and important work is now being done in areas like transition from school to work and prevention of school dropouts.

## Structuring

In this multifaceted effort involving many participants, schools needed help handling new organizational demands. In California, schools did not restructure as an end in itself, but in order to support the demands of the state's high new standards. Curriculum frameworks are the starting place for restructuring efforts at the school level.

Task forces on the readiness of pupils to enter school and to move to the next higher grade level for school were appointed for the elementary, middle, and high schools. Each group issued a report that provided a blueprint for reform, taking all of the aforementioned components (such as curriculum development, professional development, accountability) and looking at how they need to be integrated at the school level. For example, the high school report, *Second to None: A Vision of the New California High School* (California Department of Education, 1992b), calls for an education plan for every student, not just the college-bound. That report details options in curriculum planning; describes how to establish a meaningful accountability and assessment system; provides information on getting additional support for all students who need it; suggests ways to restructure the school; and reviews how to advance professionalism in the process. Hundreds of schools participate in networks that use these reports as guidelines, and they provide ongoing support to each other as they work through the complex details of systemic reform.

## The Campaign

In order to market the new ideas embodied in the curriculum frameworks and to maximize involvement in helping California students achieve new high standards, statewide public information campaigns were launched. Each was tailored to a subject area and each involved public relations experts in the design. "Arts Count," "Healthy Kids/Healthy California," and the "California Reading Initiative" were multifaceted campaigns that communicated the essence of each curricular framework in ways that reached the widest possible audience. As part of the California Reading Initiative, bookmarks with tips on reading to children were issued with utility bills, supermarkets provided space for the sale of paperbacks included on the state reading test, and the Girl Scouts created a new reading badge. Public service announcements invited parents to help their children as part of a "Parents Are Teachers, Too" effort.

All activities in the complex plan support the overall commitment to helping all students achieve at the high levels described in the curriculum frameworks. Table 3-1 illustrates the depth and breadth of the statewide plan and the attempt to bring about curriculum alignment. The strategic plan draws on support from professional organizations, such as the California Reading Association (CRA), that have been enlisted to provide assistance in the process of implementing the framework. Some of the programs listed on the chart, such as the one for demonstrations, have had their activities redirected by the Department of Education so that their objectives are consistent with those in the framework. These activities together with new projects and programs such as the California Reading Initiative make up the support system for the English-language arts framework.

The state was in the unique position of being able to convene the equivalent of a statewide town meeting on what its students should know and be able to do and keep the public's attention focused on how students were performing in relation to the new standards. Further, the state was able to use existing programs in creative ways and develop new activities in support of the curriculum frameworks, and put it all together in a comprehensive, strategic plan. The California strategy recognizes that the most important work takes place in schools and classrooms and is building an infrastructure th. supports the ongoing renewal and revitalization of education.

## HOW ARE CALIFORNIA STUDENTS DOING?

As noted previously, California schools now have a clearer sense of purpose and direction, which has been widely communicated. Many innovative programs, such as the state's advanced

Table 3-1
## California Department of Education's Publications and Coordinated Activities in English-Language Arts

| Philosophical Base for all English-Language Arts Publications and Activities | Guides and Standards to Carry Out Philosophy | Implementation Documents, Projects and Activities | Evaluation, Instruments and Activities |
|---|---|---|---|
| English-Language Arts Framework, Kindergarten through Grade Twelve | English-Language Arts Model Curriculum Guide, Kindergarten through Grade Eight | Handbook for Planning an Effective Writing Program | California Assessment Program Results |
| | English-Language Arts Model Curriculum Standards: Grade Nine through Twelve | Handbook for Planning an Effective Literature Program | District Testing Programs and Locally Developed Portfolio Assessment |
| | Recommended Reading in Literature, Kindergarten through Grade Eight (unannotated and annotated editions | Practical Ideas for Teaching Writing as a Process | Program Reports for California Schools |
| | Recommended literature, Grade Nine through Twelve | Recommendations of the Curriculum Development and Supplemental Materials Commission: 1986 Adoption | Program Quality Review for Elementary Schools |
| | Secondary Textbook Review: English | Effective Language Arts Programs for Chapter 1 and Migrant Education Students | Program Quality Review for Middle Schools |
| | Recommended Reading in Spanish, Kindergarten through Grade Eight (in process) | Celebrating the National Reading Initiative | Program Quality Review for High Schools |
| | | The Changing Language Arts Curriculum: A Booklet for Parents | Western Association of Schools and Colleges/State Education Department Joint Process for Accreditation and Program Review |
| | | California Reading Initiative | |
| | | National Reading Initiative | |
| | | CDE-sponsored Workshop and Conference | |
| | | California Literature Project | |
| | | California Writing Project | |

*continued on page 46*

Table 3-1
**continued**

| Philosophical Base for all English-Language Arts Publications and Activities | Guides and Standards to Carry Out Philosophy | Implementation Documents, Projects and Activities | Evaluation, Instruments and Activities |
| --- | --- | --- | --- |
| | | California School Leadership Academy | |
| | | California Technology Project | |
| | | Categorical Programs | |
| | | Miller-Unruh Reading Programs | |
| | | Demonstration School Project (Middle School/Junior High) | |
| | | Language Arts/ Mathematics Technology Programs (i.e., Model Technology Schools) | |
| | | Instructional Television/ Literature-based Programs | |
| | | California Instructional Video Clearinghouse | |
| | | California Software Clearinghouse | |
| | | CATE, CRA, CMLEA CABLE, and CATESOL Conferences | |
| | | County Office-sponsored Conference | |
| | | CDE Staff Development Unit and Its Programs | |
| | | Preservice Programs in College and Universities | |

accountability and assessment systems, are gaining acceptance. Still, the proof is in the product, and what inquiring minds really want to know is, How are the students doing? Here are some early results at the high school level:

- High school seniors demonstrated gains of 0.6 of a year in reading and 1.25 years in mathematics from 1984 to 1990 on the California Assessment Program (CAP).
- On Scholastic Aptitude Tests (SATs), the mean scores for all racial and ethnic groups have improved in mathematics. The average mathematics score is now above the national average, although the average verbal score is still below the national average.
- The number of students who passed challenging Advanced Placement (AP) exams grew by 179 percent from 1984 to 1991—almost double the national average.
- An additional 17,134 seniors, or 33 percent of the student population, completed the rigorous coursework required for admission to the University of California.

While the results are encouraging, much still needs to be done. For example, gaps in achievement between racial and ethnic groups remain unacceptably wide.

Administration of the state tests was cancelled in 1991 due to a veto by the governor. This may have been the biggest blow yet to school reform in the state, as it retarded development of better assessments, took the spotlight off the reform effort, created a "hole" in the data that can never be filled, and sent the wrong message to the public. The test was administered again in 1992 to eighth graders and the scores in all areas were flat or down that year. The results are still being analyzed, and some educators think that not giving the test the previous year contributed to the decline. Of course, other factors such as students' language background are being looked at. This demonstrates the importance of having assessments that are aligned to the curriculum so that conclusions can be reached on factors contributing to student achievement.

## RECOMMENDATIONS FOR RADICAL CHANGE

For almost a decade, California has been engaged in an effort to change its schools radically. While there is still much to do and the state's fiscal crisis has slowed progress, some lessons can be learned from the California education revolution:

1. Start with a vision of what students should know and be able to do. This is accomplished in California through curriculum frameworks, and these documents have become the foundation for all reform efforts. While it was unthinkable ten years ago, national standards in all subjects will be available by the mid-1990s. States like California have provided the laboratory to demonstrate the efficacy of standards-setting for guiding systemic reform. The vision of what California students should know and be able to do is a dynamic one that can accommodate new national standards and other developments as the curriculum frameworks are updated cyclically.

2. Develop a comprehensive strategic plan for change. Efforts in the past were too fragmented. Obviously, when texts and tests contradict rather than complement the curriculum, student progress will be impeded. Pushing as many levers for change as possible will make a difference.

3. Encourage autonomy at the local level. Once standards are in place, press accountability for results but do not mandate "how to's." Teachers and principals in consultation with the local community are in the best position to run particular schools. Intervention should include technical assistance and deregulation so that those closest to the students can do what needs to be done.

4. Give it time. Radical change does not happen overnight. A commitment needs to be made to a sustained effort that is multifaceted and inclusive.

5. Be flexible. Evaluate what works and what does not. Remember that radical change does not mean only doing different things; it can also mean using existing programs and resources in new ways. The process is dynamic, not static. Adjustments will have to be made so that momentum is maintained.

6. Communicate results. To maintain public support, it is

important to celebrate success and to let the public know that corrections will be made when necessary.

Revolutions, even quiet intellectual ones, are extremely complex and difficult undertakings. In California, no one announced, "Let's have a revolution," yet one came about as all those concerned about the state's education system agreed that radical changes would have to be made if all students were to achieve at a higher level. Just as the world view changed following the Copernican revolution, a deeply held belief that all students can benefit from and must have access to a rich core curriculum now influences the entire educational enterprise in California.

## REFERENCES

Alexander, Francie. "Accountability and Assessment California Style." In *Education Reform in the 90s*, edited by Chester E. Finn, Jr., and Theodore Rebarber. New York: Macmillan, 1992.

Boyer, Ernest L. *High School*. New York: Harper and Row, 1982.

California Department of Education. *Raising Expectations: Model Graduation Requirements*. Sacramento: California Department of Education, 1983.

California Department of Education. "Impact of the CAP Writing Assessment on Instruction and Curriculum: A Preliminary Summary of Results of a Statewide Study by the National Center for the Study of Writing" (Draft). Sacramento: California Department of Education, 1988a.

California Department of Education. *History-Social Science Framework for California Public Schools*. Sacramento: California Department of Education, 1988b.

California Department of Education. *English-Language Arts Framework for California Public Schools*. Sacramento: California Department of Education, 1989a.

California Department of Education. *Foreign Language Framework for California Public Schools*. Sacramento: California Department of Education, 1989b.

California Department of Education. *Visual and Performing Arts Framework for California Public Schools*. Sacramento: California Department of Education, 1989c.

California Department of Education. *Science Framework for California Public Schools*. Sacramento: California Department of Education, 1990.

California Department of Education. *Mathematics Framework for California Public Schools*. Sacramento: California Department of Education, 1992a.

California Department of Education. *Second to None: A Vision of the New California High School*. Sacramento: California Department of Education, 1992b.

Center for the Study of Testing, Evaluation, and Educational Policy. *The Influence of Testing on Teaching Mathematics and Science*. Boston: Center for the Study of Testing, Evaluation, and Educational Policy, Boston College, 1992.

Hirsch, E. D. *Cultural Literacy*. New York: Vintage Books, 1988.

Kuhn, Thomas. *The Structure of Scientific Revolutions.* Chicago: University of
    Chicago Press, 1962, 1970.
Ravitch, Diane. *The Troubled Crusade.* New York: Basic Books, 1984.
Smith, James R. *Leadership versus Control: A Strategic Approach to Lasting School
    Reform.* Washington, D.C.: Council of Chief State School Officers, 1992.

# 4

# Wild Card Educational Reform in Kentucky

## Betty E. Steffy and Fenwick W. English

One of the most popular songs in Japan in the 1990s was Stephen Foster's "My Old Kentucky Home" (Stroud, 1992, p. A1). While Toyota made the Bluegrass State its manufacturing base for the popular Camry automobile, Kentucky exported nearly two million barrels of bourbon to Nippon.

Japanese investment in "Kentakky" (Kentucky in Japanese) accounted for seventy-five manufacturing plants, fifty-five of them auto-centered and twenty more that produce an array of items from vacuum cleaners to feed additives. The total aggregation accounts for more than twenty-two thousand jobs across the commonwealth, from Fulton in the west to Ashland in the east.

The Japanese connection comes as a surprise to Americans who view Kentucky as the land of Ma and Pa Kettle, country bumpkin stereotypes sitting on broken-down front porches with their long mountain rifles, waiting for the "revenoorers" to close down their illegal stills.

Actually some of those folks are still around in the foothills, and Kentucky's politics remain squarely in the nineteenth century, at least as far as operating their public schools are concerned. This strange push-pull, exporting bourbon to Japan and

51

manufacturing one of the most popular autos in the United States with at least 80 percent native Kentuckians as the work force, produced the groundwork for the enactment in 1990 of the nation's most radical educational reform package of recent times (Steffy, 1993). That initiative was a "shot across the bow" for all of the United States and its struggling public schools, some of the best and worst of which can be found in Kentucky.

We will examine the Kentucky Educational Reform Act (KERA) as a one-group pretest-posttest snapshot, using Campbell and Stanley's (1963) classic design terminology, for the straightforward reason that no other educational "treatments" come anywhere close to the radical nature of Kentucky's; and Kentucky's educational-political problems are unlike those found anywhere else in the nation. The analysis may help to fill out the picture of diversity and complexity that make up American education. It will also enable those interested in reform of public schools to grasp the ingenuity of Kentucky's reformers in understanding some of the subtle qualities that have escaped other less sweeping mandates, as well as in coming to grips with the most difficult lesson of all to master in improving American public education: there can be no educational reform without political reform.

## MAIN ELEMENTS OF KERA

The Kentucky Education Reform Act is built on three main principles: (1) all children can learn, most of them at high levels; (2) instructional strategies to enable teachers to attain high levels of student achievement are known; and (3) what children learn should be relatively consistent across the state. To achieve these principles, the law dictates new governance and funding provisions. As depicted in Figure 4-1, these provisions are not ends, but are means to enable programmatic initiatives embodied in KERA to dramatically improve the quality of education for each student in the state. The goal is "world-class standards" for every school and high levels of demonstrated competence for every student. To ensure attainment of that goal, student performance outcomes have been identified and linked to performance assessment measures; an accountability system of school sanctions and rewards has been put in place; and teacher involvement in instructional decision making has been mandated through the formation of school councils. In addition, new state

Figure 4-1
The Kentucky Education Reform Act of 1990

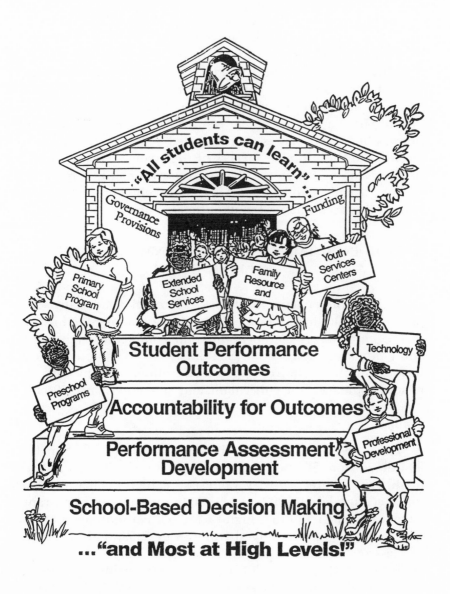

*Source*: The Prichard Committee
The Partnership for Kentucky School Reform
Lexington, KY

categorical programs have been established for professional development, preschool, technology, increased instructional time, and family and parent support.

In fulfilling the KERA mandate, schools will be judged on each student's ability to demonstrate high levels of achievement on six broad learning goals and to make a successful transition from high school to adulthood. The measure of the effectiveness of the system has shifted from course requirements and time in class to what students know and are able to do. The individual components of the reform cannot be viewed as separate; rather, each part is an integrated subset of the whole and essential to the ultimate success of the system. This comprehensive legislation recognizes that state government, communities, parents, teachers, and students are all stakeholders in the process and all are accountable for its ultimate success.

## THE INDICTMENT: MY OLD KENTUCKY HOME IS FALLING DOWN

Prior to the enactment of KERA, Kentucky had many serious problems, including a history of ranking last among the fifty states in the percentages of the population completing eighth grade and graduating high school (Sexton, 1992–93). Among the other serious problems confronting the educational system were those relating to finance, the curriculum, and local governance of schools.

### Finance

Local revenue supporting the education of children in 1989–90 ranged from $80 per pupil in property-poor districts to $3,716 in districts where property values were high (Office of Education Accountability, 1992, p. 11). State revenue per pupil ranged from a low of $1,750 to a high of $2,753. Per-pupil expenditures for teaching supplies ranged from $8 to $259, and the number of classroom teachers per 1,000 students ranged from 49.5 to 84.7. The total state and local revenue supporting education for 569,454 students in Kentucky in 1989–90 was $2,045,770,000 (Office of Education Accountability, 1992, p. 41). By 1991–92, that figure had increased by $711,459,000.

## Curriculum

Before KERA, the educational program in most schools in the commonwealth could be described as traditional. Students entered a half-day kindergarten at age five. Beginning in first grade, letter grades were given on most student report cards. The Comprehensive Test of Basic Skills was required by the state, which paid the costs of administering and scoring it. District scores were ranked by the press from highest to lowest and published in local newspapers. Grade retention was common. By the time students reached fourth grade, 20 percent of them had been retained. Of one hundred first graders entering Kentucky schools in 1975, only sixty-three completed high school. Of that number, thirty-two were college bound, with twenty-eight attending Kentucky colleges. By 1991, eleven had graduated from a Kentucky college and four were still in college (Kentucky Department of Education, 1992[b], p. 7).

The curriculum in most schools was textbook-driven, with textbooks selected from an approved state list. The state mandated the amount of instructional time per content area and monitored district compliance through an accreditation process. Accreditation standards dealt with ensuring that districts had the required number of books in the library and did not exceed class-size limits. State funds for teachers were distributed based on units (number of classes). Districts wishing to provide additional staff beyond the state unit reimbursement had to pay for them out of local funds. Consequently, districts with a low tax base or low tax structure did not staff beyond the state unit allocation.

## Governance

School administration was also traditional. Positions within districts were commonly not advertised. During the 1988–89 school year, the State Board for Elementary and Secondary Education passed a regulation requiring districts to have a listing of job openings available to the public at their central offices. It was not unusual for a local district superintendency to change after a board election. With five school board members, the election of just one new member could change a "three-two" board to a "two-three" balance. In many counties, the school district was the largest employer.

*Districts Seek Equity*

In November 1985, a group of sixty-six school districts, seven boards of education, and twenty-two public school students formed a corporation called the Council for Better Education, Inc., and filed suit in Franklin County Circuit Court challenging the equity and adequacy of the state's funding system for education (Miller, Noland, and Schaaf, 1991). Since this was a class-action suit, it could have been filed in any number of counties. Franklin County was chosen because the state capital is located there and because Ray Corns, Franklin County Circuit Court Judge, was perceived to be familiar with the circumstances of property-poor districts in Kentucky (Steffy, 1992).

The defendants named in the suit were the governor, superintendent of public instruction, treasurer, president pro tem of the senate, speaker of the house of representatives, and State Board for Elementary and Secondary Education. Positions rather than people were named as defendants because the Council felt that litigation of the case might exceed the term of office of persons filling these positions. This proved an accurate assumption. By the time the court judgment was issued in October 1988, one of the plaintiffs, John Brock, was the newly elected state superintendent of public instruction.

Former governor Bert Combs was selected as attorney for the Council. Since serving as governor, he had maintained an active role in state education initiatives. He was also quite familiar with the inequalities in funding education in the state.

Kentucky's constitution states that "The General Assembly shall, by appropriate legislation, provide for an efficient system of common schools throughout the state." In rendering his decision, Judge Corns stated that "the General Assembly had failed to provide an efficient system of common schools, and that the system of school financing was inefficient, in the constitutional sense, and discriminatory" (Miller, Noland, and Schaaf, 1991, p. 4) He further ruled that a new system for financing schools must be developed by the General Assembly.

The case was appealed to the Kentucky Supreme Court. In rendering its opinion in June 1989, the high court held that the entire system of common schools in Kentucky was unconstitutional and ordered the General Assembly to create an "efficient system." The court specified that this new system would be the sole responsibility of the legislature, available to all Kentucky children and substantially uniform throughout the state. Further, the court held that the new system should provide for equal educational opportunity, be monitored by the General Assembly, and operate with sufficient funding. Finally, the court stated that this equitable educational system was a basic constitutional right (Miller, Noland, and Schaaf, 1991, pp. 4–5). The court said, "This decision applies to the entire sweep of the system— all its parts and parcels. This decision applies to all the statutes creating, implementing, and financing the system and to all regulations, etc., pertaining thereto" (*Rose vs. Council for Basic Education, Inc.*, 1989).

## General Assembly Responds

In response to the Kentucky Supreme Court decision, the General Assembly appointed a Task Force on Education Reform in July 1989. It was composed of twenty-one members representing the leadership of the house, the senate, and the governor's office. The Task Force formed subcommittees on curriculum, finance, and governance. Each subcommittee hired an educational consultant to assist it. The General Assembly was charged with completing the redesign of the education system by the end of its next general session, which was due to convene in January 1990. However, due to the short time line, many felt the governor would convene a special session on education after the close of the regular session. When the governor announced there would be no special session on education, it was clear the legislation had to be introduced during the regular session. The Task Force approved its final report on March 7, 1990. Within a few hours, House Bill 940 was introduced. During debates in the house and senate many amendments were introduced. By the time the 950-page bill was passed, language connected to some of the hotly debated amendments was unclear. Everyone had to wait until the final bill was published to be sure what it said. The budget bill to support enactment of the reform included additional clarifying language. In order to completely understand the intent of the legislature, a review of both bills was required. On April 11, 1990, Governor Wallace G. Wilkinson signed the Kentucky Education Reform Act. It became law on July 13, 1990 (Miller, Noland, and Schaaf, 1991, p. 7).

## COMING INTO FOCUS: POSTTEST SNAPSHOT

### Six-Year Implementation Process

By January 1993, all of the finance, governance, and curriculum initiatives were in the initial stages of implementation.

Yet full implementation of KERA was still three years away. During the 1995–96 school year, two programs currently in the initial stages of implementation will be completed. The state's new performance assessment system, designed to measure student achievement on "international standards," will be fully implemented by the State Board for Elementary and Secondary Education. By July 1996, nearly all 1,366 schools in the state will be operating with school councils statutorily empowered to make policy decisions in critical curriculum areas. With the assessment system in place, and most schools operating with school councils, the last components of the Kentucky Education Reform Act will be completed.

### Finance

At the beginning of the 1992–93 school year, the SEEK (Support Education Excellence in Kentucky) formula was entering its third year. This distribution formula provides a minimum level of state support for each student. In addition to the SEEK formula, the state provides categorical funding in selected programmatic areas such as preschool programs, professional development, extended school services, and technology. By 1992, the SEEK formula was fully funded by the state. To achieve full funding and support the new KERA programs, the 1990 General Assembly passed the largest tax increase the state had ever known, increasing the biennial budget from approximately $1.2 billion in 1988–90 to approximately $2.1 billion for 1990–92. Local districts were required to levy a minimum equivalent tax rate of 30 cents per $100 of assessed property value. In addition, property-poor districts were given an option of generating additional money by increasing local taxes. Because of the new funding formula, the local options, and local tax increases, the combined state and local revenue increased 34.8 percent between the 1989–90 and the 1991–92 school year (Office of Education Accountability, 1992, p. 41).

It was not unusual for a property-poor district to experience a 50 percent increase in funds between the 1989–90 and the

1991–92 school years. More-affluent districts in the state experienced increases in the range of 15 to 18 percent. Analysis of the funding equity over the first two years indicated that the formula was working. Since it was designed to be implemented over a four-year period, it is still too early to tell whether the large influx of new money to poor districts will result in improved student achievement. Over the first two years of increased funding, however, teacher salaries in the state increased by an average of 16 percent (Office of Education Accountability, 1992, p. 44), placing Kentucky teachers twenty-ninth in the nation in teacher pay. If one measure of KERA's success is movement toward equal funding per student across the state, then success is being achieved. However, funding equity per se is not a measure of equity in educational opportunity. The state has yet to define education equity beyond equal dollars per student.

## Curriculum

By January 1993, the programmatic initiatives embodied in KERA were all being implemented. The technology program was just beginning. Others, such as the new primary program, school-based decision making, teaching to "big ideas," and authentic assessment, were starting to affect classrooms.

The new state performance assessment system began with the assessment of approximately 140,000 students in grades 4, 8, and 12 during the 1991–92 school year (Office of Education Accountability, 1992, p. 1). Results indicated that approximately 90 percent of those students tested performed below the new state standards. The state assessment system is made up of three types of student assessment: portfolio review, small-group problem solving, and open-ended responses to problems. Based on the results of the assessments, students are designated to be at one of four levels: novice, apprentice, proficient, and distinguished. Over a twenty-year period, each school in a district is expected to have all its students reach the proficient or distinguished level, yet only about 10 percent of the students tested in the spring of 1992 achieved scores at those levels (Kentucky Department of Education, 1992[a], p. 5–12).

The four descriptors of student performance used in Kentucky's assessment system are similar to those used in the National Assessment of Educational Progress (NAEP): below basic, basic, proficient, and advanced. Like the Kentucky assessment, the NAEP is administered at grades 4, 8, and 12. Kentucky eighth graders took the NAEP mathematics assessment in 1990. Of those tested, 89.5 percent scored at the basic or below-basic level (Kentucky Department of Education, 1992[a], p. 5–12). Kentucky's students' results on the NAEP and on its new state assessment system were almost identical.

State assessment results were calculated for each school where students were tested. These results are being used to determine an accountability index for each school in the state. The formula currently being used is an interim one, since the entire performance assessment system, made up of both cognitive and noncognitive indicators, will not be complete until 1996.

By 1996, the cognitive assessment system will measure student performance on six state curriculum goals. These six goals have been used to define seventy-five "valued outcomes" describing what students should know and be able to do when they graduate from high school. Presently, the cognitive assessment system assesses student performance on twenty-nine of those seventy-five outcomes. Over the next three years, it will incorporate all of them. (See Steffy, 1993, for a detailed description of the assessment system.) Noncognitive indicators include attendance, retention, reduction of barriers to learning, dropout rates, and successful transition to work or college after high school.

A school's accountability index is determined by averaging students' scores in reading, writing, social studies, science, and a combined score for the noncognitive indicators. The accountability index becomes the starting point for improving student achievement for each school. Every two years, schools will be given new targets for student achievement, called *thresholds*. Schools that exceed their threshold could qualify for financial rewards. Those that fail to meet their accountability index will be labeled "schools in crisis" and receive assistance from the State Department of Education.

Linking Kentucky's system of school sanctions and rewards to an emerging system for assessing performance, one that will change over time, seems questionable, given the limited evidence of the reliability and validity of the new tests (Office of Education Accountability, 1992, pp. 61–75). A recent study conducted by the Rand Corporation found that the "rater reliability" in scoring portfolios in Vermont was very low (Rothman, 1992, p. 1). Vermont was the first state to require portfolio assessment as part of the state assessment system. While many other states are developing authentic assessment measures to be included as part of their state assessment system, none has linked this assessment system to school scores and sanctions and rewards in the same way that Kentucky has.

## Programs to Create Success-Oriented Learning Environments

Several KERA programmatic initiatives are directed at strengthening the relationship between family and school and providing children with a success-oriented school experience during the primary years. These include a preschool program; a fundamentally different primary school; a program designed to provide additional instructional time, called the Extended School Services program (ESS); and a program to link community social services and educational services, entitled Family Resource/Youth Services Centers (FR/YSC).

*Preschool Programs.* All 176 school districts in the state are in their second or third year of implementing a preschool program for four-year-old students who qualify for free lunch, and for three- and four-year-old children identified to receive special services. Over 130 districts started this program within six months after KERA was passed. Working cooperatively with Head Start and day-care providers, these programs are currently serving approximately 80 percent of the income-eligible children in the state and 60 percent of three- and four-year-olds with disabilities (Office of Education Accountability, 1992, p. 120).

The preschool program has been one of the best-received KERA programs. There have been frequent suggestions that the program should be expanded to include all students considered at-risk, not just those who qualify for free lunch.

*Primary Program.* All districts in the state are required to "fully implement" the new primary program, based on the whole language approach and thematic units, by the beginning of the 1993–94 school year. The primary program replaces kindergarten through third grade. Each district was required to submit a plan to the State Department of Education before the end of the 1991–92 school year, outlining how it planned to achieve full implementation. The 1992 General Assembly mandated that all primary programs include seven critical attributes: developmentally appropriate educational practices, multiage/multiability classrooms, continuous progress, authentic assessment, qualitative reporting methods, professional teamwork, and positive parent involvement. Shortly after KERA was enacted, fourteen elementary schools volunteered to pilot the program. At the beginning of 1993, 830 schools were implementing action plans for primary school. But teachers across the state are beginning to register concerns about the program. Many of these concerns relate to the integration of half-day kindergarten children into the program and the requirement for multiage grouping. These concerns led the State Department of Education to establish new guidelines that permit kindergarten students to be excluded from the primary program for the first semester of school and limit the amount of time that three age levels of children can be grouped together.

A study commissioned by the Prichard Committee in the spring of 1992 found that (1) the inclusion of kindergarten in the program was the most significant problem and posed a "serious impediment to the learning of older pupils in the group"; (2) teachers did not have common planning time; (3) parents did not understand the new reporting systems that did not use grades; (4) teachers were attempting to implement many of the attributes of the program; and (5) overall, teachers' attitudes toward the program were mixed (Office of Education Accountability, 1992, pp. 157–158). The Office of Education Accountability (OEA), an agency created by KERA to monitor the implementation of reform, recommended that during the 1992–93 school year the Kentucky Department of Education was to provide more support through the state's eight regional service centers, mount a massive public relations effort, clarify the kindergarten issue, and improve collaboration between the Primary Branch and the Office of Assessment and Accountability in the Kentucky Department of Education. The 1992–93 school year was a critical year for implementation of this program. If vexing issues were not resolved, teachers would likely begin to contact their legislators regarding their concerns, which could lead to support for modifying this program during the 1994 general session.

***Extended School Services.*** Funds supporting the Extended School Services program enabled students to attend summer school and receive additional instruction outside the regular school day. Over 116,000 of the state's 574,000 students participated in this program during the spring and summer of 1992 (Office of Education Accountability, 1992, p. 89). The program was designed to "assure that students who needed additional time to achieve expected outcomes would receive it" (p. 90). State department records indicated that 84 of the 176 districts in the state used the money to support summer school programs in addition to programs that operated beyond the regular school day (p. 96). Evaluation of the program indicated that about 40 percent of the participating students improved by one or more grades, 30 percent maintained their performance, and 11 percent dropped out. Student performance data were not provided for 19 percent of the students. The highest percentages of student involvement in the program were at grades 4, 5, 6, and 9. Since the program takes place after school, attendance is voluntary, although the 1992 General Assembly passed legislation that enabled local district boards to mandate attendance. Questions have been raised regarding both the legality and the authority of local boards to require attendance in this program. This issue is currently under study. The high cost of providing transportation for students who participated in this program had also become an issue. With only 40 percent of students in the program improving their grades, its effectiveness was questioned.

*Family Resource/Youth Services Centers Program.* Schools eligible for the Family Resource/Youth Services Centers program must have 20 percent of their student population qualifying for free lunch. Initially, it was estimated that approximately 500 schools in the state would qualify for this program. Actually, over 1,000 of the 1,366 schools in the state were eligible. Family Resource Centers were designed to serve elementary students and provide the following core services: assistance with full-time preschool for children ages two and three; assistance with after-school care for children ages four through twelve; health and education services for new and expectant parents; education to enhance parenting skills; support and training for child care providers; and health services or referral to health services.

Youth Services Centers serving secondary students were designed to provide referrals to social services; health services or referral to health services; employment counseling; summer and part-time job development; substance abuse services or referrals; and family crisis and mental health services. This program was designed to be phased in over a five-year period. As the third-year implementation began, 222 centers were serving 414 of the eligible schools (Office of Education Accountability, 1992, p. 3).

Implementation of these four programs is proceeding on schedule. Three of them—preschool, Extended School Services, and Family Resource/Youth Services Centers—have been well received by districts. Because of the requirements for multiage grouping, inclusion of half-day kindergarten students, and full implementation by fall of 1993, the primary program has generated a lot of frustration on the part of teachers, administrators, and parents. Full implementation of these four programs was meant to assure that each student entering the fourth grade would demonstrate a high level of competence and would be supported by parents who provided a positive learning environment. To date, these expectations have not been achieved.

## Technology Program Delayed

Another key initiative included in KERA was the establishment of an administrative and instructional technology program. One element was to be the development of a computer network to link each school district with the State Department of Education. This network would be used to establish common accounting and reporting procedures among the districts in the state. It was projected to be in place by August 1991.

The entire technology program has been hampered by the inability of the State Department of Education and the Legislative Research Commission to agree on the components of the plan and how professional development is to be financed. The statute requires approval of a five-year Master Plan for Technology by the State Board for Elementary and Secondary Education after the plan has been approved by the Legislative Research Commission (LRC) (Office of Education Accountability, 1992, p. 2). The LRC is a legislative committee made up of sixteen members of the majority and minority leadership of the house and senate. It constitutes the administrative office of the Kentucky General Assembly. Although the initial plan was submitted to LRC in January 1991, final approval was delayed until May 1992 because of the inability of the department and the legislative committee to agree, first, on the design of the plan and, second, on the source of funds for staff development. The controversy eventually resulted in the resignation of the associate commissioner for technology in December 1992 (Lucke, 1992[a]). When fully developed, the administrative and instructional technology program, supported by $400 million, should include video and computer systems, software and hardware, and multiple delivery systems.

## Governance

Shifts in governance included the establishment of the Education Professional Standards Board (EPSB) to deal with teacher training and certification, reorganization of the Kentucky Department of Education, elimination of the elected state superintendent position and the installation of an appointed commissioner of education, antinepotism provisions for school boards and administrators, and mandating formation of school councils. With these provisions in place, local boards lost the ability to hire; this function was shifted to the local superintendent. In addition, school board members were prohibited from running for the board if a relative was employed by the school district. School principals could not have relatives working in their school. Superintendents were prohibited from hiring their relatives or those of school board members. "Relative" was defined as father, mother, brother, sister, husband, wife, son, daughter, aunt, uncle, son-in-law, and daughter-in-law. Local boards hiring a new superintendent were required to involve citizens and teachers in selection of the final candidates. Boards could not terminate the superintendent's contract without approval of the state commissioner of education.

Of these provisions, the one with the greatest impact on education governance was that calling for the establishment of school-based councils. KERA made individual school councils directly accountable for improving student achievement. At the beginning of the 1992–93 school year, approximately 500 such councils were in place (Office of Education Accountability, 1992, p. 5). Every district was required to have at least one school operating with a council by June 1991. School councils were formed when two-thirds of the faculty voted to form them. By June 1991, forty of the 176 districts in the state did not yet have a single school council. In these cases, the local board selected the school to have a council. School councils are composed of three teachers, two parents, and the principal, who serves as chair of the council. School councils have policy-setting responsibility in key curriculum and program areas, such as the selection of materials, assignment of students, use of school time and space, and the choice of specific content to achieve the state curriculum goals.

School councils have wide latitude in determining how each school will improve student learning.

## Professional Development

In order to support the massive changes required by KERA, a comprehensive professional development system was funded that is designed to provide teachers, principals, and superintendents with the necessary knowledge and skills to carry out the reforms. Professional development for teachers was funded during the 1990–91 school year with $1 per student, which was increased to $5 per student during 1991–92, and to $16 for 1992–93 and 1993–94. Eight regional service centers assist local districts in designing comprehensive professional development activities. The normal school calendar in Kentucky has four professional development days. During the 1992–93 and 1993–94 school years, districts could use up to five additional instructional days for professional development (Office of Education Accountability, 1992, p. 162). By the time KERA is fully implemented at the end of the 1995–96 school year, districts could have a total of thirty-four days each year for professional development.

## THE EMERGING PICTURE

### The Centrality of Political/Governance Issues

There can be no real educational reform without political reform. The greatest of Kentucky's education problems stems not from lack of technology, poor teachers, inept administrators, or the lack of relevant curricula, although there is evidence of all these across the commonwealth. The real problem has been that in the rural and Appalachian areas, schools are a remnant of a brand of politics and control that decides who is employed and who is not. County political machines depend on board of education positions for patronage jobs. This provides opportunities for graft—whole families can dominate access to the schools by controlling who is hired for salaried positions in classrooms and as school bus drivers, custodians, secretaries and clerks, and even school maintenance suppliers.

In the past, these school systems were largely nepotistic, placing relatives and cronies in positions of power. They used no-bid contracts and awards to disperse the spoils of that power.

A pervasive problem in the hundreds of small coal towns that dot Kentucky's Cumberland Plateau was the attitude of the miners toward outsiders and toward life in general (Offutt, 1992). The coal companies strove to isolate the miners, attaching fees to their meager wages for housing, medical attention, and even burials. There was no need to look outside the "hollers." A "live today because we might die tomorrow" attitude worked against the cause of good education. There was little evident need for schooling when death came so frequently.

The greatest corruption has been in school districts of the Cumberland Plateau. For example, one Appalachian superintendent was indicted for failure to exercise proper fiscal controls when he placed $1.1 million in non-interest-bearing bank accounts (Mueller, 1992, p. B8). As a result, the district lost from $70,000 to $80,000 in interest. An investigation found that the bank was owned in part by the Kentucky House of Representatives majority floor leader, a person who had championed education reform in Kentucky. The floor leader's extended family is one of the dominant forces in Eastern Kentucky. One elementary school in the region bears the family name, and members of the extended family work in it (see also Bishop, 1992, p. F1).

In another chronically troubled school district, the superintendent and five board members were charged with awarding a no-bid contract for construction of a high school field house, giving raises to the superintendent's wife and brother-in-law without reporting them, and skirting bidding laws in contracting for $8,136 for musical instruments (Lucke, 1991, p. A1–A12).

In this same school district, a $1.3 million account was discovered in a bank over one hundred miles from the school district. This account was inappropriately labeled "construction" instead of "general fund." Few people knew of its existence. After finding this money, the state canceled a bond sale because the "found money" pushed the district's reserves to over 10 percent of the annual budget, an amount considered excessive in lean financial times. The chairman of the state school board committee overseeing operations in this district commented, "What I don't understand is how there could not have been a clear money trail within the records. . . . That kind of money should never be a matter of surprise to discover it's on hand. You have to wonder why there was no clear record" (Lucke, 1992[b], p. B2).

The record of public corruption in some of Kentucky's school systems was not dealt with directly in the educational reform law. However, four indirect provisions stand out. The first was outlawing nepotism by prohibiting board members from serving if relatives are employed in their school systems. Yet, some board members have defied this provision, which prompted the state attorney general's office to consider how to deal with them in December 1992, some thirty months after enactment of the law.

The second thrust was to remove all hiring power from elected school boards, save for the superintendent. This adjustment, however, simply removed a board from directly hiring personnel. If enough pressure can be brought to bear on the superintendent to cause him or her to fear that noncompliance will jeopardize his or her re-employment, board patronage can still prevail. Since the enactment of KERA, over 50 of the state's 176 districts have replaced the superintendent (Office of Education Accountability, 1992, p. 192).

The third thrust was to establish the Office of Education Accountability (OEA) to conduct independent investigations of misconduct and fraud in school systems, and to monitor the implementation of reform. The OEA reports directly to the legislature, whose members represent the epitome of patronage from the same political system that controls the schools. A 1992 FBI investigation of the Kentucky legislature included a sting operation to uncover influence peddling for intertrack betting on horse races. The investigation brought down the speaker of the house, an influential backer of educational reform (see Jordan, Wagar, and Estep, 1992). Just how far the Office of Education Accountability will be permitted to delve into real Kentucky politics remains conjectural.

The fourth thrust was to limit contributions to board member campaigns to $100 from individuals and $200 from political action committees. Board candidates were not permitted to solicit money or services from school employees.

Despite these features, it must be said that KERA has only nibbled at the edges of Kentucky politics. It did not outlaw or even curb student fundraising to pay for fixing school roofs or using magazine drives and candy sales to purchase school supplies. Kentucky's schools are littered with junk food and soda machines, even in the principals' offices. Profits are used to support educational programs and student activities. KERA did not take the schools out of partisan politics. It did not remove the schools from the spoils system, although it attempted to curb certain excesses.

The problem is one not only of reform in governance, but also of economic development by which alternative sources of jobs are created in areas where the schools, and what is left of the mines and fields, remain the principal source of employment. Education is part of the cycle of poverty and politics. Poverty, illiteracy, and cultural insulation work to keep business out, and as a result reinforce the political system that feeds on them. Kentucky's schools cannot produce high-quality graduates. Businesses of the twenty-first century require a trained workforce that is well enough educated to keep learning new skills as technology improves (Holusha, 1992, p. C5). Graduates do not have the skills to get these jobs, and such jobs do not exist in these geographical areas anyway. A kind of "chicken-egg," either/or scenario is the result. Which comes first, new jobs that require new skills or graduates with new skills that will make them employable by prospective new companies?

To partly fund KERA, reformers recognized that changes were required in the state's system for collecting property taxes. The new law requires that all property be assessed at open market value. The ensuing clash at the county level, where taxes are paid, has produced some bizarre results. In the state's largest county, the tax assessor took property assessed at $87 million off the rolls in 1987 for friends and business associates. Four years later, even after state investigations, $56.4 million was still not being assessed. In many counties, it is impossible to trace the methods used for determining the rate of assessments.

The state's agency in charge of tax collections, called the Revenue Cabinet, declared an emergency in twenty-five counties where tax assessment practices were in disarray. In many of these counties, the delinquency rate was near 20 percent (Wagar, 1992).

The massive transfusion of previously unimagined sums of money into public education has severely challenged the old premise that more money alone would really improve public education. In three county school districts where the State Board for Elementary and Secondary Education has taken action to remove the superintendent from office, new money from state and local sources has increased the local school budget by more than 40 percent during the first two years of reform (Office of Education Accountability, 1992, pp. 232–233). The public has become restless and impatient for results, "proof that their tax investment is paying off," because "the political clock runs faster than real time" (Sexton, 1992–93, p. 2).

## Issues of State Leadership

KERA downgraded the old constitutionally designated post of state superintendent to a position paying only $3,000 per year. In the past, Kentuckians had refused on several occasions to approve of such a change in statewide elections. KERA simply removed the electorate from the matter. While it could not change the constitution without electoral approval, it could change the remuneration and alter the job duties. In the place of the old elected State Superintendent of Public Instruction, a new Commissioner of Education position was created, responsible to a reformed State Board of Education.

Since that new State Board of Education did not yet exist, KERA provided that the new commissioner was to be hired by a special screening committee composed of representation from the legislature and the governor's office. A search was conducted but no in-state candidate for the new post made the list of finalists. A new commissioner was selected from California.

The new commissioner brought with him some friends and associates from California, so many that some Kentucky observers called them "the California mafia." Outsiders filled many of the top positions. In time, some worked out; others did not and returned to California or went elsewhere. For a time, an underground newspaper appeared within the Kentucky Department of Education, criticizing the new bosses for their lack of understanding of Kentucky politics and ways, and derisively pointing out the outsiders' lack of finesse and their bumbling efforts to be accepted by the natives. In the beginning of the third year of reform, an underground newsletter was sent from somewhere in Kentucky to all superintendents in the Commonwealth, criticizing the commissioner and parts of KERA that dealt with the Act's provisions relating to testing and eliminating grading in primary schools. At least one major newspaper printed portions of the critical letter, as did *Education Week* (Harp, 1992).

## School Governance and Local Site Councils

KERA mandated the creation of individual school site councils as the means of breaking away from systemwide gridlock caused by bureaucratic red tape and political influence exerted at the board level. A clash over money and power has come between local school boards and local site councils. In such disputes, the state has served as arbiter, supplying the leverage to resolve the issues.

The Kentucky School Boards Association has fought hard to retain school board hegemony over the fledgling site councils, and reacted bitterly to a stinging defeat over shifting financial authority to them by calling a state board regulation that embodied the change "taxation without representation" (Lucke, 1992[c], p. B1). The KSBA charge drew a response from a leading Kentucky legislator, who said, "School boards are a child of some previous General Assembly. In 1990, we created another child, school councils. Our intent was clear" (Lucke, 1992[c], B1).

Even as the struggle between school councils and local boards intensifies, legislators have been disappointed that fewer than 4 percent of the parents in Kentucky are participating in site councils, and that teachers have voted to form councils in only 506 of Kentucky's 1,366 schools (Office of Education Accountability, 1992, p. 5). There has been much speculation as to why more parents and teachers are not anxious to share in decision making at their schools. The tepid response of these major constituencies poses a real dilemma for reformers who insist that teachers and parents are important participants in reform at the local level.

### Curriculum and Assessment

The shift in curricular practices in Kentucky was decidedly toward increased state control of curriculum. The Council on School Performance Standards created seventy-five "valued outcomes" based on six learning goals (Pankratz, 1992, p. 141). These outcomes were used to redesign the state's assessment system toward authentic assessments, that is, experiences that have intrinsic merit for learners. During the summer of 1993, the State Board for Elementary and Secondary Education approved a state curriculum framework that includes benchmarks of achievement for students in elementary, middle, and high school, suggested activities to integrate the curriculum across grade levels, and ideas for using community resources to assist in teaching the curriculum. While KERA did not mandate that local school districts follow this framework, it is clear that a decision not to use it as a guide for instructional planning could prove disastrous when the new rewards and sanctions package is fully in place.

As the commonwealth has lurched toward a new curricular core, the assessment program has become a source of controversy and some embarrassment. A multimillion dollar contract was awarded to a small New England firm for development of the authentic assessment program. Designing quality assessment items and providing the necessary training to assure reliability and validity has proven difficult and costly. A request by the new commissioner for an additional $50 million to supplement the mandated testing program was subsequently denied by the legislature, which had already provided $10 million more than the original estimate to develop the program (Gregory, 1991, p. A1). This conflict illustrated that no matter how comprehensive an educational reform may appear to be—and few, if any, are as comprehensive as Kentucky's—situations and unforeseen problems still come up that are never imagined by the reformers. It is simply impossible to anticipate all of the major consequences of engaging in broad-scale educational reform, let alone the minor glitches that are always part of change.

Kentucky educational reform is both complex and unique. The crucial battleground is not the green grasslands of Lexington, with its quaint Southern mansions, mint juleps, and horse farms, nor the burgeoning suburban housing tracts in Northern Kentucky opposite Cincinnati, Ohio, but the nineteen hard scrabble coal counties in the Cumberland Plateau. Harry Caudill's (1962) prophetic voice still rings out from his mountain grave:

> Exhaustion is apparent on every hand—exhaustion of soil, exhaustion of men, exhaustion of hopes.... The nation—engulfed in its money-making and international politics—has paid no noticeable heed to its darkest area. The plateau, almost unnoticed, continues to lurch toward a day when perhaps 80 percent of its inhabitants will be Welfare recipients—charges on the national purse. [P. 394]

If KERA fails, it may signal the last major effort to carve out of Kentucky's mountains a better world for its children in the twentieth century. Educational reform in the heartland is a tough business, harder than the hardest coal still mined in its "hollers."

## REFERENCES

Bishop, William. "Stumbo Shows Real Colors on Reform." *Lexington Herald Leader*, October 11, 1992.

Campbell, Donald T., and Stanley, Julian C. "Experimental and Quasi-experimental Designs for Research on Teaching." In *Handbook of Research on Teaching*, edited by N. L. Gage, pp. 171–246. Chicago: Rand McNally, 1963.

Caudill, H. M. *Night Comes to the Cumberland*. Boston: Little Brown, 1962.

Gregory, Eric. "Boysen Seeks $80 Million to Test Students." *Lexington Herald Leader*, July 30, 1991.

Harp, Lonnie. "Reform Law Meets Rear-guard Reaction in Eastern Kentucky." *Education Week*, December 9, 1992.

Holusha, J. "Working as Learning, Learning as Working." *New York Times*, December 30, 1992.

Jordan, Jim; Wagar, Kit; and Estep, Bill. "FBI Widens Scope of Investigation." *Lexington Herald Leader*, April 2, 1992.

Kentucky Department of Education. *Ed News* 32, no. 6, August, 1992(a).

Kentucky Department of Education. *Kentucky Teacher*, December 1992(b).

Lucke, Jamie. "Superintendent, Board Face Accusations of Misconduct." *Lexington Herald Leader*, November 8, 1991.

Lucke, Jamie. "Kentucky Schools' Technology Chief Forced to Resign." *Lexington Herald Leader*, December 12, 1992(a).

Lucke, Jamie. "'Lost' $1.3 Million in Harlan May Go for Labs, Repairs." *Lexington Herald Leader*, June 22, 1992(b).

Lucke, Jamie. "Education Panel Head Urges Boards to Avoid Bickering with Councils." *Lexington Herald Leader*, December 4, 1992(c).

Miller, Mary Helen; Noland, Kevin; and Schaaf, John. *The Kentucky Education Reform Act of 1990: A Citizen's Handbook*. Frankfort, Ky: Legislative Research Commission, 1991.

Mueller, Lee. "Auditor Urges Floyd Board to Make Changes." *Lexington Herald Leader*, February 12, 1992.

Office of Education Accountability. *Annual Report: Measuring Progress*. Frankfort, Ky: Legislative Research Commission, December 1992.

Offutt, C. *Kentucky Straight*. New York: Vantage Books, 1992.

Pankratz, Roger. "Political Realities in Setting State Standards," *International Journal of Educational Reform* 1, no. 2 (1992): 139–148.

*Rose v. Council for Better Education, Inc.* KY. 790 S.W. 2d 186 (1989).

Rothman, Robert. "RAND Study Finds Serious Problems in Vt. Portfolio Programs," *Education Week* 12, no. 15 (1992): 1.

Sexton, Robert. "Viewpoints: School Reform Is Not a Spectator Sport," *Perspectives* 3, no. 4 (Fall/Winter 1992–93): 2.

Steffy, Betty. "The Last of the Breed in Kentucky: An Interview with John Brock," *International Journal of Educational Reform* 1, no. 1 (1992): 46–49.

Steffy, Betty. *Kentucky Educational Reform: Lessons for America*. Lancaster, Penn.: Technomic Publishing, Inc., 1993.

Stroud, Scott. "Japan, Kentucky Becoming Lands of Rising Cooperation." *Lexington Herald Leader*, December 27, 1992.

Wagar, Kit. "School Reform Producing Fairer Tax System." *Lexington Herald Leader*, November 22, 1992.

# II
# DISTRICT-LEVEL CHANGE

# 5

# Raising Standards in Charlotte-Mecklenburg Schools

## *John A. Murphy*

I arrived in Charlotte, North Carolina, in the summer of 1991 to assume the school superintendency. Charlotte was a city on the move, the epitome of the New South. But public education, a key ingredient of any rising urban star, was not moving with her.

While the details differ, the problem with education in Charlotte is the same as that in school districts across the country. All objective measurements say that Charlotte schools are average at best. Academic indicators are fair to poor. Trend lines for test scores are flat. The gap between black and white achievement is grim. The dropout rate hovers around 25 percent. Student violence is up. Low-level courses abound.

No standards, too little time, anemic content, and irrelevant tests are to blame. Times have changed; schools have not. Technology, telecommunications, and their infinite offspring have spread like wildfire through our culture, revolutionizing almost

---

This chapter draws upon an analysis of reform efforts in the Charlotte-Mecklenburg Schools as reported in Denis P. Doyle and Susan Pimentel, "A Study in Change: Transforming the Charlotte-Mecklenburg Schools," *Phi Delta Kappan* 74 (March 1993): 534–539.

every aspect of our lives, except for what happens in school. Schools of the 1990s are schools of the 1890s with a fresh coat of paint. They are pony-express institutions trying to make it in a high-tech world. In the competitive market, that is not nearly good enough.

While some educators maintain that graduates of our schools today are as well-educated as graduates of a century ago, that news— if true—is hardly comforting. Evidence from international comparisons is consistent and alarming. Standing still while competitor nations make giant strides puts us sorely behind. Given our standard of living and salary requirements, we will not be doing the job more cheaply than others worldwide, so we are going to have to do it better. No doubt we will have to scramble to keep up with the competition. More of the same is a recipe for disaster. Nothing less than the reinvention of public schools will do.

But that is a tall order for any school system. Districtwide transformation and renewal do not just happen on their own. The path to better schools is fraught with pitfalls and peril. Good will and hard work are not enough. The proponents of systemic change are few. Those with a vested interest in the current system number many more. They tend to be ferocious defenders of the status quo who have to be dragged kicking and screaming into the future. The rest wait to see which way the wind blows before committing themselves—they follow success.

There are, however, some simple and straightforward steps a community can take to blaze the trail. The story that follows describes how one community, Charlotte, has taken the plunge.

## THE CONTEXT

Charlotte-Mecklenburg is the nation's twenty-ninth largest school system, with about 80,000 students, 4,000 full-time teachers, and 109 schools in which to house them.

Fortunate for the school system, Charlotte has a civic culture devoted to growth and harmony. The city is home to one of the country's most dynamic and aggressive business communities and has a Board of Education to match. The nine-member board— elected at-large on a nonpartisan basis—has a lively mix of personalities and talents. The city and its surrounding community is still a low cost-of-living-area—at least by the standards of most large metropolitan areas—and is a beacon to new companies.

Race relations, while not perfect, are more harmonious than in most American cities. Unlike many communities in the North and South that equivocated and dragged their feet, Charlotte dealt with the busing order fairly and directly, making the city one of the most successful integrated large school systems in the nation. The *Swann* decision—the decisive 1971 Supreme Court ruling sanctioning the constitutionality of busing—heralds from Charlotte. A consolidated city/county school system restricted "white flight" to the suburbs. Today, the school system is 56 percent white and 39 percent African American.

Despite progress on these and other fronts, Charlotte-Mecklenburg schools did not measure up to the demands of the modern postindustrial economy. Business leaders were the first to register complaints. Their concerns did not fall on deaf ears. In the spring of 1991, under the leadership of the board chairman, the Reverend George Battle, a highly regarded black pastor, the board began a national search for a new superintendent. The undertaking proved difficult. A sharply divided board met past midnight two nights in a row, a total of twelve hours, before deciding to make a contract offer. In my mind, the vote for me was a vote for radical change. I had told board members to expect as much if I was hired. My job would be to make people feel uneasy and to raise expectations. There would be no leniency: educators who did not do the job would be finding other work.

## THE CHALLENGE

I took the helm on July 1, 1991, greeted by newspaper headlines that had introduced me to the community as a "head-knocker," "gunslinger," a "bureaucracy-bashing educator." Two assistant superintendents from my former posting, Dan Saltrick and Jeff Schiller, and one consultant, Susan Pimentel, an attorney and former aide to Maryland's Governor Schaefer, joined me. Tough, smart, and well-versed in my management philosophy of "applied anxiety," they would join with the Charlotte talent to form the nucleus of my executive team.

The power structure, longing for immediate change, extended a warm welcome and unequivocal support—for two years. After that, support would hinge on results. Goals had to be set and met. My feet were to the fire, but much was at stake. The community had entrusted me with the minds and futures of 80,000 of its young citizens. I told them I could do the job. I also told them that if we did not hit the system benchmark, then do not lower the standards, fire the superintendent.

My first official pursuit as superintendent was to initiate two districtwide information-gathering missions: one internal, one external. Both revealed significant problems and substantial opportunities.

The internal probe was straightforward. It confirmed my worst suspicions. Like so many other school districts, the administrative imperatives in Charlotte were all bureaucratic. Central management had become slack, top-heavy, and ponderous. No one in the system was held to high standards—not students, not teachers, not administrators. To the contrary, self-protection and back scratching were the orders of the day.

The data revealed a lousy set of student outcomes—nothing to warrant the kind of dollars being spent. Yet administrative review of personnel files revealed that almost without exception, principals had been given glowing evaluations by area assistant superintendents—in utter disregard of the academic performance of their students. We plotted the findings on a single graph. The results were astounding: the students appeared below the median line while their principals showed up in the superior range. Either the evaluation process was a farce or we had pretty dumb students in Charlotte.

There was nothing to suggest that Charlotte students were not every bit as capable as their counterparts any place else in America or the world. If children fail in our schools, it is not due to what they bring, but is due to what they encounter when they get there. My conclusion: the organization had begun to serve itself— the employees—rather than its customers—students and parents.

The external reconnaissance was no less sweeping and just as consequential. I got out from behind my desk (and the piles of data) to listen to what was on the minds of Charlotte citizens. We initiated a round of town meetings—five over a period of six months. I asked them to tell me what they wanted changed, what they wanted left alone, what they would support, and what they would fight. I learned that the citizens of Charlotte wanted schools that were disciplined and safe; schools that were racially integrated (but without forced busing); and above all, schools that were accountable to students, parents, and taxpayers for solid academic results.

The twin reconnaissance forays reinforced my conviction that the schools were failing because they were not changing. The education profession had been far too cautious. Academic standards had to be defined and measured; students had to be held to them; professional staff had to be held to them; and the delivery of education, from central headquarters to the classroom, had to be reinvented. I was convinced that the organization chart should be flat, reflecting the primacy of instruction—decision making should be delegated as far down the line as possible. The dilemma was that it must be delegated to people who had no experience of it, little taste for it, and high anxiety.

Charlotte's challenges were two: identify and legitimize the substantive changes needed to bring Charlotte-Mecklenburg schools into the twenty-first century and build constituencies for change that would support change in the first instance and also stay the course.

The pivotal decision was whether to take on a set of interlocking problems simultaneously, or to take a problem at a time and solve it before proceeding to the next. I chose the first strategy. While such boldness invites every single force of opposition to mobilize at once, to do otherwise all but assures failure. Innovations do not have a prayer for survival unless the old and tired ground rules—the long-entrenched habits, policies, constraints, and power relationships—are replaced with new ones that are synchronized. In large, complex organizations everything affects everything else. While this might sound more like particle physics than education, a serious change in one important area of schooling inevitably requires changes in others. They are joined at the hip. They live and die together.

## WHO ARE WE? WHAT ARE WE DOING HERE?

Being certain of one's destination is the only sure way to find one's way. And in education, there must be general consensus as to the direction. History is our guide. Despite almost a decade of agitation, change in the field is barely perceptible. That is because those at the heart of the learning enterprise—teachers, principals, parents, and students—have had little say-so.

Determined to do it right, we organized a giant rally one month into my term. Charlotte's 10,000 school employees—teachers, principals, bus drivers, support staff—came from the four corners of the district to hear first hand about what was in store.

It was the first time in nearly three decades that they had met as one. U.S. Deputy Secretary of Education, David T. Kearns, came to lend his support. Some dubbed it a "call to arms." There was plain talk about our strengths and weaknesses, and staff were challenged to develop an appropriate set of standards that would heed the challenges of today's society and prepare students for tomorrow's.

A key message was that all youngsters have a natural aptitude to succeed; that schools have the responsibility to find out how to nurture, develop, and encourage that innate talent. No excuses would be allowed, no "blame-the-victim" analysis in which we excuse students' failure by their poverty or other life circumstances. All students can learn; if they fail, it is our fault. That is what would be expected. In return teachers and principals would get professional running room, the right to take risks. I gave them my personal guarantee: the central office would not be a command post barking orders to its subjects; teachers and principals would call the shots, with central office in their service. The place erupted.

The event, covered in depth by the *Charlotte Observer* and local television and radio, ushered in our long-term strategy to transform the school district. And it laid the groundwork for our most ambitious plan—to impanel ten distinguished educators of varying backgrounds and interests to help us identify the elements of a "world-class" school district. What would it look like? How would it work? What kind of results would it produce?

## A PLAN OF ATTACK

In December 1991, leading education experts from across the nation gathered in Charlotte to help us plan the revolution. We selected ten men and women to serve on the world-class schools panel* who shared the conviction that change was nec-

---

* Panelists included William Bennett, former U.S. Secretary of Education; Ernest Boyer, president of the Carnegie Foundation for the Advancement of Teaching and former Commissioner of Education; James Comer, author and professor of child psychiatry at Yale University Child Study Center; Denis Doyle, education writer (co-author with David T. Kearns of *Winning the Brain Race*); Chester Finn, Jr., Vanderbilt University professor and former Assistant Secretary of Education (now part of Chris Whittle's Edison Project brain trust); Patricia A. Graham, president of the Spencer Foundation and former dean

essary but held widely divergent views on just what change would involve. Each knew of the others by reputation and several knew each other personally, but never had the group been assembled at one time. The only rule was that there would be no rules. Everything would be up for grabs. Nothing—no policy, position, structure, organization, or program—would be off limits.

The panel agreed to meet three times over a six-month period for a day and a half each session to hammer out a consensus document that would establish the framework for lasting reform.

Attended by a small audience, the first discussion was closed to the public—not for secrecy but to protect the caliber of the deliberations and to encourage frank, open, and informal discussions. But restricting the public was a mistake. Community attention and anticipation ran high. We had underestimated both the public's interest and the abilities of panel members to protect the authenticity of their deliberations. We therefore videocast subsequent meetings live.

We were dedicated to giving the larger community a real voice in these deliberations, because plans, no matter how grand or well thought out, do not work unless they are shaped by the people who have to carry them out. Without support, any plan developed is worth only the paper it is written on. The community must be convinced that change is both necessary and desirable, and that means keeping open lines of communication.

Over the course of the panel's deliberations, we sought and received input from nearly 10,000 people. We started with four day-long community forums: one for principals and teachers, representing all 113 schools; one for parents and concerned citizens; one for business and civic leaders; and one for over two hundred high school students representing each of the district's seventeen high schools.

Opening with a context-setting plenary session led by Denis Doyle, a world-class school panel member and noted education author, these meetings quickly broke into small groups to discuss the same issues the world-class school panel was examining: student performance standards, the organizational changes needed

---

of the Harvard Graduate School of Education; Matina Horner, vice-president of TIAA-CREF  and former president of Radcliffe College; James Kelly, president of the National Board for Professional Teaching Standards; John Slaughter, physicist and president of Occidental College; Donald Stewart, president of the College Board; and Susan Pimentel, study director to the panel.

to meet them, and barriers to implementation. Each group carried its findings back to its constituents. Interestingly, the students were the toughest of all, demanding higher standards, meaningful assessments, an end to tracking, and administrators with backbone.

The panel finished its work in April 1992. A preliminary plan that reflected both the panel's thinking and the thoughts of thousands of Charlotteans ran in the Sunday edition of the *Charlotte Observer*. Astonishing even the panelists themselves, the product was an unparalleled report—they reached virtual unanimity on a fourteen-point plan—entitled *The Charlotte Process: Reclaiming Our Legacy*.

One week after the panel's report appeared in the newspaper, a communitywide summit was held. Jointly sponsored by the Greater Charlotte Chamber of Commerce, the *Charlotte Observer*, and the schools, two thousand citizens came out to register their preferences and lend their voices to the effort. In that setting, Charlotte's "fourteen points" were ratified, the necessary first step in transforming the city's public schools.

## DARE TO CHANGE

The panel's deliberations and conclusions can be captured by a single tenet: it is time to do more than rearrange the deck chairs. Higher expectations for students and greater autonomy for schools got top billing, but the panel's recommendations went far beyond, challenging several fundamental conventions and traditions of American education.

### Challenged: The Preoccupation with Making Every Student Feel Good

This is the American education curse of the century. What sense does it make to organize thresholds around the lowest common denominator—usually defined as what every sixth grader should know? We wanted everybody to feel good but we did it at the expense of excellence. Young people, like most adults, do enough to get by. Minimum requirements fast turn into maximum goals. The reason most students are not learning very much is because we are not teaching them very much. A Charlotte teacher summed it up, "No one rises to low expectations. Aim high, achieve a lot. Aim low, achieve a little."

The solution: to develop a set of performance standards that describe what academic performance is both expected and possible for students in each subject area—rigorous yet achievable by the masses provided they work hard and long enough. International baccalaureate and advanced placement programs—"top of the line" American standards that compare favorably to the advanced standards of competitor nations—would set the pace.

### Challenged: Calibrating High School Diplomas to Carnegie Units

"Graduation requirements are a joke," a Charlotte student charged. Right he is. Carnegie units represent little more than hours of course credits on transcripts. Most high school diplomas mean only that a student has accumulated seat time in an approved location—more a clue to patience than evidence of any authentic academic achievement. Though the diploma remains a necessary credential for employment and college admission, employers do not trust it to reflect what students know and students realize it has little bearing on their future plans. Students are not stupid—they learn early on that it does not much matter what courses you take or how well you do, just that you take enough courses and pass.

Why continue to measure courses in hours? Why not develop profiles of competency that describe a student's path to a diploma in units of accomplishment rather than in units of time? To exit, why not also require students to write a serious essay, present it orally, and defend it under cross-examination from their peers and teachers? An exit essay is one measure that cannot be faked. It reveals students' grasp of vocabulary, their prowess in integrating thoughts and expressing ideas clearly and cogently, and their capacity to apply ideas to an issue of consequence. The quickest way to improve schools is to make what you do in them count. These two proposals fit the bill. They will enable every employer and education institution to know with precision the body of knowledge and skills that students have mastered.

### Challenged: The Prevailing American Attitude That We Cannot Educate Everyone of Normal Intelligence to High Levels

This nation was built on the belief that anything is possible if you work long and hard enough—except in matters of schooling.

There, curiously, effort and hard work count for little. Innate ability is considered the key to school success. What a message! Being uninspired is one thing. That is curable. Being labeled innately unable, on the other hand, is terminal. Children respond accordingly. Why work harder if success is not related to effort? Alternatively, if tagged as "high ability," why not relax, rely on your talents, and breeze through?

The poor, the disadvantaged, and racial minorities have borne the brunt of these paltry expectations. If the moral affront does not convince that a change in attitude is essential, then good old-fashioned self-interest should. In the days of an industrial economy, when semiskilled jobs were a dime a dozen, this exclusive approach could be tolerated in a purely economic sense. But this is no longer true in today's knowledge-based economy that is desperate for employees who are broadly and deeply educated, steeped in the traditions of a liberal education. The bottom line is that everyone deserves—and the nation needs everyone to get—a hefty dose of the very best. What we must vary is the means—not the ends—of education, and do so in ways that respect the particular differences of children.

### Challenged: The Curricular Tracking System That Gives "Good" Students One Curriculum and "Poor" Students a Watered-Down Version

Curricular tracking strikes early, sorting students into separate groups for fast, medium, and slow learners. Once sentenced, there is no escape. Students remain in these ruts through high school. Those unfortunate enough to be dumped into the general or vocational tracks—holding pens characterized by unchallenging courses and the accumulation of low-level skills—find themselves wholly unprepared for either postsecondary education or meaningful work. It perpetrates a cruel hoax on students. Whatever a student's destination, the real currency in this economy is solid academic grounding.

### Challenged: The Prohibition Against Teaching "Values" in School

Americans have taken the aversion to teaching values in schools to ridiculous lengths. Can we be serious when we tell kids, "Do your own thing. Anything goes. There are two sides to every story"? Are there two sides to the Holocaust? slavery? murder?

If we do not understand why the world is as it is today, if we are ignorant of people's struggles for freedom, if we are oblivious to the villains of history and their ideologies, how can we know what to fight for or against on a personal or a national level? There is such a thing as right and wrong, and values such as liberty, equality, and justice are some of those on which we all can agree.

### Challenged: School Assignments, Made on the Basis of Geography, That Presume That Children Are Interchangeable and Parents Have No Stake

What is fair about creating one kind of school and one kind of teaching style when children's interests, passions, and learning styles differ so vividly? People do not learn alike and to run schools one way with one style is itself profoundly prejudicial. It makes enormous sense to offer students a choice of venues—a variety of distinctive pedagogical and academic specialty schools. What better way to capture the minds of young people than to enroll them in schools they want to attend, tailored to their particular educational and career aspirations? Choice celebrates the differences and uses them to good effect.

### Challenged: The Conclusion That All Youngsters Can Learn the Same Amount During the Six-Hour, 180-Day School Year

The extent to which the clock and calendar determine school organization must give way to more enlightened thinking. It does not make sense to give the fastest student and the slowest student identical time to master the same material. Why must the school day and year be the same length for everyone, anyway? Why not measure students by what they learn, and give them the hours and days they need to master the material?

### Challenged: The Presumption That All Children Born in a Certain Year Are Somehow Exactly Alike

Teach them the same stuff in the same way at the same time. Even to the untrained eye of the noneducator, this defies common sense. Since when are all seventh-graders or eleven-year-olds the same? Youngsters grow at different rates with unpredictable starts, stops, and surges along the way. Grades and classrooms are an administrative convenience embraced for the sake of grown-ups. Grades and classrooms are how we keep track of students. They create a mirage of homogeneity and allow teachers to develop one lesson plan—too often one that works well for just a fraction of the students.

Why not instead adopt a flexible mastery curriculum where the skills and knowledge that young people need to acquire are arranged into broad levels of learning where students advance as they master the material without regard to age or grade? That way, a student—in relation to his or her individual strengths—can advance quickly through some subjects and more slowly through others.

### Challenged: The Belief That Too Much Emphasis Is Placed on Tests

No one likes tests much, but without them we flunk. Academic standards are relegated to pretty words on a page. Until we decide what our schools are trying to accomplish, and develop ways to determine whether they are doing so, we can not know whether we are headed in the right direction, whether we ought to adjust our course, or whether we are succeeding at all. Only by chance will targets be hit and results be better.

Tests are powerful tools. A good test keeps everyone—grown-ups and youngsters alike—focused on the right stuff. What gets measured, gets taught. What gets tested, gets emphasized. Tests keep instruction on track. So long as the test does a first-rate job examining the knowledge and skills we want students to acquire, teaching to the test can be an exalted thing.

That is how most educators in competitive nations view testing. Teachers are expected to prepare their students for them. It is through preparation that youngsters learn a great deal about the particular subject.

Cynics argue that tests are flawed; that many things defy assessment. But if it can be taught, it can be measured in some fashion. The challenge is to develop tests with loftier expectations and higher stakes.

### Challenged: The Belief That Education Means Formal Schooling

Children hardly wait for formal instruction to speak, think, and write. In fact, there is universal agreement that the learning that takes place in the first five years of children's lives, before they ever walk through a schoolhouse door, is the most consequential. So why wait until a child is five years old and on our doorstep? Why not strike while the iron is hot and forsake the mind set that education means formal schooling; that what happens in the earlier years is none of our business? That means making connections at birth to let parents know what is needed to prepare their children for school.

By the same token, what stops us from thinking about the 365-day block of time instead? Schools cannot afford to continue to be silent on all but the 180 days children are in their custody. Learning can take place in a variety of different settings: at home, with computers, in museums, in libraries, at zoos, or at work. Schools can take a lesson from the girl and boy scouts where the objectives for earnings badges are set internally, but students do the bulk of the work elsewhere under the watchful eyes of parents and community members. Scouts engage children directly for only a portion of the time. Schools could follow suit.

## *Challenged: The Conviction That Public Responsibility for the Education of Children Begins and Ends at the Schoolhouse Door*

To the contrary, the public stake in children begins at birth and continues after the school day and through the summer. It does not begin and end at the schoolhouse door.

Estimates are that school casts a direct shadow over only 9 percent of children's lives. The rest—a full 91 percent—is spent outside school. Parents, churches, social welfare organizations, employers, and a variety of other institutions are the custodians of that time. Their beliefs—the principles and values by which the community lives—set the tone for much of what goes on inside schools. In fact, a surefire way to improve schools is for the community to signal in everyday ways that learning matters— that there is a real and legitimate future in the community for students who do well and that there are real life consequences if they do not learn.

As things stand, young people know that no matter what they do in school they can still get hired and into college. Few employers ever ask to see high school transcripts. Even fewer take time to investigate what courses students took or what grades they received along the way. Business and colleges hold the real goods—jobs and college acceptance. The younger watch the older to gather clues about what's important in life. They learn best when the community signals in everyday ways that learning is valuable and that there are consequences if they do not learn.

Employers could encourage students to work hard in school by, for instance, paying a dollar more per hour for work performed by high achievers, issuing a list of courses or—better—a list of competencies that future employees must have, or making it clear that those with the strongest transcripts and test scores will get the better jobs and nicer working conditions. Once it is clear that new hires will be treated according to their educational preparedness, word will spread quickly.

## A POWER SHIFT

Teaching is a job that requires judgment. Yet, teachers' worlds are governed by someone else's rules. Legions of highly paid personnel who hold nonteaching jobs, unaccountable to the people on whose behalf they ostensibly labor, churn out an inexhaustible supply of prose and policy about how to teach—leaving little to the imagination or discretion of those on the front lines.

The panel's plan would be dead in the water unless those power relationships and governing arrangements were fundamentally altered. Reform requires that teachers work harder and be smarter. But teachers—people in general—will not work harder in places they feel are hostile.

In Charlotte, we made a change. So long as goals are reached, school-house professionals will be trusted to do right by their students. We will govern by outcomes, not rules and regulations— a far more efficient system than micromanaging schools from afar. A whole level of management was wiped out as a result. Dozens of veteran instructors were sent back into the schools. Far fewer central office staff were needed to check up on whether schools were following the rules.

The most important point is that rules do not teach. If children do not learn, it does not much matter that regulations and guidelines are followed or even that the public's money is spent according to law. Outcomes are all that really matter. When central office staff dictate every move, teachers and principals are not responsible for the results. They have a perfect excuse for poor performance.

The goal is to work the central office staff, including the superintendent, out of a job.

## AN ACCOUNTABILITY PLAN WITH A BITE

Like any business, schools have a profit line—student outcomes. What is happening to students in our schools? Are they learning what they should?

Educators have always been accountable—just not for the right things. Schools have long been judged by their efforts, good intentions, compliance with rules, orderly procedures, and resource allocations. Shifting the focus to the efficacy of their efforts means judging schools by the quality of their results. Student competency over challenging subject matter, enrollment in demanding classes, low suspension and expulsion rates, high completion and college acceptance rates, and strong parent-home connections must become the prime indicators of success.

To be responsible for outcomes includes knowing that consequences, pleasant or not, will follow from one's success or failure. As things stand, however, public education is an enterprise that pays its best employees the same thing as its worst employees. Whether you do a good job educating students or a bad job, nothing different happens to you either way. Salaries are determined by arbitrary measures. Pay is awarded solely on the basis of paper credentials and seniority. If you take college courses—almost any course, relevant or not—you are paid more. If you live longer and do not get fired, you are paid more, too. Job performance is irrelevant, and incompetents are rarely fired. It is hardly a system to inspire people to great accomplishment. The high achiever gets penalized while the low achiever gets rewarded.

The education profession needs to rethink its position on salaries and job performance. Major results will evade us until the day we as a profession join the rest of the modern world and move to a well-conceived, profit-sharing system. The recipe for success is simple: reward staff when they succeed, shape them up when they falter, and replace them when they fail.

Deciding not to wait for the rest of the country to agree, I instituted a $5 million employee bonus incentive plan. If they increase the "profits"—meet certain student outcome standards—they get a bonus at the end of year. Goals are set for each school. If all markers are met, all staff, regardless of their personal performance, share in the rewards at the end of the year. Allowing the entire school to benefit encourages teamwork. Good teachers have an incentive to help poorer ones. Poorer teachers have an added incentive to do better, for other people's salaries depend on their performance. For the future, teachers who perform exceptionally will be eligible for personal bonuses as well.

To be effective inducements for change, honors and rewards must be outlined in advance. They must be simple, clear, and certain, as must the interventions in the cases of failure. Otherwise, these inducements are not likely to make a great difference in people's behavior. The problem is, in the school system, for better or worse, most employees have tenure. You just cannot call someone in and say, "You're fired," no matter how poor their performance. This is especially so when the file holds twenty-two "average or above" evaluations for the twenty-two years the administrator or the teacher has been in the system. There are legal constraints against firing. It takes times to build a contrary record.

In spite of the constraints, by the end of our first year, forty-one CMS central office staff had been dismissed or reassigned to front-line positions. As well, thirty-two principals retired, resigned, or were dismissed. Forty-nine teachers did not have their contracts renewed or had resigned due to performance issues. I had one principal say to me, "When you came here I felt safe because I knew there were thirty principals who were worse than me. . . . Now I'm really worried." The expectations are clear: every adult in the system is expected to keep uppermost the obligation to improve student outcomes.

These numbers are not offered to gloat. We all know there are teachers teaching who should not be. They have talents, but not in education. We have got to get tough both for the sake of the misdirected adult and for the children. We help no one by taking twenty years to show them the door.


## OUT WITH BUSING, IN WITH CHOICE

Judging by the percentages, Charlotte's forced busing program is one of the best in the country. Children of all colors come together daily to study peaceably in the same schools. But scratch the surface and a depressing array of African-American student achievement indicators reveal themselves. Despite good intentions, black students trail white students on standardized tests by a disturbing forty percentile points. They have sharply lower grade-point averages, higher school suspension and drop-out rates, and fill the ranks of lower-level courses. Children, integrated by school, are resegregated into separate classrooms. More often than not, African-American children are relegated to the worst classes—the least challenging, the least interesting, and headed by the least experienced and least motivated teachers.

Unfortunately, busing programs all over the nation have fallen short of expectations. That is because their sole focus has been on obtaining numbers that look good. Once students are bused cross-town, the decrees of *Brown vs. Board of Education* and *Swann* are considered fulfilled; no further attention is necessary. The true purpose of integration—equal opportunity to learn—got lost in the statistics.

To make matters even worse, in the name of leveling the playing field, schools across the nation lowered their standards. It is a critical and costly mistake for minority children, and a cop-out for schools. African-American children—like all others—benefit from clear goals, lofty expectations, expert teachers, and rigorous study. Without those, they are doomed to dim futures. Serious work is required of everyone once they hit the real world. It is no wonder a larger portion of African-American children act out, tune out, and drop out. We set them up for failure.

Rather than continue a costly and unproductive busing program, we proposed to integrate through a choice program, thereby dedicating the millions of dollars used to ferry children around the district to improving instruction instead. Inner-city schools would be the venue. They would be given additional resources to develop their own distinctive academic personalities, to become schools that would attract students from different neighborhoods. The decision met with mixed reviews: relief to be out from under *Swann*, combined with trepidation that racial balance might not be met, causing *Swann* to be reapplied.

There are now in place fourteen specialized magnet programs—ranging from creative and performing arts to science technology. Parents clamored to sign their children up. There were four applicants for each magnet school seat. The only complaints are from those parents and students who did not get in. Another seven are planned for school year 1993–94.

Beyond racial balance, choice acts as a bridge that reconnects parents and children to schooling. Experience reveals that schools striving to survive within a magnet system become more responsive. That is because they have to vie for customers. Respect and confidence are apt to flourish because the relationship is voluntary. They have to work harder to provide better quality. A consumer-dependent enterprise can slip for only so long before customers vote with their feet to take their business elsewhere. Choice programs—good for racial balance—give the entire district a shot in the arm. The goal is to make Charlotte's 113 schools all magnets by the end of the decade.

## LESSONS LEARNED

School reform is like changing the tires on a car going eighty miles per hour. Several bumps and scrapes later, I know only that the organization has been fundamentally altered, that incentives and disincentives have been changed, and that public confidence is beginning to grow. Charlotte's 1992 enrollment was higher than had been predicted. Twenty-five hundred newcomers enrolled rather than the five hundred expected; nearly one thousand came from private schools. But it would be a mistake to simply settle on a new, equally rigid bureaucracy. For that is the ultimate lesson of restructuring. Reform is not an end or even a goal in and of itself. Reform is a process. It confronts a moving target. While it may have a beginning, it has no end.

# 6

# Radical School Reform in Chicago: How Is It Working?

## *Edgar G. Epps*

In this chapter, I examine the results of Chicago school reform in the context of the effective schools model, which emphasizes the role of the principal as the key factor in school effectiveness; high achievement expectations for students as well as high performance levels for teachers; commitment to student achievement as the focus or mission of the school; and a safe and orderly environment for students and teachers (Clark et al., 1984), and the school restructuring model, which emphasizes choice and voice for parents; empowerment for teachers; school-based management involving parents and teachers; and changes in the teaching-learning process (Murphy and Hallinger, 1993). But first, I provide a brief description of the Chicago reform legislation.

## CHICAGO SCHOOL REFORM

In a recent book, I wrote:

The reforms of the 1980s can be characterized as a movement in three waves. The first wave emphasized the increasing influence of the states in determining curricula, monitoring achievement, evaluating

95

and certifying teachers, and setting goals and standards. The second
wave used the language of school restructuring, with an emphasis on
reducing the isolation of teachers, increasing the role of teachers in
formulating and implementing school policy, sharing decision making at the local school level, and devolving authority from the central bureaucracy to the local school. The third wave, which is still a
minor ripple on the broad surface of reform, emphasizes empowering the major actors at the school-site—teachers, principals, and *parents and community*. [Epps, 1992, p. 152]

How radical is the Chicago School Reform Act of 1988 (P.A.
85–1418)? Nationally recognized scholars (Katz, Fine, and Simon,
1991), in an article in the *Chicago Tribune*, referred to Chicago
school reform as "radical," "a social movement," "historic." Michael
B. Katz (1992) characterizes it as "a process of school reform
that transcends the historic limits that have constrained the potential for change in urban education" (p. 56). Fred G. Newmann,
director of the Center on Organization and Restructuring of
Schools at the University of Wisconsin, Madison, stated that "since
1988, the 600 schools in Chicago have been operating under
the most extensive effort in restructured school governance in
U.S. history" (Newmann, 1992, p. 2.).

The legislation provided for the election of local school councils
(LSCs) at each of the schools in the district. The law also stripped
principals of tenure, placing them on four-year contracts renew-
able by the LSCs. The councils consist of six parents, one of
whom *must* be LSC chair; two community representatives; two
teachers, and the principal. High school LSCs include a nonvot-
ing student member. It is clear that power has been shifted formally from the education professionals to the lay members of
the LSC. But are the lay members of the councils really empowered? Moncrief Cochran (1987) defines empowerment as

> an interactive process involving mutual respect and critical reflec-
> tion through which both people and controlling institutions are
> changed in ways which provide those people with greater influence
> over individuals and institutions which are in some way impeding
> their efforts to achieve equal status in society, for themselves and
> those they care about. [P. 11]

The Chicago School Reform Act (P.A. 85–1418) provides *legal empowerment* for parents and communities. Whether it results
in *de facto empowerment* in the form of "mutual respect," "critical
reflection," and shared decision making is problematic. Since

LSCs, consisting of a majority of parents and community representatives, have the power to hire and fire the principal, to negotiate a performance contract with the principal, and to evaluate the performance of the principal, it is clear that the power relationships between the school's chief administrator and representatives of its client population are, or should be, substantially more equal than they were under the centralized form of administration.

Now that LSCs have the authority to approve the school's budget, help develop and approve a school improvement plan, and make decisions about curriculum, facilities, and other matters that affect the operation of the school, the wishes of the local constituency should be paramount in the planning and operation of the school's program. Public Act 85–1418 clearly legitimized parent and citizen power in Chicago schools. For the first time in the history of the Chicago Public Schools, principals and teachers in schools that serve economically disadvantaged minority children are legally accountable to parents and communities. Kent Peterson (1991) has observed that empowerment of local school councils has meant a drastic change in the way principals must view their work. Rather than attending primarily to central office or subdistrict demands as in the past, principals are now required to negotiate daily with LSCs about every aspect of school policy and procedure. Principals must now exercise leadership in a way that at least gives the appearance of shared authority and power. One result of the Chicago school reform effort is likely to be a change in the role of the principal. Gary Gottfredson and Lois Hybl (1987) reported on a nationwide survey of public school and private school principals that found that the jobs of public school principals involved more interaction with higher levels of authority than did the jobs of private school principals. Private school principals appeared to have more authority to make personnel and other administrative decisions and to view these aspects of their jobs as more important than did the public school administrators. Early research suggests that Chicago principals are beginning to view their roles as more like those of private school principals since school reform has become institutionalized (Bennett et al., 1992).

Both national and local observers of the implementation of reform in Chicago are optimistic about its potential for improving the quality of education, especially in schools serving minority children (Clements and Forsaith, 1991; Katz, Fine, and Simon,

1991). However, as Charles Payne (1991) noted, some principals may try to create the appearance of collaborative decision making while retaining real power in their own hands:

> They will create committees they can manipulate, influence decision making by controlling the flow of information, judiciously use rewards and punishments to influence teacher members of the LSCs, curry favor with parent members, and so on—the familiar catalogue of techniques by which executives maintain democratic forms without democratic substance. [P. 20]

Payne (1991) also points out that the Chicago reform process has taken place in an atmosphere of political conflict, and that while the Illinois legislature gave "power to the people, [it] saw no need to give them any significant new funding" (p. 16). However, some new financial resources did flow to the schools as a result of P.A. 85–1418. Changes in the use of state compensatory education funds permitted many schools serving disadvantaged students to receive considerably more discretionary dollars and gave them greater freedom in choosing what to do with these resources. In six schools studied intensively, the amount of discretionary funds ranged from $400 per pupil to $1,600 per pupil (Bryk et al., 1993, p. 31.).

During October 1989, the first year of Chicago school reform, elections for LSCs were held in 540 schools. The law required one-half of the schools to decide whether to retain their principals or to select new ones during the first year; the remaining schools would make this decision during the second year of reform implementation. LSCs were also required to approve the school budget and a school improvement plan. All of this was undertaken with little training and little assistance from the central office. Outside agencies, including universities and nonprofit organizations that supported the reform movement, attempted to fill the void, but most councils reported that they had not received the amount or type of training needed for them to operate effectively under the pressure of "unreasonable" deadlines.

Despite the haphazard way in which reform was implemented, interviews with seven hundred LSC members conducted in October 1990, one year after the beginning of reform implementation, indicated that most council members perceived their schools to be operating better than they were a year earlier (Leadership for Quality Education, 1990). Parents (especially black parents) were more likely than teachers or principals to say that their schools had gotten better in such areas as safety and discipline, interaction between parents and school personnel, and planning the learning process. Overall, all constituencies expressed optimism about school improvement in 1990–91. Two-thirds of the respondents said that volunteer and parent involvement in the school had improved. It appears that Albert Shanker's opinion (Lederer, 1968) that decentralization and community control are programs designed to produce parent and community *satisfaction* is supported by this survey. At least LSC members appear more satisfied with their schools now that they feel empowered. We do not know how other parents and community residents feel about the effects of reform. To this observer, there has been only modest improvement in overall parent and community participation in most schools. Teachers share this rather pessimistic assessment. In responding to a survey conducted by the Consortium on Chicago School Research, only 51 percent of teachers said they receive support from parents for their work, 46 percent thought community members made efforts to help the school, and 59 percent felt that parents respect teachers in their school. However, 78 percent of teachers believed that their school makes an effort to reach out to the community (Easton et al., 1991, p. 9). The survey results suggest that schools will find it necessary to find means of improving their efforts to increase parent involvement and community support.

Observations of seventy-four local school council meetings in twelve schools by staff of the Chicago Panel on Public School Policy and School Finance (Easton et al., 1990) indicated that average attendance at meetings for LSC members was 70 percent in elementary schools (8 of 11) and 78 percent in high schools (about 8.5 of 11). Principals (97 percent), teachers (88 percent), and LSC chairpersons (88 percent) had the highest attendance rates. Community members (67 percent) and parent members (62 percent) had lower attendance rates. A similar pattern emerged for participation in discussions during LSC meetings. Absence of members was a concern in at least two of the councils observed. Charles Payne (1991) estimates that there has been a possible 30 percent dropout rate among those elected to councils in 1989. Some schools are unable to attract substantial numbers of parents to LSC meetings, and some have difficulty obtaining a quorum of LSC members to conduct business at scheduled meetings (Obejas, 1991).

The impact of this "radical" empowerment of parents and

communities on the performance of schools as "communities of learning" is being monitored by academic researchers and members of organizations that advocate reform (Rothman, 1991). One such collaboration, the Consortium on Chicago School Research, which includes representatives of Chicago-area universities, advocacy agencies, and the Chicago Public Schools, has published surveys of teachers (Easton et al., 1991) and principals (Bennett et al., 1992), and an overview of school reform in elementary schools (Bryk et al., 1993). Whether the reforms will result in long-term positive effects on schools cannot be determined until longitudinal evaluation of the effects of reform is available. However, the recent publications of the Consortium and observations of other academic and nonacademic informants do provide a basis for estimating the early impact of Chicago's school reform on school governance and school climate. It is possible to estimate what proportion of councils are functioning well and how many are experiencing difficulties. It is also possible to estimate how many councils are operating collaboratively and how many are dominated by the principal or have been ineffectual because of political, racial and ethnic, or personality conflicts. A recent opinion poll of 705 LSC members conducted for Leadership for Quality Education (cited in Bradley, 1993) found that every group represented on LSCs was positive about the effects of school reform in Chicago. Principals (82 percent), teachers (68 percent), parents (87 percent), and community representatives (80 percent) reported seeing school improvement. It is not surprising that teachers are less positive about school reform than other LSC members. The reform legislation empowered all other groups except teachers. While it did mandate the establishment of a Professional Personnel Advisory Committee (PPAC) at each school, the PPAC has advisory authority only. Many teachers resent the fact that "lay" persons who may know nothing about education are in a position of authority over "professionals." Nevertheless, the most recent poll of Leadership for Quality Education shows that LSC members are substantially more positive about school reform than they were when polled in 1990.

### Summary of Progress Reports on Chicago School Reform

The Consortium on Chicago School Research (Easton et al., 1991) sponsored a survey of 12,708 Chicago Public School elementary school teachers. They found that a majority of teachers are "moderately positive" about how school reform has affected them and their schools. Less than one-fifth of the teachers experienced negative consequences, such as increased conflict among students, staff, administration, and parents due to school reform. In 62 schools, teachers see reform as "really working." In another 241 schools, teachers are moderately positive. Teachers are more positive about reform in small schools (those with 350 or fewer students); teachers are more negative in larger schools. However, teachers expressed concerns about the level of order in their schools, and also indicated that they had a relatively low amount of influence on decisions in their schools that affect them. *More than one-half of the teachers said that reform has not had an effect on their classroom practices.*

The Consortium also surveyed Chicago Public School principals (Bennett et al., 1992). A total of 457 (out of 550) elementary and high school principals (83 percent) responded to the survey. The majority of respondents who were principals prior to the beginning of reform in 1989 (83 percent) believe their schools are getting better since reform. Only 29 percent of these principals report increased conflict in the school. However, only 41 percent of the principals say they feel better about working in schools since reform. According to this report, while many positive things are happening, principals feel that their work and their role have become more difficult. Generally, most principals report that their relationships with their LSCs are satisfactory. Slightly more than half of the principals consider their LSCs to be effective policymaking bodies, about 20 percent do not consider them to be effective, and about one-quarter give neutral responses.

Perhaps the most important function of the LSC in the Chicago School Reform Act is the selection or retention of the principal. The survey of principals revealed that, of the current principals, 43 percent have been hired since reform (94 percent are new to the principalship, but almost all previously held jobs in the Chicago Public Schools). The changes appear to have opened up the principalship to younger persons and to a larger proportion of women and minority aspirants. However, the transfer of hiring authority to local constituencies appears also to have increased the likelihood that a principal's race or ethnicity will match that of the majority of students in his or her school. In other words, greater local choice in selecting principals is almost certain to result in an increase in considering race and ethnicity when hiring principals.

How do principals view the effects of reform on school restructuring? The Consortium on Chicago School Research constructed composites of principals' responses to individual survey items to develop categories that are useful in summarizing principals' attitudes toward school reform. The principals' responses indicate that about one-fourth of the schools had begun restructuring efforts before reform began. Most of these schools had stable, professional leadership from both principals and teachers as well as consistent contacts with external educational organizations. Another one-fourth of the schools are described as "recently restructured." In these schools, the key factor seems to be new leadership from principals who believe that they can make a difference in the academic development of their students. Some schools (19 percent) are categorized as complacent; they were doing relatively well before reform and see no need to make significant changes. Finally, there are the schools (32.4 percent) that "reform left behind." They tend to serve low-income students (87 percent), and many are racially isolated (61 percent predominantly African American; another 18 percent predominantly minority). The principals of these schools report minimal or no restructuring. The results of this survey as well as the results of case studies (Bryk et al., 1993) suggest that these "left-behind" schools either retained a principal who was resistant to change, selected a new principal who did not know how to move the school toward restructuring, or became involved in internal power struggles leading to conflictual relationships between principals and LSCs. The research results clearly support the effective schools model's emphasis on the importance of the principal's leadership role.

The Consortium (Bryk et al., 1993) also looked at what they called the "Experiences of Actively Restructuring Schools" (EARS). The close look at six successfully restructuring schools supported the results of the principals' surveys in finding that "the key feature that stands out in EARS schools is principal leadership" (p. 27). Background characteristics such as race, ethnicity, and gender did not appear to be a factor. However, previous experience in the Chicago Public Schools central office was a common factor. Interviews with these principals revealed that they made effective use of their knowledge of "how the system works" as well as their personal contacts with central office administrators. Members of the schools' communities, students, parents, teachers, and ancillary staff all commented on the dedication and commitment of the principals. All six principals were reported to have high energy levels, spending long hours at the school and on school business when not in the building. The principals were also characterized as persons who believed that they could make a difference in the effectiveness of the school, that inner-city children could learn, and that teachers could teach these children much more effectively than had previously been the case.

The key elements of successful restructuring in Chicago elementary schools include (1) an active local school council that selected or retained a principal committed to students and parents and that supports the principal's efforts; (2) facilitative, inclusive principal leadership that reaches out to both parents and staff to get them more involved; (3) a highly visible principal who creates a "new image" of the school as a place where students learn and teachers teach; (4) a longer-term focus that includes strengthening the technical instructional core (including replacing ineffective teachers, recruiting new staff, providing sustained schoolwide staff development, and promoting professional community among the faculty); (5) strong external connections to support school development (universities, social service agencies, reform organizations, etc.); and (6) strategic use of discretionary resources. All of the EARS principals exhibit characteristics of entrepreneurs in the sense that they vigorously seek out resources from external agencies and incorporate programs from a variety of sources. Some principals who become adept at acquiring outside resources do not, however, address the core operations of their schools in a systematic fashion. These are "showcase schools" with many new programs that are uncoordinated and have little effect on the organizational core of the school. Anthony Bryk and colleagues (1993, pp. 14–15) refer to this type of school as a "Christmas Tree School." However, in the EARS schools, unlike the "Christmas Tree" schools, the changes are coherent with the school's vision and affect most classrooms and teachers.

What has been the impact of reform on students and teachers in EARS schools? The evidence from observations and interviews strongly suggests that these schools are well on the way to developing the type of community of learning that is stressed in both the effective schools model and the restructuring model. Teachers and students enthusiastically praise the efforts of the principals and spontaneously refer to positive changes in the schools' climates. Attendance is improved, disruptions and disorder have been reduced, students and teachers feel that safety has been improved, teachers and students appear to have a serious commitment to the academic program, and there is general optimism about the future of the schools.

Bryk and colleagues (1993) estimate that of the schools most in need of change, one-third are involved in successful movement toward restructuring and another third are making some progress. That estimate suggests that about a third of the most needy schools will require some type of substantial intervention from external sources if they are to be successful in the restructuring effort. The reform legislation placed the responsibility for monitoring the progress of schools on the central office of the Chicago Public Schools. However, severe budget limitations, plus a lack of enthusiasm for "reform" on the part of some administrators, have impeded the development of a monitoring capacity within the Chicago Public Schools. Chicago *Sun-Times* columnist Vernon Jarrett (1993b) contends that the central office has been decimated deliberately as part of a political agenda designed to eliminate the Chicago Pubic Schools as a public school system.

### *Reactions of Reformers and News Media*

Local newspapers have recently chronicled the progress of the LSCs with headlines such as "School Is Lifted from Squalor," "Reform Working, School Council Study Told," "New Public School Opens to Oohs, Aahs" (*Chicago Tribune*, February 10, 1993; January 27, 1993; February 2, 1993). Political leaders, parents, community representatives, and reformers have praised the work of selected LSCs. For example, *Chicago Tribune* reporter Paul Sloan describes Hefferan Elementary School (also selected as an EARS school) as a site where parent empowerment through the LSC has transformed the school.

> Walking into Hefferan Elementary School on the West Side, it's easy to forget the stark streets just outside—the abandoned, burned-out buildings, the graffiti, the cars left to rust, the restless people on the street corners.
>
> Step inside and see a school that bears the marks of a sort of mini urban renewal: freshly painted halls, new desks, a fully equipped computer lab, and a recently built science lab where students take a hands-on approach to a subject that just a few years ago never left the textbooks. . . .
>
> And inside the classroom and out, you're likely to find parents participating—helping in classrooms, the lunchroom or on field trips. [Sloan, 1993]

LSCs appear to have been most effective in the area of improvements to the physical plants of schools and in the area of improved safety. On the other hand, they tend to defer to the principal and other professionals in matters of instruction, curriculum, and the like (Bryk et al., 1993, pp. 25–27).

Another EARS school was highlighted in the Business and Professional People for the Public Interest (BPI) *Newsletter* (James, 1992b). The Eugene Field Elementary School, led by principal Nelda Hobbs, has embarked on an ambitious plan to transform a very large school into five small schools. The principal says she could not make it work without the support of the teachers; the teachers give credit to the principal for leadership; both principal and teachers give credit to the assistance they received from an external relationship with the Center for School Improvement, of the University of Chicago. The principal has participated in a summer leadership institute directed by the Center, and she and her staff have benefited from ongoing staff development, including a retreat, facilitated by Albert Bertani, Director of Leadership Development at the Center for School Improvement.

Reformers and local news media illustrate the benefits of local school empowerment by frequently publicizing the success of some schools in adopting innovative instructional programs. Mary Galloway James, writing in the *BPI Newsletter*, cited the following:

- Coalition for Essential Schools, a national program, helps high schools develop long-term answers to their own unique problems (eight Chicago high schools are involved).
- Comer Plan, a national program, deepens parents', teachers', principals' understanding and interaction and provides and coordinates extraordinary resources for schools serving low-income, low-achieving children (four West Side elementary schools are involved; the inclusion of ten more is planned). [James, 1992a, p. 6]

Chicago Public Schools operated an extensive magnet school program (Options for Knowledge) as part of a desegregation agreement long before the current reform began. The "Options" schools selected a variety of specializations (Agriculture High School, elementary and secondary foreign language academies, science and mathematics secondary schools, technical schools, vocational schools, and the like). Some of the Options schools had already become involved in curriculum and instructional innovations before 1988. For example, the Paideia Program operated in both elementary and secondary schools, the Reading Recovery Program was available to selected schools, and cooperative learning was tried at some schools. However, nonmagnet schools had few options, only those available through Chapter 1 and other compensatory programs, with decisions about program participation being made at the central office of the Chicago Public Schools. Reform opened up the full range of options to individual schools. The only restrictions are the availability of funding and the imagination of the principal, teachers, and LSC. Now many additional schools are attempting to implement cooperative learning, Reading Recovery, the University of Chicago School Mathematics Program, and other instructional innovations. Success for All, the widely acclaimed instructional program developed by Robert Slavin of Johns Hopkins University, has recently been adopted by the Terrell Elementary School on Chicago's South Side (Plath, 1993, p. 9). A recent article in *Catalyst* (Forte and Shore, 1993), a newsletter that reports on Chicago school reform, reported that during the 1992–93 academic year, eleven Chicago high schools were part of the Coalition of Essential Schools; seven elementary schools and three high schools had adopted the Paideia Program; seventy-four schools used Reading Recovery; and four Chicago schools were involved in the Accelerated Schools Project. Whether a program developed by experts in another context can be successfully transplanted to a system as diverse and complex as that of Chicago remains to be seen. The following section describes some of the difficulties in bringing to Chicago one such model, the Comer School Development Program.

*Bringing the Comer Model to Chicago.*Youth Guidance, a social service agency in Chicago, in a project funded by the Chicago Community Trust, Citibank, and the MacArthur Foundation, is attempting to implement the Comer School Development Program (SDP) in Chicago (Youth Guidance, 1990). In 1990, four elementary schools—Riis, Dodge, Brown, and Jefferson—on Chicago's near west side were chosen as pilot programs for the SDP. Schools selected were those where academic achievement was among the lowest in the city and where principals were eager for change and open to sharing power. Phase I implementation of the SDP in Chicago began in the four pilot schools in fall 1991. In Phase II, four more schools—Ryerson, Smyth-Joyner, Herbert, and Prescott—were added in fall 1992 (Johnstone and Loseth, 1993). By the third year of the program, it is anticipated that all fourteen elementary schools in the community will be included in the program.

Principals of the pilot schools, their key staff, and Youth Guidance staff spent two weeks at Yale University in an intensive orientation to the SDP. They observed the SDP in operation in New Haven schools, and talked with parents, teachers, and children involved in the process. They learned what worked for those involved, what did not, and the "growing pains" associated with social change. A two-day retreat is planned for other members of the Chicago school teams so that those who visited Yale can share their experiences. Parents at the pilot schools have expressed enthusiasm for the program and a willingness to become involved in the process.

The core element of the SDP, *the governance team*, is charged with the goal of creating a good climate in the school. Representatives of all stakeholders (administrators, parents, the principal, union representatives, curriculum specialists, and counselors) should have a voice on the team. Decisions on the governance team are made by *consensus* to avoid a winner/loser situation. The team must learn to work cooperatively on the problems common to the school. Its major task is to formulate a comprehensive school plan aimed at developing social and academic skills.

Creating governance teams in the pilot schools was surprisingly easy. Comer originally suggested that the LSC serve as the proxy for the governance team in order to avoid conflict. The four schools, however, chose to create their own teams, called School Management and Planning Teams (SMPTs). The rationale given by all four was that the LSC disproportionately represents the interests of parents, and that the SMPT should represent each stakeholder group equally. Members of the LSC are on the SMPT at each school, but the LSC itself is not involved in the day-to-day management of the schools. This has caused conflict between the SMPT and the LSC at some schools, which the Youth Guidance Team is attempting to mediate and resolve. By 1993, the schools in both Phase I and Phase II had also established parent programs to enhance parental involvement, and mental health teams to reduce behavior problems and encourage the development of a cooperative, nonconflictual social climate within the schools. Youth Guidance has been joined in the project by two local universities. DePaul University's Center for Urban Education provides staff development for curriculum improvement and parent involvement. Two members of the Urban Teacher

Corps from DePaul will be based at each school, with experienced teachers at each of the four schools acting as their mentors.

The SDP is being evaluated by a team of researchers from Northwestern University. The evaluation will examine both the process and outcome. The process evaluation will focus on the functioning of the three teams at each school in order to observe the decision-making process and quality of participation. In addition, changes in school climate and parent-teacher relations will be examined.

Whether the SDP will be successful in Chicago depends on the ability of the school teams, Youth Guidance, and the affiliated universities to create a climate at each school that meets the criteria of the Comer model. The Youth Guidance School Development Team has identified three major implementation problems at the end of the second full year of operation. First, there continue to be negative attitudes from some school staff. Some of the resistance appears to stem from an unwillingness to be open to change. Second, at times the leadership from the principal is tentative. The Youth Guidance SDP Team attributes this tentativeness to a fear of the Chicago Teachers Union because of contractual rules and possible negative reactions from the Chicago Public Schools bureaucracy. Third, some of the principals in the Comer schools have limited expertise in curriculum development and are not able to provide effective instructional leadership. The Youth Guidance SDP Team plans to provide or arrange for continuing staff development for participating schools in these problem areas. The SDP Teams will also add a curriculum/instructional specialist to work with principals and teachers. The March 1993 Quarterly Summary of the Youth Guidance Comer School Development Project concludes: "Several of the [eight Comer schools] are well on the way to internalizing the model and will need less and less direct support from the Youth Guidance SDP team facilitators and administrators" (Johnstone and Loseth, 1993, p. 14).

Independent evaluation of the program will be available in the future. When the results are made public, we will be better able to assess the success of the implementation. I selected the Comer Program for discussion here because it is a complex comprehensive model that attempts thorough restructuring of schools, and because the attempt to implement it illustrates the difficulties encountered when schools attempt to apply a model developed in another context in a large, politically and socially complex school system. If this model can be successfully implemented in Chicago, the outlook for reform will be very bright indeed.

If the problems cited above and the conflictual nature of Chicago school reform (Payne, 1991) cannot be resolved, the SDP will have a difficult time in Chicago. However, I would caution against forming quick conclusions about the effectiveness of the program in Chicago. It took nearly ten years for the New Haven program to demonstrate its value to the satisfaction of the skeptics. It may take several years for the management teams to learn how to work together consensually and to develop ways of obtaining resources and cooperation from the Chicago central administration as well as from other agencies.

## DISCUSSION AND CONCLUSION

The community-control movement, which began in the 1960s, attempted to move decision making from a centralized, and unresponsive, bureaucracy to local schools or local districts. The political response to community control was *decentralization*. Decentralization defused the community control movement by shifting *limited* decision-making powers to local school districts. However, some of the most important decisions continued to be made by the centralized bureaucracy. This included developing the systemwide budget, negotiating with representatives of employee unions, and the awarding of most major contracts. In Chicago, in spite of the "radical" nature of school reform, these major functions continue to be the responsibility of the Chicago Board of Education, the General Superintendent of Schools, and the central office staff.

Linda Grant (1985) concludes: "Schooling experience, for the most part, seems to contribute to socialization of each race-gender group in a manner consistent with prevailing societal norms about appropriate roles for adults of each ascribed-status group" (p. 73). In the context of Chicago's school reform, this statement implies that the success of this reform must be assessed in terms of the adult roles the "reformers" envision for African-American and Hispanic children. Tim Black (1992), co-chair of the African-American Education Reform Institute, a coalition of African-American and community leaders of Chicago, has pointed out that the first two and a half years of reform focused on governance, but it is now time to refocus and consider first the needs of and goals for children at the point of intervention, the classroom. Anthony Bryk and Sharon Rollow (1992) have noted that African Americans are skeptical of the motives of the politicians, the leading reform organizations (for example, Designs for Change, The Chicago Panel, Business and Professional People for the Public Interest, Leadership for Quality Education), the business community, and the white citizens of Chicago and the state of Illinois. African-American political leaders fear that the reform is designed to fail so that local communities can be blamed for its demise. This, according to their beliefs, would set the stage for the initiation of a market-based voucher system that would spell the end of the Chicago Public School system. (This view is also expressed by some white politicians. See State Senator Arthur Berman's letter to the editor of *Catalyst* [Berman, 1992].) At the root of the desire to eliminate the Chicago Public School system, African-American political leaders assert, is a belief on the part of Democratic and Republican party leaders and the business community that the Chicago Public Schools are too important economically and politically to permit control to remain in the hands of local African-American educators (Jarrett, 1993a, 1993b). Some minority leaders believe that the continued struggle between Chicago's Mayor Richard M. Daley and Illinois' Governor James Edgar is nothing more than a contest for control of a $2.4 billion budget and control over the awarding of major contracts. At any rate, many African Americans believe that political and business leaders of the white community do not care enough about the education of nonwhites to provide adequate funding for the Chicago Public Schools. I agree with Jonathan Kozol (1991) that these leaders would not tolerate the physical deterioration of facilities or the absence of basic educational materials that now exist in Chicago if the majority of the children served by the system were white.

The political coalition that pushed the Chicago School Reform Act through the Illinois state legislature was an uneasy alliance. African-American leaders remain skeptical about the school reformers' "hidden agenda" (Bryk and Rollow, 1992). Chicago *Sun-Times* columnist Vernon Jarrett wrote:

> The purpose of the seductive language of school reform, as it was used by City Hall and its operatives on the School Board, was to, in fact, undermine the spirit of community control. . . . "Reform" also was a device to avoid state and local responsibility for the financing

of public education in a city where black enrollment is more than 61 percent and white enrollment is less than 12 percent.

Let's face the hard fact that we're a society that has a problem spending money on any education, not to mention black education.

Remember, school reform was passed by the Illinois General Assembly and a Republican governor. So why can't they find more money for Chicago? In the name of reform? [Jarrett, 1993b, p. 33]

This is not an isolated viewpoint. In a recent issue of *Catalyst*, Linda Linz (1992) provides an excellent summary of Chicago's school funding crises from 1971 to 1991. The Chicago Panel on Public School Policy and Finance (1993) contends that "The major threat to the effort to reform Chicago Public Schools comes not from the classroom, but from the fiscal crisis which may shut down the school system next fall and justify impatient politicians lusting to regain control of the public schools and their 45,000 jobs" (p. 1).

As of early September 1993, the state legislature had provided neither funding nor authorization to borrow money that would enable the Chicago schools to operate for the 1993–94 school year. Nevertheless, the schools did open in September when a federal judge issued a temporary restraining order that prevented closing of the schools. In November, however, the legislature approved a controversial financial package that enabled the school board to borrow funds needed to keep the schools open for the next two years. This continuing uncertainty about funding has had a very negative effect on the morale of parents, teachers, administrators, and the general public in Chicago. Until the funding issue is resolved, reform efforts will lose much of the momentum that has been gained during the past four years. It will be extremely difficult to recapture the enthusiasm for change that has been developed in the most forward-looking schools.

In addition to funding problems, not all participants in the reform process are favorable to school-based management and school restructuring. Some teachers continue to express concern about the quality of the home environments of inner-city children. Thus, they worry about the educational disadvantages of their pupils, and what they perceive as lack of support for education among parents and lack of ambition among students. They frequently express excuses for low academic achievement that "blame the victim" rather than seeking to examine the policies and practices of the schools that victimize economically disadvantaged children. Approximately three-fourths of the teachers surveyed by the Consortium on Chicago School Reform feel that they are instructionally proficient (Easton et al., 1991). Therefore, persuading the teaching force that successful restructuring of schools depends on their willingness to make major changes in their instructional practices will be a difficult task. It is also a very complex process that requires an enlightened principal who creates a "strong democracy" governance structure (Bryk and Rollow, 1992), and the support of the total school community. Even in such an environment, many things can go wrong that might prevent a successful transition to systemic restructuring. (See, for example, the case study described by Julia Aguirre [1993].)

A positive note from the Chicago Teachers Union is the implementation of the QUEST Center for staff development. The union's efforts in creating the QUEST Center is an acknowledgement from union leadership that teachers are an important part of the problem of low achievement in Chicago schools. Perhaps the union is responding to the widespread views of other observers of Chicago school reform. The *Catalyst* survey of Chicago Teachers Union delegates and 34 percent of Professional Personnel Advisory Committee (PPAC) chairs found that nearly 29 percent of union delegates and 34 percent of PPAC chairs said that difficulty in removing poor teachers was a definite or serious problem at their school, as did 53 percent of local school council chairs (Forte, 1993).

Principals report that they need greater control of school staff, including building engineers, custodial personnel, lunch room staff, and other unionized ancillary personnel. The survey of principals (Bennett et al., 1992) also revealed that foremost among principals' concerns is their desire to be able to remove ineffective teachers more easily than is now possible. Surprisingly, teacher leaders agree with principals that ineffective teachers are a major hindrance to the implementation of reform at the classroom level (Forte, 1993).

After four years of school reform in Chicago, I would give the project a mixed report card. By the lowest standards of evaluation, the effort has been successful. All schools have elected LSCs; all LSCs have selected or retained principals; all schools have submitted School Improvement Plans (of widely varying quality). At a slightly higher standard, it appears that most schools (probably 80 percent) have made some effort to improve school-community relations and increase parent participation. At the level of systemic restructuring, perhaps one-third of schools are making substantial progress and another third are beginning to make progress. That still leaves about one-third of the schools lagging behind, and needing considerable assistance in making movement toward systemic reform.

Whether the new superintendent, Argie Johnson, can provide the kind of leadership needed to help the most needy schools will depend to a great extent not only on her own vision, but also on the willingness of the state legislature and the local political community to make a serious commitment to the goal of effective schools for minority inner-city children.

Chicago school reform has the potential to revolutionize urban education. I can envision nearly six hundred schools with imaginative principals who collaborate with teachers and other staff to work closely with parents and community residents to bring about systemic restructuring of the schools. These visionaries would bring the most exciting and effective instructional resources into their schools and organize them for maximum effectiveness. I am not dreaming alone. In May 1992, the Chicago School Finance Authority, an oversight body established by the state legislature, convened a panel of teachers, principals, and local school council members from twenty-six schools to dream about reinventing Chicago's public school system:

> Divided into four "focus groups," they dreamed big: Local school councils would set principals' salaries, principals would hire school engineers and maintenance staff, teachers would work on year-to-year contracts, and schools would control all professional development and building repair funds. [Forte and Klonsky, 1992, p. 1]

The report generated considerable controversy, especially from the Chicago Teachers Union and other employee unions concerned about loss of job security. Others complained that many of the recommendations were illegal or unworkable. What is important here, in my view, is that someone in a position of authority realizes that school reform is serious business that requires the best thinking and good will of a diverse constituency. What is required is a commitment to the proposition that African-American and Hispanic children in Chicago deserve the very best system of education that the best available minds can devise. That commitment is sadly lacking among the political leaders who have the power to finance and support such a visionary system of education (Chicago Panel on Public School Policy and Finance, 1993). It is not likely that the promise of Chicago school reform can be realized without that type of commitment. As Tim Black (1992) stated: "Our goal is increased achievement and an efficient system of delivery of services" (p. 14). Anything less I would consider to be a failure of school reform in Chicago.

## REFERENCES

Aguirre, Julia M. "Case Study Evaluation of an Intensive Staff Development Initiative to Improve Mathematics Instruction in an Urban Elementary School Setting." Master's Paper, Department of Education, University of Chicago, 1993.

Bennett, Albert; Bryk, Anthony S.; Easton, John Q.; Kerbow, David; Luppescu, Stuart; and Sebring, Penny A. *Charting Reform: The Principal's Perspective.* Chicago: Consortium on Chicago School Research, 1992.

Berman, Arthur. "Amendment Opponents Really Want Vouchers," *Catalyst* 4, no. 3 (November 1992): 16.

Black, Tim. "Don't Lose Sight of Classrooms," *Catalyst* 4, no. 1 (September 1992): 13–14.

Bradley, Ann. "Poll Highlights Positive Responses to Chicago Reforms," *Education Week*, 10 February 1993, p. 5.

Bryk, Anthony S., and Rollow, Sharon G. "The Chicago Experiment: Enhanced Democratic Participation as a Lever for School Improvement." In *Issues in Restructuring Schools.* Madison, Wisconsin: Center on Organization and Restructuring of Schools, School of Education, University of Wisconsin-Madison, Issue Report no. 3 (Fall 1992): 3–7.

Bryk, Anthony S.; Easton, John Q.; Kerbow, David; Rollow, Sharon; and Sebring, Penny A. *A View from the Elementary Schools: The State of Reform in Chicago.* Chicago: Consortium on Chicago School Research, 1993.

Chicago Panel on Public School Policy and Finance. "Budget Deficit Threatens School Reform Gains." *Panel Update* 8, no. 4 (Spring 1993): 1, 8–9.

Clark, David L.; Lotto, Linda S.; and Astuto, Terry A. "Effective Schools and School Improvement: A Comparative Analysis of Two Lines of Inquiry." *Educational Administration Quarterly* 20, no. 3 (Summer 1984): 41–68.

Clements, Stephen K., and Forsaith, Andrew C., Eds. *Chicago School Reform: National Perspectives and Local Responses.* Proceedings of a conference sponsored by the Educational Excellence Network and the Joyce Foundation, Chicago, November 19, 1990. Washington, D.C.: Educational Excellence Network, 1991.

Cochran, Moncrief. "The Parental Empowerment Process: Building on Family Strengths," *Equity and Choice* 4, no. 1 (Fall 1987): 9–23.

Easton, John Q.; Storey, Sandra; Johnson, Cheryl; Qualls, Jesse; and Ford, Darryl. *Local School Council Meetings during the First Year of School Reform.* Chicago: Chicago Panel on Public School Policy and Finance, November 1990.

Easton, John Q.; Bryk, Anthony S.; Driscoll, Mary E.; Kotsakis, John G.; Sebring, Penny A.; and Van der Ploeg, Arie J. *Charting Reform: The Teachers' Turn.* Chicago: Consortium on Chicago School Research, 1991.

Epps, Edgar G. "School-Based Management: Implications for Minority Parents." In *Restructuring the Schools: Problems and Prospects*, edited by John J. Lane and Edgar G. Epps. Berkeley, Calif.: McCutchan, 1992.

Forte, Lorraine. "Bad Teachers Worry Teacher Leaders," *Catalyst* 4, no. 8 (May 1993): pp 1, 3–5.

Forte, Lorraine, and Klonsky, Michael. "Focus Groups Target Laws, Union Contracts," *Catalyst* 4, no. 1 (September 1992): 1–3.

Forte, Lorraine, and Shore, Debra. "New Ideas for Reaching Kids Who Lag Behind," *Catalyst* 4, no. 5 (February 1993): 14–17.

Gottfredson, Gary D., and Hybl, Lois G. *An Analytical Description of the School Principal's Job*, Report no. 13. Baltimore: Center for Research on Elementary and Middle Schools, Johns Hopkins University, May 1987.

Grant, Linda. "Uneasy Alliances: Black Males, Teachers, and Peers in Desegregated Classrooms." Paper presented at the Annual Meeting of the American Educational Research Association, Chicago 1985.

James, Mary Galloway. "I Came. I Saw. I Was Conquered!" *BPI Newsletter* (April 1992a): 1–7.

James, Mary Galloway. "Field of Dreams," *BPI Newsletter* (Fall 1992b): 1–9.

Jarrett, Vernon. "Bad News about Schools: Then Good News about a March," Chicago *Sun-Times*, 18 May 1993a, p. 29.

Jarrett, Vernon. "The School Reformers' Hidden Agenda," Chicago *Sun-Times*, 20 May 1993b, p. 33.

Jarrett,Vernon. "Scapegoat Search Targets Teachers Union," Chicago *Sun-Times*, 1 August 1993c, p. 39.

Johnstone, Nancy, and Loseth, Vivian. "Youth Guidance Comer School Development Program: Quarterly Summary, March 1993." Chicago: Youth Guidance, 1993.

Katz, Michael B. "Chicago School Reform as History," *Teachers College Record* 94, no. 1 (1992): 56–72.

Katz, Michael B.; Fine, Michelle; and Simon, Elaine. "School Reform: A View from Outside," Chicago *Tribune*, 7 March 1991.

Kozol, Jonathan. *Savage Inequalities*. New York: Crown, 1991.

Leadership for Quality Education. *A Survey of Members of Chicago Local School Councils*. Chicago: Richard Day Research, Inc., 1990.

Lederer, Joseph. "Interview with Albert Shanker," *Urban Review* 3 (November 1968): 23–27.

Linz, Linda. "Decades of Finance Tricks Create Annual Crisis," *Catalyst* 4, no. 1 (September 1992): 17–19.

Murphy, Joseph, and Hallinger, Philip. "Preface." In *Restructuring Schooling: Learning from Ongoing Efforts*, edited by Joseph Murphy and Philip Hallinger. Newbury Park, Calif.: Corwin Press, 1993.

Newmann, Fred M. "Director's Introduction." *Issues in Restructuring Schools*, Madison, Wisconsin: Center on Organization and Restructuring of Schools, School of Education, University of Wisconsin-Madison, Issue Report No. 3 (Fall 1992), p. 2.

Obejas, Achy. "Getting Down to Business: Councils Chalk up Small Gains," *Catalyst* 2, no. 6 (March 1991): 13–15.

Payne, Charles. "The Comer Intervention Model and School Reform in Chicago: Implications of Two Models of Change," *Urban Education* 26, no. 1 (1991): 8–24.

Peterson, Kent D. "The New Politics of the Principalship: School Reform and Change in Chicago." In *Chicago School Reform: National Perspectives and Local Responses*. Proceedings of a conference sponsored by the Educational Excellence Network and the Joyce Foundation, Chicago, November 19, 1990. Washington, D.C.: Educational Excellence Network, 1991.

Plath, Karl H. "New Way of Learning," Chicago *Tribune*, 25 July 1993.

Rothman, Karl H. "Chicago's Grassroots School Reform Provides Irresistible Laboratory for Dozens of Scholars," *Education Week*, 30 October 1991.

Sloan, Paul. "School Is Lifted from Squalor," Chicago *Tribune*, 10 February 1993.

Youth Guidance. "Near Westside Elementary School Development Program." Grant Proposal. Chicago: Youth Guidance, 1990.

# 7

# Comprehensive School Services in San Diego

## Thomas W. Payzant

As our society has become more diverse, the demands placed on the public schools have steadily increased. It has been many years since the academic mission was the single focus of public education. While it is true that most public school districts began providing some limited health and counseling services in the 1930s and 1940s, in recent years the level of these programs has grown dramatically. Further, a much greater variety of services is now provided. Schools routinely give underprivileged youngsters free or reduced-price lunch and breakfast, provide special classes for pregnant teens and school-age mothers, educate students about AIDS and drug and alcohol abuse, and reach out to help parents become involved in their children's education. As the gap between the haves and have-nots widens, the demand for social services for children and families continues to grow with it.

Paralleling this growth has been a steady expansion of special education programs as well. The passage in 1975 of the Education for All Handicapped Children Act (Public Law 94–142) heralded a major increase in special services for students. The legislation requires all schools to provide free, appropriate individualized education programs for all handicapped children from birth to twenty-one years of age. The number of children receiving special education services is increasing, and all projections indicate it will continue to do so for some time to come. The problems are exacerbated by the growing numbers of babies born addicted to drugs or to very young mothers who have given them little or no prenatal care.

The condition of children in America is worsening. According to a recent report published by the Children's Defense Fund (1992), one out of every five American children lives in poverty. We have more poor children—14.3 million—than we have had since 1965, and contrary to popular myth, the majority of them are not African American and are not on welfare. They live in working families in rural, suburban, and urban America. The fund reported that the median income of parents under age thirty fell 32 percent between 1973 and 1990. About 2.7 million children were reported abused or neglected in 1991, and 429,000 were in foster homes or institutions. Poor children with problems will most likely grow to be teenagers with problems. In 1990, a joint commission was formed by the National Association of State Boards of Education and the American Medical Association to study some of the problems of adolescents. In its report, the commission warned that America is raising a generation of adolescents plagued by pregnancies, drug and alcohol abuse, violence, and suicide (National Commission on the Role of the School and the Community in Improving Adolescent Health, 1990). The commission pointed out that today's young people are less prepared to take their places in society than were their parents. Among other things, the study found that alcohol-related accidents are the leading cause of death among teenagers; the suicide rate for teens has doubled since 1986, making it the second leading cause of death among adolescents; teenage arrests are up thirty-fold since 1950; and homicide is the leading cause of death among fifteen- to nineteen-year-old minority youths.

The commission stressed that inattention to these problems has left thousands of young people doomed to school failure, which for many is a precursor to a life of crime, unemployment, or welfare dependency. It is clear that more and more children and young people are bringing more than educational needs to the classroom. Many public school educators resent the additional responsibilities the schools are assuming by default. They bemoan the failure of families and other institutions in the society that traditionally have accepted the primary responsibilities for the upbringing of children, but now seem distracted by the harsh realities of economic survival. In many families, children are left to their own devices.

Only a generation ago, parents could rely on others in the neighborhood to help oversee the safety, health, and behavior of all the neighborhood's children. Relatives often lived close by and were available to help out. Except in rural America, most children could walk to school. It was not unusual for a child to go home for lunch because mother was at home. As families have changed, neighborhoods also have changed, and in far too many places there is no longer a sense of community grounded in the values of shared responsibility. Most parents want to do what is right for their children. They care about their children's well-being and want them to be healthy, safe, and successful. Most people who work in schools and in other agencies that provide services for children, youth, and families care about the people they serve. However, each agency has its own policies, rules and regulations, funding sources, political pressures, and traditions that all tend to create barriers to interagency collaboration and set up frustrating hurdles for their clients to clear in order to receive the services they need.

We must do better than that. We have to stop blaming the children for conditions over which they have no control. Poor children are very capable of learning. Poverty and the conditions it breeds raise serious questions about fairness and equity, but there is no justice in stereotypes that characterize poor children as human beings with a deficit. The present system results in great loss in human terms and an enormous waste of public and private resources as well. We cannot afford these losses for long and expect to remain a strong nation. A comprehensive, collaborative approach to providing services for children, youth, and families must be developed and established across the country. That may sound simple, but in actual fact, it is a very radical proposal. Major reform does not come easily, and bureaucracies are notoriously resistant to change. During the past few years, a number of communities have initiated projects designed to bring together the various human service agencies in order to transcend artificial agency boundaries and serve their mutual clients more efficiently and humanely. Many of these collaborative efforts are based in schools. What follows is an overview of the development of one of these collaborative efforts.

# NEW BEGINNINGS IN SAN DIEGO: DEVELOPING AN
# INTERAGENCY COLLABORATIVE

About five years ago, the San Diego City School District became involved in the development of an innovative approach to providing social services to low-income families. It had been recognized for some time that the schools and local family service agencies served the same families with limited resources and fragmented efforts. Little systematic communication or collaboration existed among the various entities.

In the summer of 1988, informal discussions began among the local social service agencies and the school district to see if things might be done differently. Among other things, there was concern that most resources in the system were being used to deal with crises, and very little was being done to help children and families whose problems had not reached crisis proportion. Also, as one might expect, there was considerable duplication of effort in gathering information, certifying eligibility, and keeping records. Many of the families being served did not know of the existence of or how to contact the several public assistance agencies charged with helping them. The situation was getting worse with no consistent or coordinated efforts being made to improve it.

It was clear from the beginning that addressing these concerns would be difficult, if not impossible. Conflicting regulations, problems of confidentiality, and questions about areas of responsibility could be overwhelming. However, the need to do something was clear, and the leadership of the local agencies agreed there should be greater cooperation among the different agencies serving the same children and families. There was also agreement that this should not be an effort to develop a project to accomplish a single given idea. Rather, the goal was to find a long-term strategy for systemic change in the way services were provided—to create one system out of many systems. This is a lofty goal created with serious intent and strong conviction. The indications of our early expectations for reaching this goal have been tempered by the hard political and economic reality of our experience with implementation.

Four local agencies were the nucleus of the initial work. They were the county of San Diego, the city of San Diego, the San Diego Community College District, and the San Diego City School District. The group has since been expanded to include the San

Diego Housing Commission, the University of California at San Diego Medical School, and Children's Hospital and Health Center of San Diego. The collaborative was given the title "New Beginnings." From the start, it was seen that it was critical for all the participants to agree on exactly what interagency collaboration meant. It was obvious that difficulties could arise if the participants had different perceptions of the collaborative effort they wanted to initiate. In his very helpful book *Thinking Collaboratively* Charles Bruner (1991) defines collaboration this way:

> Collaboration is a process to reach goals that cannot be achieved acting singly (or, at a minimum, cannot be reached as efficiently). As a process, collaboration is a means to an end, not an end in itself. The desired end is more comprehensive and appropriate services for families that improve family outcomes. . . . Collaboration includes all of the following elements: jointly developing and agreeing to a set of common goals and directions; sharing responsibility for obtaining those goals; and working together to achieve those goals, using the expertise of each collaborator.
>
> Because collaboration involves sharing responsibility, it requires consensus building and may not be imposed hierarchically. It is likely to be time-consuming, as collaborators must learn about each other's roles and responsibilities, as well as explain their own. Collaborators must also acquire expertise in the process of group goal setting and decision sharing, which may not be part of their other work. [P. 6]

We have found that partners easily embrace the rhetoric of collaboration, but that developing a collaborative process that results in a consensus on strategies to use to change partner institutions in fundamental, systemic ways is very ambitious and time-consuming work. Competing demands for partners' time, resources, and undivided attention constantly test the commitments necessary to develop and implement action plans. As the participants in the New Beginnings project continued to meet and talk, a set of shared assumptions emerged:

- San Diego faces complex problems, including a large and growing population of Indochinese and Latino immigrants, inadequate public transportation, inadequate low-cost housing, and high mobility among families and children.
- All agencies are experiencing serious financial constraints. Attention must be focused on doing better with existing resources, rather than on developing more costly solutions.
- It is more effective to provide assistance early in a child's life than to wait until adolescence.

- Interventions that focus on individuals rather than family systems are unlikely to be effective.
- Staff members in many agencies are unfamiliar with and mistrustful of the services provided by other agencies.
- Interagency collaboration must be led from the executive level.

## Conducting a Feasibility Study

These discussions led to an agreement to pursue the possibility of conducting an action research project to study the feasibility of a one-stop coordinated service center located on a school site. In July 1989, the collaborative received a $45,000 foundation grant to help fund the study, which began with staff and services donated by each participating agency. It was agreed that the study would focus on early intervention and ask such questions as:

- How many families receive services from the county, city, or community-based agencies funded by the city or county?
- What services do they receive?
- Are they eligible for services that they are not currently receiving?
- Is there a relationship between a family's use of social and health services and the academic and social success of children?
- What barriers do the families encounter when they try to get help from the present system?
- What barriers exist within the system, as seen by agency staff members?
- Can the service delivery system be made more responsive to the needs of low-income families in a way that is integrated and cost effective?

The study included five elements: interviews with families and students; interviews with front-line providers from the participating agencies; a data-sharing plan to investigate the number of families the agencies served in common; a study of the migration patterns of the school's families; and, finally, an action-oriented component that called for placing a social worker at the school to work directly with families, and for establishing a cadre of agency liaison people to help outside agencies become more accessible to families and to the school staff.

The school selected for the study is located in San Diego's City Heights community. The attendance area is a densely populated, highly transient, ethnically mixed neighborhood. It has one of the city's worst crime rates and highest reported incidence of child abuse. The school, which is on a multitrack, year-round schedule, has an enrollment of about 1,300 students. It has one of the highest mobility rates in the district. The student body is 42.6 percent Latino, 25.0 percent Indochinese, 21.3 percent African American, 8.2 percent white, and about 3 percent from other racial or ethnic groups. Twenty-three languages are represented at the school, and more than half the students do not speak English as their native language. A majority of the school's students are from single-parent families. The selection of this school as a study site gave the collaborative an opportunity to study the problems of poor families and students in an overcrowded school located in a high-crime, low-income area.

The study began in January 1990 with off-duty county public health nurses conducting in-home interviews with thirty-two families in the school's attendance area. These interviews were designed to determine the needs of the families; learn what barriers exist to receiving services; identify the services that the families deemed most helpful and available; investigate the effects of the assistance from the family perspective; and consider the barriers to service from the interviewer's perspective.

For the second element of the study, interviews with the service providers, the County Department of Social Services contributed two trained facilitators to conduct nine focus-group interviews. These sessions involved a total of seventy-seven workers representing all of the agencies. The interviews attempted to examine the workers' perspective of the needs of the school's students and families; identify barriers to service from the workers' point of view; and identify services they thought were most helpful and available.

The data-match study was conducted by the County Department of Social Services with data tapes provided by the school district, the County Department of Social Services, the County Department of Juvenile and Adult Probation, and the City Housing Commission. The data match was designed to determine current levels of service provided to the school's families by the major agencies; examine the extent of the multiple use of services by families; compare the use of services by families of different racial or ethnic backgrounds and other factors; and determine the total financial resources allocated to the families by the participating agencies.

The social worker placed at the school was a bilingual

(Spanish/English) professional from the County Department of Social Services. He conducted a case-management study to examine the impact of the current system on families in a school setting; determine the effects of case-management services on twenty selected high-risk families; document the needs of families for services; identify the barriers they encountered in the system; and document the extent of services provided by the school staff.

To accomplish the fifth element of the study, one liaison person was appointed by each agency to expedite referrals and share pertinent information about eligibility and the availability of services with members of the school staff. The liaison study was designed to increase access by the school staff members and students to agency services; increase agency staff awareness of the needs existing at the school; identify agency and family barriers to receiving services; and identify areas of potential change within agencies that would enhance services for families.

For the migration study, data were gathered by the Research Department of the San Diego City School District and analyzed by a member of the New Beginnings team. The purposes of the study were to determine patterns of student and family mobility in and out of the school attendance area, and to determine the characteristics of the mobile and stable student populations. All of the study field work was completed by the end of April 1990, and the final report was released in July 1990.

## Findings of the Feasibility Study

The study produced valuable findings: many reinforced our previous ideas and biases, and others led us in new directions. What follows are some highlights from the report of the study (San Diego City Schools, 1990.)

It was found that most families are unaware of the services available to them. They need help finding help. There must be basic, fundamental reform in the way schools and governmental agencies deliver services to families. Such reform requires new ways of thinking about the needs of families, the roles of agency workers, eligibility determination, the focus and process of service delivery, and the allocation of funds. Families see the school as a place to get help. Being identified with the school during the study helped the family services advocate and the county public health nurses gain initial access to families. However, schools can quickly become overwhelmed by the multiple needs of families. Without question, the school setting is an excellent primary contact point for working with families, but a school-governed integrated services program is not advisable. Governance by any one agency could inhibit maximum cooperation. The study pointed out that differences in philosophy make cooperation among agencies difficult. For example, schools are required to report all suspected incidents of child abuse, but the Child Protective Services cannot share information about a child's placement with the schools. The school thus often loses contact with the child if he or she is removed from the home. School officials estimate that because of this, 40 percent of the school personnel underreport suspected child abuse.

The study reinforces the concern that the system is too fragmented. It found that families must carry their life stories around to several places, and that each agency wants only one part of the story. Eligibility procedures that are complex and specific to each agency create barriers for families, and the lack of data sharing among agencies, workers, and families complicates the system. The report recommends that a common eligibility process be developed, with one central point of contact for families. Funding should be flexible enough to allow for appropriate services, whether specialized or general. Waivers, policy changes, and staffing changes may be necessary to provide appropriate funding flexibility. Legal means must be developed to allow workers to share pertinent information about families with the staff members of other agencies.

Interestingly, the study found that the families see themselves in better overall condition than the agency personnel see them, but they do feel plagued by short-term problems. However, the service providers are more likely to see the families as having many long-term needs. Clear discrepancies exist between the perceptions of the families and those of the workers. The study also found that most social service providers are frustrated with the narrowness and inflexibility of their roles. They say they feel dehumanized in their jobs. They report that they see generations of recurring problems in a family and feel helpless and unable to "break the chain." The report suggests that workers should become family advocates, working more intensively with fewer families. They should be given more authority and flexibility to determine when cases are opened, what services are rendered, and when cases should be closed.

## Establishing a Demonstration Center

The findings of the feasibility study made it clear that an integrated approach to the delivery of social services had potential. The report outlined a proposal for establishing a demonstration social services center at a school on a three-year pilot basis. Its goals would be to deliver combined, comprehensive services to children and families in the school's attendance area, and the center would be a vehicle for the continued study and development of a strategy for interagency collaboration. In July 1990, the governing boards of the participating agencies each adopted the report and its recommendations, and plans to establish the demonstration center were put in motion. The center was established at the school where the feasibility study was conducted and began serving clients in September 1991.

An expanded student registration, screening, and family-assessment process has become one of the center's primary activities. All families who enroll children in the school have an opportunity to become familiar with the services available to them, and the center's staff can make an initial assessment of the family and student needs. Also provided at the center are social services planning for families, ongoing case management, and various health services for families who need professional intervention. It is hoped, however, that increasingly the center's emphasis will be placed on prevention, not primary care. The collaborative must seek to change the nature of the services provided to families. We must get beyond merely responding to crises and find ways to help alleviate a family's long-term problems and allow children to naturally develop educationally, socially, and emotionally.

One interesting innovation at the center is an interactive video system that allows clients to access information about services available to them. By touching the screen, an individual can, in many cases, achieve a self-referral. The information is available in English, Spanish, and Vietnamese. This equipment was donated to the center by IBM, with the labor for the software development provided at no cost by North Communication. The center is now in the process of linking the data bases of the participating agencies together to create a single management information system. When this system becomes operational, the interactive video will be integrated into it, which will greatly expand its capability.

The school is a primary source of referrals. Classroom teachers refer children who are experiencing academic, behavioral, attendance, or health problems. Teachers receive training in problem identification and supportive techniques. They also gain awareness of the roles of other agency staff members and the services they provide. There is regular communication between the teachers and the workers at the center to constantly assess whether the services are helping the child. Staff members at the center, called family services advocates (FSAs), assure sustained contact with families in the system. They provide information about available services, help determine eligibility, and work with families to create and follow a plan for moving toward self-sufficiency. The FSAs also provide some direct counseling and work on behalf of the family with the agencies. Because the FSAs know their own agencies well, they are able to act as advocates for families to help them traverse the system. Each advocate works with thirty to forty families on a continuing basis.

New Beginnings also has an extended team of service providers to address needs in the community and do other work that cannot be performed at the center. For example, some agency workers have specialized tasks such as direct service and agency administrative activities that cannot be conducted within the center's facilities. In other agencies, the number of staff hours allocated to the school's families does not justify assigning a full-time staff person to the center. As members of the extended team, some workers continue at their home agencies and in their usual jobs but modify their case load to focus on families from the center.

The governance structure at a collaborative is difficult to create. Care must be taken not simply to establish a new bureaucracy. New Beginnings is led by an executive committee of eleven top-level administrators from the five participating agencies. This committee is complemented by an eleven-member implementation team, which is a working group made up of professionals from the New Beginnings Center or of people who represent their agencies in its New Beginnings involvement. These people must establish a meaningful collaborative relationship if New Beginnings is to realize its vision and develop a workable strategy for interagency collaboration and change. They form a vital link between the vision of what we want to accomplish and the action plan for making it happen. The center coordinator reports to the executive committee, but that is sometimes difficult to do each day. The executive committee leadership must remain accessible. The director, especially in the initial stages of the development of the collaborative, needs support and direction. There is always the problem of reporting to two or more masters. We chose to make one of the partners, San Diego City Schools, fiscal agent for New Beginnings. When the first director was hired from outside, she became an employee of the school district and was covered by the district's personnel policies and procedures. She was reporting directly to the executive committee and to a supervisor in the school district who is a member of the implementation team. If the coordinator was on loan from another partner institution, the same problem of a dual reporting relationship would exist. One solution would be to establish New Beginnings as a separate entity, but this approach has its limitations in the areas of governance and finance.

### Addressing Some Initial Problems

We have found that moving from improved communications and cooperation to actual interagency collaboration is the most critical step to be taken. It is also a very difficult one. It involves such issues as turf and control, decisions about leadership, agreements about group decision making, honest self-evaluations of the effectiveness of existing systems, gaining full understanding of how the other agencies in the group operate, and a willingness to overcome the complications of differing and sometimes redundant rules, regulations, and procedures. It is easy to find reasons not to attempt to establish a collaborative effort.

Success can be achieved only when everyone involved recognizes that things can be done much better by working together, and that it must be done to improve services to children and families. In short, there must be a common vision. That vision must be discussed thoroughly and be accepted by all participants. In their book on interagency collaboration, *What It Takes: Structuring Interagency Partnerships to Connect Children and Families With Comprehensive Service*, Atelia Melaville and Martin Blank (1991) say this about a common vision:

> A practical vision requires that members move beyond generalities, come to terms with the assumptions underlying their vision, and consider the accommodations that may ultimately be required. Members must participate in a self-conscious process that asks not only what has brought them together, but where they hope to go, and most important, what they have to lose. Calling for a comprehensive

system of child-centered and family-oriented services, for example, sounds good, but its creation will require changes and trade-offs in how, where, and by whom resources are distributed. It also will raise difficult issues of quantity vs. quality in service delivery, and equality vs. equity in determining who should receive limited resources. If these issues are anticipated and resolved early on, conflicts at the implementation stage will be minimized. [P. 22]

When the New Beginnings effort began, California was in reasonably sound financial shape and the partner institutions were not pitted one against the other in the fight for state funding. Late in 1990 when fiscal conditions changed for the worse, an extended period of austerity began. This serious shortage of funds continues to threaten the commitments to collaboration as each partner faces the pragmatic necessity of acting in one's own interest. However, when working with the center's budget, it is essential that the partners cooperate. Also, it is critical to break away from the traditional pattern of keeping score. Some agencies will contribute more in-kind services than will others. External constraints that are difficult to eliminate may prevent some of the partners from contributing their fair share of resources at the outset. A top-level person from each participating agency, preferably the chief executive officer, must, through his or her actions, demonstrate the commitment to the collaborative both through rhetoric and personal involvement. This is a prerequisite and gives those of other levels in the organization permission to make the same commitment. It should be pointed out that while start-up and operating costs are being paid by the participating agencies, it is very important that support from foundations continue as well. These funds are critical to enable us to experiment and grow.

One of the first issues to be addressed was the question of confidentiality. There was disagreement and misunderstanding about moving confidential information across the lines of various publicly funded programs. It was decided a study was needed to identify what barriers blocked the exchange of confidential information among agencies and to propose solutions. An extensive staff study was undertaken, and a comprehensive report was issued in July 1991 (County of San Diego Department of Social Services, 1991). The report, which is thought to be the first of its kind in California, provides practical guidance to program managers and offers concrete technical assistance. Interestingly, one of the principal findings of the study was that the law is not the sole or even the major barrier to the exchange of confidential information. The study found that most barriers to the safe and open exchange of confidential information are not legal questions at all—they are mainly management issues. A great many of the impediments can be overcome relatively easily when agencies work together collaboratively. The report also makes recommendations for some modest changes in the law and state regulations that would further facilitate interagency exchanges but not compromise confidentiality. The study resolved most concerns about the exchange of information among agencies.

Another significant problem that required early attention was the conflicting, overlapping, and often confusing eligibility requirements of the partner agencies. Valuable staff time was being spent determining client eligibility, and families were being required to tell their stories again and again to meet various agency requirements. As the feasibility study report recommended, a common eligibility process needed to be developed. The group decided to investigate the development of a preliminary system for determining eligibility for multiple programs with one application and verification process. A management consultant conducted an extensive review and developed a detailed set of recommendations for each of the participating agencies. Many of the recommendations have been implemented and are resulting in significant cost savings, making agency contact much easier for applicants, and enhancing the collaborative efforts.

For example, the county of San Diego and the San Diego City School District have worked out an agreement to share data and meet legally mandated confidentiality standards. Data are being matched on students enrolled in school who are from families who qualify for Aid to Families with Dependent Children (AFDC) and/or food stamps. These children automatically are declared eligible for the school district's free or reduced-price lunch with the signature of the parent. No longer will many parents or guardians be required to fill out the detailed school district application to qualify their children for the free or reduced-price lunch program if they are already receiving AFDC and/or food stamps. For the 1991–92 school year, 40.2 percent of the students receiving free or reduced-price lunches were directly certified. This is a clear example of a cost-effective result of a major systemic change in the way the agencies now deal with eligibility for an important service for children. The county's Department of Social Services and the school district had to be tenacious in convincing state and federal officials that what was being proposed made sense and was legal.

The health component has been difficult to establish at the center, reflecting the fragmentation and underfunding of health services for poor children in our country. The primary goal is to provide health screening, initial diagnosis of medical conditions, treatment of common health problems, and referral for major treatment health services. The medical school of the University of California at San Diego is now providing the health services at the center. One problem yet to be fully resolved is the matter of billing for Medicaid and MediCal payments. Many of the children and families receiving services are eligible for health insurance payments, but which agency can do the billing and how the money is dispersed are questions that have been difficult to resolve. We are hoping for new regulations from the federal and state level to help clarify the issue.

Another major challenge has been the training of the family service advocates for the center. These are professional people who have very different backgrounds—school counselors, social workers from the welfare department, probation officers, and so on. Very few have been trained to work with the entire family for an extended period. Most have dealt primarily in crisis management. It takes time and patience to help them develop the necessary attitudes and skills required to become an advocate for the family and assist in meeting a wide variety of needs, not just the needs they have addressed based on their prior training and job requirements. Our tendency is to underestimate the amount of time required to train people to become family service advocates.

There have also been problems with the relationship between the regular school staff members—the principal, teachers, and others—and the professionals at the center. The professionals are not seen as school people, and credentials are sometimes questioned. Greater understanding needs to be developed and a more common language established. There are employee union concerns as well. When people from different agencies are brought together, professionals who perform similar jobs are mixed and problems can easily emerge. One example took place in the health clinic and involved the nurse practitioners. The doctor from the medical center who supervises the nurses could only work with nurses from the doctor's hospital because of the requirements of the liability insurance. Consequently, the regular school nurse was transferred to another school. As a result, the nurses' union has filed a grievance against the district.

Because of the multidisciplinary nature of the program, it has been difficult to find anyone to agree to evaluate it. It was necessary to bring a team together with representatives from the education, medical, and social welfare communities to design a formal evaluation. Evaluation of the demonstration center and what is and is not working is possible because of foundation support. The evaluation also addresses the issues of collaboration, the effectiveness of the partnership, and the extent to which the institutions involved are changing the way they do business based on what is being learned from the demonstration center. Just as the feasibility study gave us important information to use in designing the demonstration center, the ongoing evaluation will provide data to inform future policy direction.

## SOME PRELIMINARY CONCLUSIONS

It seems clear that there must be a catalyst for change and leaders must provide it. Different communities may find that the leadership emerges in different ways. In San Diego, the initiative came from staff. Elsewhere it might come from elected officials and policymakers. In either case, staff and policymakers must develop a shared commitment to the goals of the collaborative effort and find ways to facilitate implementation plans. An early concern that did not materialize was that elected officials from one or more of the governmental agencies would attempt to control the early deliberations in order to gain visibility and recognition for political purposes. At the outset, staff members made the commitment to keep the elected officials informed about their efforts and to coordinate the simultaneous approval of policy statements by each of the participating partners.

Also, the amount of time necessary to work on process issues should not be underestimated. In our initial meetings, we quickly learned that it would take time for educators, social service providers, housing experts, law enforcement officials, and health professionals to understand each other. An important early decision was for each agency to provide a detailed report of all services provided and dollars appropriated for children, youth, and families in one of our high school attendance areas. All were amazed at what we individually were spending, the lack of communication among us, and the fragmentation of services. This reality check was critical in convincing us that we had a great deal to gain by trying to find a way to work together to improve services to children, youth, and families. It provided the cornerstone for the emerging commitment to undertake a major collaborative effort.

Policymakers and staff members must have patience. Results based on traditional indicators will not be immediate. Public agencies are under tremendous pressure to trim bureaucracies, improve the quality of services, stretch resources, become more cost-effective, and be accountable. The hope is for quick, tangible evidence of success, but the complex needs of today's children, youth, and families cannot be met with simple solutions. Prevention is a long-term strategy, not a short-term fix. Policymakers and professional service providers across the country are eager to discover what works. There is lots of good talk, certainly a necessary precursor to action, but probably no perfect model will emerge from local efforts such as New Beginnings. Efforts have to be community-specific, although, as suggested here, we are learning about some generic issues to be addressed. We hope that local efforts such as ours will push those at the state and federal levels to eschew their traditional turf battles and find new ways to work in collaborative, nonpartisan ways. The challenge to policymakers at all levels is to revise the system of incentives and rewards to encourage this change.

Governmental agencies cannot be satisfied only with the successes resulting from their early collaborative efforts. The private nonprofit sector also has many organizations that provide services for children, youth, and families. Community-based organizations and their leaders have advice and resources to bring to collaborative efforts. It is not easy to keep adding participants as equal partners to a collaborative effort without raising questions about governance, decision making, communication, and accountability. For true collaboration to occur, each agency must change the way it does business. School restructuring, community-oriented policing, and automating lengthy eligibility processes are examples. It is not wise to attempt the involvement of all potential partners from both the public and private nonprofit sector at the outset, but we continue to look for more new ways to expand our collaborative work.

Finally, those who come together to collaborate must know a lot about children, youth, and families. They must have professional training and years of experience to support their attitudes and practice. However, it is dangerous to rely on professional and political expertise alone. Our feasibility study taught us an important lesson—the users of our services know things that we do not know. No effort will succeed without regular opportunities for users to inform providers about their experience and assessment of what is and is not working. One requirement of effective leadership is a willingness to ask for, receive, and act positively on information the leader would rather not hear.

## CLOSING THOUGHTS

We have reached a crucial crossroad of public education in America. For public education to survive, it cannot be business as usual. Schools must radically extend their purposes and operations and become integral parts of our increasingly diverse communities. Reform must be systemic in order to meet the needs of all students. The pressure and fears associated with dramatic demographic changes will threaten our commitment to universal public education if we forget that it resists both the development of an elite class and the emergence of a large permanent underclass.

Our efforts to reform public education will fail if the responsibility for leading reform rests alone with the interest groups that have been the traditional proponents and opponents of renewal and change. Strong, effective public schools are in the best interest of us all. We all have a responsibility to help keep children's issues and public education high on the political agenda at all levels of government. While responsibility for outcomes must be shared by many, accountability must be targeted for change to occur. Experience has proven that when everyone is responsible, often no one is truly accountable. The question of who is responsible is not easy to answer. The current experience of educators is that the schools are asked to do more and more to meet the needs of children, while the general public judges the school's success or failure based on school achievement. Few argue that the school's primary mission is to provide a sound academic education for all students. The dilemma for educators is how to meet the reasonable expectation when resources are scarce and increasing percentages of available dollars are diverted for services traditionally provided by the family and other institutions. As schools assume additional responsibilities in these nontraditional areas, it must be acknowledged as part of an accountability system that clearly defines who is responsible.

The issue of accountability is complex enough when a single institution confronts it. When multiple partners in a collaborative effort try to agree on an accountability system, the task seems overwhelming. Education of elected policymakers and the general public is critical. The conversation in schools about accountability seems to be leading toward a consensus that educators, parents, students, and the community have shared responsibility. The conflict is over who has what portion and what happens if one or more of the responsible parties fails to perform. Are the others released from their obligations or expected to assume a greater share? These same daunting questions apply when the number of partners involved increases. The challenge is to eschew traditional ways of thinking about targeting responsibility and defining new ways of thinking about groups sharing it. New rewards and incentives must be devised to support this kind of thinking and the practices it may generate.

The result will be a radical restructuring of schools and other institutions that provide services for children, youth, and families. It will require leadership from the professionals and public policymakers in federal, state, and local government. It will require a policy agenda that focuses on the conditions of children first and how institutions can devise new working relationships to provide education, health, and other social services. It will not be such a radical idea to make schools the centers where services are provided. What will be radical is the change that must occur in all of the institutions that must be partners in this effort.

People must understand that public education that works for the common good is in the best interest of all Americans, not just those who have children in school. It is no longer sufficient for educators alone to reach out to their communities and people of all ages urging them to become involved and support our schools. The nation must be convinced that we can no longer tolerate 20 percent of our children living in poverty. All who work with children, youth, and families should come together to establish ways to improve the conditions that define the lives of children. Collaboration is not an option. It is a necessity, something much greater than the sum of our individual efforts. The arguments are powerful. Every American has a stake in the success of our children. That success will determine the future strength of our democracy, the vitality of our economy, and our individual quality of life.

## REFERENCES

Bruner, Charles. *Thinking Collaboratively: Ten Questions and Answers to Help Policy Makers Improve Children's Services.* Washington, D.C.: Education and Human Services Consortium, 1991.

Children's Defense Fund. *The State of America's Children.* Washington, D.C.: CDF Publications, 1992.

County of San Diego Department of Social Services. *Tackling the Confidentiality Barrier: A Practical Guide for Integrated Family Services.* San Diego, Calif.: County of San Diego Department of Social Services, 1991.

Melaville, Atelia I., with Blank, Martin J. *What It Takes: Structuring Interagency Partnerships to Connect Children and Families with Comprehensive Services.* Washington, D.C.: Education and Human Services Consortium, 1991.

National Commission on the Role of the School and the Community in Improving Adolescent Health. *Code Blue: Uniting for Healthier Youth.* Alexandria, Va.: National Association of State Boards of Education, 1990.

San Diego City Schools. *New Beginnings: A Feasibility Study of Integrated Services for Children and Families.* San Diego, Calif.: San Diego City Schools, 1990.

# III
# GENERIC APPROACHES

# 8

# Charter Schools in Minnesota

## *John A. Cairns*

The establishment of charter schools in Minnesota was authorized by state legislation passed in 1991. The legislation enables school districts to negotiate contracts with individual public schools that are to be characterized by new and innovative programs. The contract states the standards that the school and its students are expected to meet and contains assurances that the efforts of the school will be supported over an extended period of time in order to allow its innovations a chance to succeed. The school is to be managed by a board on which certified teachers are a majority. Teachers in the school have responsibility for its program and are accountable for results. The school is supported financially by the school district on the same per-capita basis as other schools in the district. The legislation exempts charter schools from state laws and regulations. The school, however, must observe federal rules regarding desegregation and it must also abide by local regulations pertaining to health and safety.

In effect, by chartering a school, the school district has an opportunity to hold the teachers accountable for whether or not students learn. Combined with a waiver from rules, regulations, and statutes, a contract negotiated under the charter law allows the school district to negotiate what is expected of students (i.e., what they should know or be able to do at specific points in time) and gives the professionals in charge of learning—the teachers—control over the instructional process and holds them accountable for results. Without charter authority and the protection afforded by the negotiated contract binding the sponsoring authority, effective continuing reform and restructuring could be severely compromised.

I begin this chapter by summarizing some of the developments in educational policy in Minnesota that preceded the legislation authorizing the creation of charter schools.

Beginning in the late 1960s, Minnesota policymakers initiated a major rewrite of laws, rules, and regulations governing the K–12 education system in the state. Much of the early impetus for change stemmed from financial considerations: too much reliance on property taxes, resistance to proposals of local school boards to increase funding for schools, and a clear public demand for more and better schools.

Major lobbying efforts on these matters were initiated by the organizations representing teachers, administrators, and school board members. While there was substantial tension between and among these groups over management of the K–12 system, there was unanimity on the funding problem. All lobbied regularly and effectively for more money to be allocated to the system from the state's levy of broadly based taxes other than the property tax and for higher income and sales taxes.

While there was general consensus that more money should be allocated, there was underlying disagreement on other matters, most of which can be placed in the general category of "control." Local school boards resisted broadening state mandates; legislators insisted on requiring local boards to do more and different things as a condition of receiving more state money; teachers developed their unionization plans; and the courts were stepping in as well, largely on matters pertaining to desegregation in the urban districts and to equalized funding.

By the mid-1970s, the Minnesota K–12 system had been radically changed. Control by the state and by local boards and funding relationships were completely redesigned. The connection between raising revenues and making spending decisions was ruptured. The state raised the money by expanding sales and income taxes, but local boards continued to make most spending decisions. Politically, both levels of government avoided accountabil-

ity: the local board could blame the state for not making resources available, and the state could blame the local boards for
not making the right decisions on how to spend the money.

Meanwhile, teachers' unions were growing stronger, since all
certificated personnel were required to belong to the teacher
union favored by a majority of teachers in each district. To some
observers, union goals appeared to be stressing the protection
of seniority rights, the treatment of all teachers alike regardless
of skills and performance, lock-step salary increases, and compli-
cated and time-consuming administrative procedures for questioning the competence of individual teachers.

By the end of the 1970s, the public monies being spent on
K–12 schools had increased tremendously. Politicians and the
organizations representing educational professionals had effectively convinced most of the public that more money would bring
better schools.

Outside the legislative arena, however, forces were starting
to question whether or not, in spite of favorable comments about
the high quality of Minnesota's public school system, students
were really learning more than their counterparts in other states.
Many asked whether students were learning what they really needed
to know, who was accountable for whether they were learning,
and what standards should be used to measure performance.

The concerns about what students were really learning came
from many sectors. Leaders in minority communities, especially
in the urban areas, correctly complained of inadequate education for minority children, citing alarmingly high dropout rates,
disproportionate employment of minority youth, high incidence
of criminal involvement, and other factors. Commentators on
national test results began to point out that scores were flatten-
ing out and even declining for Minnesota students.

Nationally known educators began to publish research pointing out that students have many different learning styles and
that many of them were not learning well in traditional classrooms. Others published commentaries on the use and effectiveness of different pedagogies. Still others developed projects to
demonstrate that students could learn more if the teacher's efforts were supplemented by technology and by paraprofessionals
in the classroom who would perform many nonteaching functions.

Perhaps critical to the change in views about education were
two additional phenomena. An economic slowdown, even reces-
sion, in Minnesota and in the nation dramatically reduced the

funding available for schools. Second, the world's economic system changed radically in many respects. Business leaders began to question the effectiveness of the U.S. educational system relative to education in other nations.

The public demand for better K–12 education and better-prepared workers grew as the economy slowed down and as public resources became constricted. The new reality thus conflicted directly with the policymaking patterns of the 1970s. No longer could more money be provided, and no longer did the public accept the proposition that public schools were adequate to provide what was needed.

The public was further troubled by the consequences of the newly unionized management systems that had been created. Seniority rules required that the highest salaried (almost always the older) teachers be retained and that the youngest (and least expensive) teachers be cut. No consideration was permitted as to whether the best teachers were retained and the least effective eliminated. Class sizes grew, while it was clear from most research and instinctively known by parents and students that such a change would not result in better education.

The public rightfully demanded more. It was apparent that different skills were needed for employment in the 1980s and beyond. Too often, the traditional public school system responded by doing less of what was already perceived by many to be inadequate. Classrooms looked just like they did in the first part of the century at a time when nearly every other aspect of society had changed radically. Although technology had emerged as an essential element of the economic system, few technological improvements were found in the public schools. Yet teachers' salaries continued to escalate even though to many it was increasingly clear that students were not learning what they needed to know.

Two essential courses were available to force significant change. Those pushing for reform and restructuring could go to the legislature and become a lobbying force to counteract the lobby of the educational establishment, and a concerted effort could be made to change the system from the inside. These efforts proved to be overwhelmingly frustrating, since political loyalties developed in the 1970s blocked any moves to bring about change. Notwithstanding their historical differences on everything except spending more money, the organizations representing the educational establishment found new common ground in their resistance to pressures for change.

As an alternative, change-minded people could work from outside the system. New private and quasi-public projects evolved. Newly developed schools created the hope that new techniques could result in significant improvement in learning.

Business leaders determined that they could not wait for the evolutionary changes that would come from confronting the existing system directly. They encouraged experimentation and reform by urging their company foundations to become involved. And the private foundations began to do the same, often motivated by their perception that poor education was associated with nearly all the social problems on which they regularly spent their resources.

Initial school reform efforts actually began in Minnesota with the Southeast Minneapolis Education Alternative (SEA) program in the late 1960s and early 1970s, one of four such pilot projects funded by the federal government. The SEA effort involved creation of an independent, greatly deregulated "district within a district." Its key characteristics were distinctive learning programs in each of six separate schools, choice among those schools for area families and students, and greatly increased community input into school management. From this successful effort emerged a series of "magnet" schools that are now firmly established in the Minneapolis system. They were precursors as well of the interest in school-based management and other reforms.

Many leaders in the SEA program continued to be involved in promoting alternative school choices in Minneapolis and St. Paul and policy changes that would make such opportunities more widely available. The impetus for change was enhanced as well by the success of schools funded under the Model Cities program. These schools were developed for students, mostly of color, who had dropped out or were otherwise not being served by the traditional urban school districts.

In fact, both the Minneapolis and St. Paul school districts quietly but actively encouraged the development of such alternative schools in order to serve students known to be doing poorly in the traditional system. Many of these schools were managed by private vendors who believed that these students, given more appropriate support in their learning, could also become effective students and citizens. The school districts entered into contracts to support these efforts.

The contract schools emerged as a practical, but not specifically authorized, means of educating hard-to-teach students. Their successes were widely known to many people who followed schools closely and believed that the traditional model was ineffective even for gifted and motivated students.

Yet another phenomenon occurred in Minnesota that helped to set the stage for the charter school effort—public support for private sectarian K–12 schools. Here the motivation was a bit different, but it was based on the premise that these schools delivered a quality of education at least similar to that found in the public schools. Supporters of public aid to private sectarian K–12 schools relied on the idea that all Minnesota students, whether in public or private schools, should have equal support, for example, for transportation and books. They also believed that a savings to the public treasury results when students attend private schools. That is, the parents of children in private schools paid their local property taxes as well as their state income and sales taxes. But no per capita aid was going to the private schools. This was seen as a kind of indirect subsidy of public education by families whose children attended private schools.

Similar concerns about other public service delivery systems were emerging at the same time. The seminal work on the topic of new delivery systems came from a publication by the Twin Cities Citizens' League (1972), which recommended wider use of private vendors for traditional public services. The study provided convincing evidence that alternative delivery systems often led to better results for the people served. Such alternatives also served as models for the traditional systems to adopt. The point was made that government could do many things better by being a "provider" of service but not necessarily a "producer."

By the early 1980s, then, momentum for educational reform was building. Add to that the emerging national concern about how U.S. high school graduates compare with graduates in other cultures. This concern, of course, received national attention with the publication of *A Nation at Risk* by the National Commission on Excellence in Education (1983).

Charter school legislation in Minnesota was preceded by other legislation growing out of a concern of parents and legislators that high schools were failing to challenge their most able students. This concern resulted in legislation designed to let certain eleventh- and twelfth-grade students complete some or all of their credits by taking classes in postsecondary institutions. This early variation of "choice" and the availability of alternative education was made possible by the passage of the Postsecondary Enrollment Options Program in 1985. The legislation was strongly opposed by those in the educational establishment who argued that the option would cause top students to leave and that high schools would be left with only the weaker students. They also argued that the program was improper interference with local decision making. Notwithstanding these arguments, the policy was adopted. Most supporters saw clearly that the traditional high schools were simply not providing the higher-level courses that parents and students were demanding.

A major impetus for change and more effective schools emerged in 1982 with an announcement by the Minnesota Business Partnership (MBP) that it would undertake a major study of the effectiveness of Minnesota's K–12 system. The study was motivated by two primary concepts: first, that Minnesota graduates were not learning what they needed to know, and second, that the historic pattern of spending more money to secure better education was no longer possible. Economic conditions dictated a permanent slowdown in the growth of state tax revenues, yet a better educational system was essential.

The MBP study (Berman and Weiler, 1984) recommended several major changes. It made the convincing point that traditional schools no longer served most students well and that a major restructuring was called for. Its primary method was to open up choice for families. It also called for changing most of the traditional systems for managing schools and delivering the service.

The MBP study became the essential building block of an effort by Rudy Perpich, then governor of Minnesota, to promote educational reform as his major initiative in the 1985 legislative session—a program to make Minnesota the "brainpower state." His motivation was to enhance the Minnesota economy by developing a strong educational system with a focus on what students were really learning and what skills they were developing. This was a radical departure from the system then in place, which measured success by how much time students spent in class and how many credits were taken.

The debate in 1985 focused on broadening choice for families and on encouraging the development of new management systems. Persistent resistance from the educational establishment blocked much of the effort, but the momentum for change continued to develop.

The Twin Cities Citizens' League (1988) was back to work as well. A committee chaired by John Rollwagon, then chief executive officer of Cray Research, studied the management of the K–12 system for over a year. It concluded that the institutional resistance to change for better education was too intense to limit continued efforts to change schools only to strategies designed to change from within. Rather, the League proposed creating authority for the establishment of entirely new public schools to be managed primarily by teachers. And just as important, these "charter" schools were to be exempt from all state laws and regulations governing the traditional schools. Additionally, the proposed legislation provided that a performance contract be entered into between the sponsoring district and the school. For the first time, schools would become recognized legal entities with contractual assurance that they could not be arbitrarily terminated as charter schools.

The resistance to the legislation to create charter schools came mostly from the teacher associations. They resisted even though the legislation recognized the primary importance of the role of the teachers in the charter schools. As a result of this resistance, certain compromises occurred in the legislative process that weakened the recommended approach.

For example, the legislation provides that schools can be chartered only by school districts, whereas the original proposal was that any local governing unit (city, county, school district) should be able to authorize charters. Also, persons able to seek charters were limited to teachers, whereas the initial proposal was to authorize any interested group of sponsors to seek charters so long as the schools were outcome-based and teacher-managed.

Nonetheless, the following essential characteristics of the proposal for charter schools (technically called "outcome-based" schools) were incorporated in the legislation:

- State laws and regulations for managing the schools were completely waived except for those pertaining to desegregation, health, and safety.
- The school is operated under a contract with the sponsoring school district that defines expectations and allows the school board to meet its obligations to oversee the delivery of educational services in the district.
- The nonprofit or cooperative entity formed to run the school must have a board with a majority of certificated teachers.
- The teachers have the freedom to manage the resources to provide the best education possible, including the ability to hire other certificated or noncertificated personnel and to acquire technology. This authority is coupled with

enforceable assurance that the sponsoring authority cannot arbitrarily end the project (i.e., the contract creates rights in the school that cannot be taken away).

- All operating funds available to any public school on a per-capita or categorical basis move to the charter school based on the number of students attending. Capital funds are not available.

Progress with charter schools has been promising in Minnesota. To date, charters have been granted for the following schools:

- A K–12 school in northern Minnesota with a curriculum based largely on environmental studies and experiential learning. The program will be affiliated with several regional institutions of higher learning in Minnesota and Wisconsin.
- An apprenticeship-oriented vocational school (grades 7 through 12) co-managed by the Minnesota Teamsters Service Bureau and a suburban Twin Cities school district.
- A private Montessori elementary school converted into a public magnet school.
- An elementary school in an urban neighborhood with a diverse student population.
- A school for hearing-impaired students with a curriculum based on signing.
- An alternative program for students in grades seven through twelve located at the corporate headquarters of a major Minnesota grocery store group in a former suburban junior high school building.

Two other contracts for charter schools in Minnesota are in the final stages of negotiation. Recent legislation calls for expanding the number of charter schools in the state from eight to twenty.

It is anticipated that deregulated schools managed by teachers and other stakeholders seriously committed to accountability for student outcomes will be shown to be a better alternative than the traditional structure of schooling and that more schools will convert to the charter school model. In fact, legislation permitting the establishment of charter schools has also been adopted in California, where several charters have already been granted. Charter school legislation has also been enacted in Georgia, Colorado, New Mexico, Wisconsin, and Massachusetts. Similar legislation is pending in Arizona, Tennessee, and New Jersey, and is under consideration in other states.

# REFERENCES

Berman, Frank, and Weiler, Daniel. *The Minnesota Plan: A Design for a New Education System.* 2 vols. Minneapolis: Minnesota Business Partnership, November 1984.

National Commission on Excellence in Education. *A Nation at Risk.* Washington, D.C.: U.S. Department of Education, 1983.

Twin Cities Citizens' League. *Why Not Buy Services?* Minneapolis, Minn.: Twin Cities Citizens' League, September 20, 1972.

Twin Cities Citizens' League. *Chartered Schools = Choices for Educators + Quality for Students.* Minneapolis: Twin Cities Citizens' League, November 17, 1988.

# —— 9 ——

# Free Market Choice: Can Education Be Privatized?

## Joseph L. Bast and Herbert J. Walberg

"Radical," the *Oxford English Dictionary* tells us, means "going to the root or origin; touching or acting on what is essential and fundamental." What is "essential" or "fundamental" about education in America today? What is the "root or origin" of its shortcomings?

It is difficult, in this age of academic specialization, for "experts" to rise above their disciplinary walls in order to see the larger context in which their research takes place. Education researchers, it seems, are surrounded by particularly high walls. They spend their days examining issues of curriculum, child psychology, school management, finance, and evaluation, but they only rarely contemplate the context in which schools operate. Their ideas of what constitutes a "radical" reform might begin and end with a change in curriculum, an adjustment to job descriptions, or (always a favorite) an infusion of funds from somewhere "outside" those walls.

A view from outside the walls of educational research presents a very different vision of what is essential and fundamental to schooling in America. When entrepreneurs look at our schools, the most noteworthy features they see are that government owns the buildings, government employs the teachers, government discourages private competitors, and government tries to supervise and manage this entire enterprise. Why do these aspects of public education stand out? Because as we search for other undertakings organized in similar fashion, we find only the U.S. Postal Service and the U.S. Armed Forces (Adie, 1989). We are struck that we would use this same organizational model to deliver services that are so obviously dissimilar. We cannot help but wonder why we chose this peculiar model, and whether today, if we were to start anew, we would make the same choice.

With the global collapse of communism, the retreat of socialism in most countries, and the U.S. trend toward "privatizing" public services, America's public education system is becoming more peculiar with every passing day. Most other nations in the world encourage the creation and operation of private schools either by making grants directly to the schools or by giving financial support to parents who choose private schools for their children (Glenn, 1989; Ignas and Corsini, 1981). For example, as few as three dozen parents are required to start a new school, eligible for state funds, in Denmark and Holland (James, 1984). Even Poland now has a voucher plan for parents enrolling their children in private schools (*Wall Street Journal*, 1992a).

Education experts do not like to dwell on these aspects of their enterprise. They say that "what goes on in the classroom is what matters," not issues of governance and finance. They contend that the right people, given the right tools, can get the job done; that well-intentioned people elected to school boards and state legislatures can effectively oversee this vitally important enterprise; and that there is no alternative to government financing, operation, and management of schools. Reason and experience, however, tell another story.

We have tried spending more money, 89 percent more money in real terms in the past two decades alone (National Center for Education Statistics, 1991, p. 49), but student achievement has not improved. We have tried different curricula so often that many teachers despair of ever discovering a program that works. Some of our best educators are using twenty-year-old textbooks and McGuffey Readers (see Collins and Tamarkin, 1982, pp. 51–60). We have hired superintendents of every ethnicity and gender recruited from inside and outside our districts; devolved power to local councils and concentrated power in education "czars"; torn down walls between classrooms and then put them back up; taught self-esteem and gone back to basics; adopted schools and mentored students. It is difficult to imagine, amid all this trial and error, what has not been tried. Yet test scores and international comparisons reveal that our efforts have not paid off. Why is this? Could it be our reforms have failed to reach to the root of the problem?

Moving education out of the public sector and into the private sector would be a "radical" change in the true sense of that word. It would strike at the very root of the problem by rescuing our schools and our children from an institutional model that cannot, even with the best-intentioned people, efficiently produce effective outcomes. *How* and *why* privatizing education would work is the subject of this essay.

## PRIVATIZATION

The term "privatization" was coined in 1968 by management guru Peter Drucker (Drucker, 1968, p. 234). The first article advocating privatization as a strategy appeared in *Harper's Magazine* in 1971 (Savas, 1971). The first book on the subject was Robert Poole's *Cutting Back City Hall*, published in 1980 (Poole, 1980). Since then, dozens of excellent books have been published on the subject.

Privatization is the practice of transferring responsibility for producing part or all of a service from the public to the private sector (Savas, 1987). It typically takes one of three forms: contracting out, sale of assets, and load shedding. Contracting out involves soliciting bids from potential providers, reviewing them, then signing an agreement with the qualified bidder with the lowest bid. Selling assets can be either simple divestiture—the sale of unneeded equipment or properties—or a lease-back whereby a government agency sells an asset but then leases it from the new owner. Load shedding means government not only stops delivering a service itself, but also divests itself of any responsibility for ensuring that the service is delivered by a private party.

The actual practice of privatization is far older than either the term or the movement. In 1492, King Ferdinand and Queen Isabella of Spain contracted with a sailor named Christopher Columbus to find a Western passage to India. His price: 1 million *maravedis* and 10 percent of the transactions generated within his admiralty—an advance and a commission. (Would the New

World have been discovered as quickly had the royal couple used the Spanish Navy rather than an independent contractor?)

Most services that are now publicly provided, including education, were once privately performed (Beito, 1988). They were transferred to the public sector for a variety of reasons, many of them no longer compelling. For example, most urban mass transit systems were built and initially operated by private firms. They were taken over by government agencies after government-imposed price controls undermined the industry's profitability (Lave, 1985). Urban sewage systems were routinely privately designed and built until the turn of the century (Beito, 1988), and the first traffic lights in Chicago were bought and installed by the city's taxicab companies (Gilbert and Samuels, 1982). Government is a relative newcomer to these and scores of other services we commonly identify as "public services."

Like other services now considered "public," most schooling in the United States was provided privately, often with public subsidies, prior to the 1840s (Spring, 1986). The decision to deny public funds to private schools and expand public schools in the second half of the nineteenth century was not the result of some new appreciation for the First Amendment, nor was it out of concern for the poor, who by contemporary accounts were receiving quality education at very low cost (Smith, 1982; High and Ellig, 1988). Instead, the decision was driven by nationalism, an admiration for a barely understood and antiindividualist Prussian model, and anti-Catholicism following the Irish immigrations of the 1850s (Spring, 1986; Smith, 1982).

Similarly today, whether a service is produced by a government agency or a private enterprise is more likely to stem from historical accident than from any essentially "public" character of the service. Literally hundreds of "public" services are handled by private firms in some cities and by public agencies in others. They range from street cleaning and waste disposal to providing security for public buildings and managing parks and recreation facilities (Stevens, 1984).

## PRIVATIZATION IN ACTION

Privatization is a bona fide "megatrend" in the United States and around the world (Savas, 1987; Naisbitt and Aburdene, 1991). According to the World Bank (1992), governments around the world raised $50 billion in 1991 alone by selling state-owned firms to private investors. Surveys of municipal officials in the United States find that nearly 80 percent already use some privatization techniques, and most of these officials report that such techniques lead to reduced costs or provision of higher-quality services, or both (Touche Ross, 1987).

Extensive empirical research has shown that, other things being equal, private organizations perform significantly better and at lower costs than do public agencies. This has been demonstrated in the United States by studies of airlines, banks, bus service, debt collection, electric utilities, forestry, hospitals, housing, insurance sale and processing, railroads, refuse collection, savings and loans, slaughterhouses, water utilities, and weather forecasting (Fitzgerald, 1988; Reason, 1990; Savas, 1987; Bast and Bast, 1990). Such favorable experiences have led governments to experiment with broadening the role of the private sector in such traditionally "public" sectors as prisons (Logan, 1990), police, and fire protection.

Privatization works for several reasons (Cox and Love, 1991). First, it allows government to separate the roles of *providing* and *producing*. In providing, government sets policies and objectives concerning services to be provided. If government then attempts also to produce the service itself, it finds itself caught in a conflict of interest. Ted Kolderie and Jody Hauer (1991) described the conflict as follows:

> In the administrative arrangement typical of the public sector, the unit of government and its principal executives play double roles: as policymakers they are buyers who think about the interests of the taxpayers and consumers. On the other hand, they are sellers who think about the interests of the organization and the facilities they have built and run. This can sometimes lead to problems.... [T]he "purchase of service" (i.e., privatization) arrangement separates these functions and helps reduce the inherent conflict between the two.... By its nature the contract arrangement forces the "buyer" to be clear about objectives, and the "seller" to be clear about performance and accountability.

Peter Drucker (1968) comes to the same conclusion: "The purpose of government . . . is to govern. This, we have learned in other institutions, is incompatible with 'doing.' Any attempt to combine governing with 'doing' on a large scale, paralyzes government's decision-making capacity" (p. 233).

A second reason privatization works is because it empowers consumers in relation to producers. Government agencies, including public school districts, typically are given near monopolies over their service areas. People in the service area cannot refuse to fund the government agency, nor can they patronize a different service provider. Because its funding and patronage do not rely on the quality or efficiency of its operation, a government agency is able to do what private firms in a competitive environment never could: ignore the wishes of consumers, allow costs to escalate, and be slow to implement quality-enhancing or labor-saving innovations. The U.S. Postal Service is a notorious example of how a government agency can deliver deteriorating service at ever higher costs (Ferrara, 1990); America's public schools, regrettably, are another.

But are not consumers of public services empowered at the ballot box? Cannot they testify before their local school boards, say, to call for greater efficiency and accommodation of their special concerns? Such opportunities do exist, but they are clumsy and ineffectual compared to the marketplace. "In the political democracy," wrote Austrian economist Ludwig von Mises, "only the votes cast for the majority candidate or the majority plan are effective in shaping the course of affairs. The votes polled by the minority do not directly influence policies. But on the market no vote is cast in vain. Every penny spent has the power to work upon the production processes" (Mises, 1947, p. 271).

Chubb and Moe (1990) linked the absence of choice in education to the powerlessness of consumers when they wrote:

> Lacking feasible exit options, then, whether through residential mobility or escape into the private sector, many parents and students will "choose" a public school despite dissatisfaction with its goals, methods, personnel, and performance. Having done so, they have a right to try to remedy the situation through the democratic control structure. But everyone else has the same right, and the determinants of political power are stacked against them. Democracy cannot remedy the mismatch between what parents and students want and what the public schools provide. Conflict and disharmony are built into the system. [P. 34]

Some of this "mismatch" derives from organizational advantages that teachers and school administrators have over parents (see Olson, 1971). Teachers and administrators are relatively small and easily organized groups that stand to reap huge, concentrated benefits for themselves by investing in the political process. Parents, in contrast, are a much larger group, more diverse and more difficult to organize. Individual parents stand to benefit much less by cooperating with one another than do teachers. The typical, rational parent, then, will not invest nearly as much time attempting to influence a school board or state legislature as will the typical, rational teacher.

Privatization rescues parents from this uneven competition by moving the consumer-producer relationship outside the political arena. Privatization empowers consumers by giving them choices among different providers of a service. Consumers can "vote with their feet and dollars" for the best service provider, which will then grow at the expense of less efficient competitors. This natural discipline of the marketplace—what Adam Smith referred to some two hundred years ago as the "invisible hand"— is what ensures that the food we eat, the clothes we wear, and even the homes we live in are produced as efficiently as possible. It is far more effective than the clumsy once-a-year voting for or against elected officials who may or may not represent our specific views or do what they promise once elected. The absence of a natural discipline in the public sector is responsible for much of the waste, inefficiency, and stagnation found there.

## PRIVATIZING EDUCATION

Privatization can be applied to education in several ways. Some of the activities of public schools, such as maintenance, cafeteria service, and transportation of students, can be contracted out. Overall management of schools also can be contracted out, or instruction for particular subjects or grades can be contracted out to teachers in private practice (Lieberman, 1989). This kind of "incremental privatization" can gradually relieve public schools of the many services and activities they must *provide* but not necessarily *produce.* Cost savings then can be translated into higher cost effectiveness. Unfortunately, incremental privatization does not remove public schools from a political environment that tolerates waste and inefficiency. School administrators and school board members still do not face strong incentives to pursue cost savings.

Another and more dramatic kind of privatization entails giving the public funds that now go to schools to parents in the form of scholarships or vouchers. Parents would then take these scholarships to the schools, public or private, of their choice, and use them to pay tuition. Schools would have to convince the newly empowered parents that their facilities and faculties are better than those of other schools in the neighborhood, creating a healthy competition among schools and an incentive for parents to become more actively involved in their children's education.

This kind of privatization will be immediately familiar to most readers: it already exists in higher education. Government-financed scholarships are issued directly to students, not to schools, and colleges and universities must compete for students and the funding they bring with them. By funding students rather than schools, the scholarship approach sidesteps possible constitutional dilemmas involving direct government support of religious institutions while empowering the consumer and fostering a wide range of competitive choices.

We can call this kind of privatization "comprehensive" education choice to distinguish it from public-school-only choice, which is only a timid step in the direction of comprehensive choice. Comprehensive choice is realized when funds that now go directly to public schools are given instead to parents or their chosen advocates in the form of certificates or scholarships, or possibly as deposits to "Education Savings Accounts" (Blum, 1958, 1967; Coons and Sugarman, 1978a, 1978b, 1992; Friedman, 1962; Bast and Bast, 1991). Parents can redeem these certificates or make withdrawals from the accounts to pay for tuition at participating public and private schools or, with the assistance of education service coordinators, can purchase education programs provided by multiple providers.

The design of comprehensive educational choice programs can take many forms. Legislation and initiatives that have been proposed in recent years have put the value of the certificate at amounts as low as $1,000 and as high as the average public school per-pupil spending level; some would allow children from only low-income families to participate at first, while others would be open to all children; some include sectarian schools, others do not; some would require participating schools to set aside a certain portion of their enrollments for low-income or minority students, while others would require only that participating schools not violate federal civil rights laws. The specific design of a choice program depends on design principles, local circumstances, and the preferences of coalitions that support the cause.

Allowing parents to use their education taxes to pay for tuition at private schools constitutes a kind of contracting out for educational services, not load shedding. Public funding of education would remain intact, and with it public oversight of the kinds of schools and instruction that qualify for public support. Still, educational choice extending to private schools would be a significant departure from the current method of financing and managing public schooling in the United States. It would open the way for further experimentation, perhaps requiring middle- and upper-income families to pay tuition directly and limiting the use of vouchers to low-income families, much as food stamps are used by only the poor.

## WOULD PRIVATIZING EDUCATION WORK?

What evidence do we have that privatization would have the same positive effects on education as it has had on other public services? We can look for evidence in three areas: experiments with comprehensive educational choice programs, comparisons of public and private school outputs, and research on effective schools.

### The Milwaukee Parental Choice Program

The Milwaukee Parental Choice Program, enacted in 1990, allows up to 1 percent of students in the Milwaukee Public School system to receive state aid of approximately $2,500 per student to attend private schools. The program is available to low-income students only, and sectarian schools are not allowed to participate.

Although often called a "voucher" program, the Milwaukee Parental Choice Program does not give parents certificates or vouchers with which to pay tuition. Instead, funds go directly to schools that sign up for the program and report qualified student enrollments. The present program is limited in other ways: no more than 49 percent of a private school's enrollment may consist of pupils attending the school with state aid, and only newly enrolled students or students who qualified for aid in the previous year are eligible to receive the voucher. Participating schools may not charge tuition higher than the $2,500 state grant, and they are required to submit reports on academic achievement, daily attendance, percentage of dropouts, percentage of suspensions and expulsions, and evidence of parental involvement in the schools' programs. Thus, they share some of the regulatory and reporting burdens of public schools but must get by on about half of the funding that public schools receive.

The first in-depth study of the Milwaukee Parental Choice Program (Witte, 1991) found that "rather than skimming off the best students, this program seems to provide an alternative educational environment for students who are not doing particularly well in the public school system" (p. iv.) Moreover, "Choice families appear to be considerably less well off than the average MPS [Milwaukee Public School] family in terms of employment, income, and being on public assistance or AFDC. They are also less likely to come from two-parent families" (p. 5).

Regarding student achievement, Witte found little change in test scores that could be attributed to the choice program. Students in the Choice Program improved slightly relative to a national population on reading but fell slightly in mathematics; on the same tests, MPS and low-income students declined slightly in both areas. "If there is any firm conclusion from these results," reports Witte, "and we are not sure if there is much of one, it is that when students begin as far behind as the students apparently did in the first year of this program, seven or eight months will not produce dramatic changes in test scores" [p. 19].

Though they came from poorer socioeconomic backgrounds, Witte found that students in the Choice Program had slightly higher attendance rates than their MPS counterparts. He also found evidence that choice was motivating students and parents: "Student attendance, parental attitudes toward Choice schools, opinions of the Choice Program, and parental involvement were all positive" [p. iv]. Involvement by Choice parents at home and at the school was higher in "every category of parental involvement except belonging to a parent/teacher organization" (p. 16), with the exception explained by the absence of formal parent-teacher organizations at some of the schools participating in the Choice Program. Witte concludes his report by recommending that the legislature remain committed to the principle that "parents can best exercise accountability and determine the adequacy of educational outcomes by making free choices among schools" (p. 24).

After only two years, the Milwaukee Parental Choice Program could hardly have been asked to provide definitive evidence to "end" the educational choice debate. But already the Milwaukee experiment has answered some critics of educational choice. Specifically:

- A carefully designed choice program need not "skim" the best students from the public schools, leaving the children of less sophisticated parents behind in even worse learning environments. In fact, choice can have just the opposite effect, benefiting the students who need help the most.
- A choice program can inspire and motivate students and their parents. The private schools participating in the Milwaukee program involved parents more extensively in school activities than did their public school counterparts. Parents and students responded by valuing the schools and having more positive attitudes toward the learning process.
- Private schools that participate in a choice program will not all be perfect—witness the closing of Juanita Virgil Academy (in Milwaukee) because of "severe difficulties" in its first year—but they tend to be "more than adequate educational institutions" that create an environment of close cooperation and trust among teachers, students, and parents. Many parents and educators will recognize "the cultural emphasis" that Witte discerned as a very valuable component of a successful classroom, and something often missing in public schools (p. 17).

### Educational Choice in Vermont

Vermont has had a little-known "voucher" program for over a century involving thousands of students each year (McClaughry, 1987). Like the Milwaukee program, it sheds some light on how educational choice works in practice.

Approximately 95 of Vermont's 246 communities have no public high schools. They choose instead to pay tuition for their high school students to attend either private high schools or public high schools operated by another town. Thirty-five towns offer this choice to K-6 students, either because they have no public elementary schools or because the public schools do not offer every grade. This program originated in 1869 as a way to enable small and geographically distant communities around the state to provide a high school education for the students without incurring the expense of building their own public schools. Minimum tuition amounts are set at the average cost of tuition at a Vermont public high school, with parents usually responsible for paying any additional tuition charges and transportation.

Prior to a Vermont Supreme Court ruling in the 1970s, sectarian schools were allowed to participate in the choice program; since that time, those schools have been excluded. The state requires private schools participating in the program to offer specific courses, maintain attendance records, assess progress regularly, issue a public statement of school objectives, maintain a faculty with adequate training (though not necessarily certified), support the U.S. Constitution and laws, immunize students, and submit to periodic approval by the state.

Has the Vermont program worked? We are not aware of any attempt to compare the achievement of students in Vermont who use the program with the achievement of those who do not. Anecdotal descriptions invariably mention strong parental support for the program and popular opposition to attempts to end it. Bryan and McClaughry (1989), for example, report that "educators may disapprove, but from all accounts parents love it. In some cases parents have chosen to move into a town simply because it gives them the right to choose their children's school" (p. 195).

Given the great variety of schools that participate—parents are free to "add on" to the tuition with their own funds, and students can even attend schools outside the state—and the self-selection nature of the program, an evaluation of Vermont's system would be difficult to perform. However, the very fact that the program is so little known outside the state suggests that the many problems predicted by opponents of vouchers have not occurred. On its face, this program appears to be providing an efficient and popular solution to the problem of delivering quality education in areas with low population densities.

Vermont ranked sixth in the nation in 1989 in SAT scores, seventh in the percentage of high school graduates taking the test, and thirteenth in high school graduation rate (U.S. Department of Education, 1990). Once a relatively low-income state, by 1989 Vermont ranked twenty-fifth in the nation in income. Which of these statistics, if any, can be attributed to Vermont's choice program cannot be known, but it is known that about a quarter of Vermont students participate in the choice program.

## Public Versus Private Schools

While no large-scale experiment with comprehensive educational choice has been conducted in the United States, an unintended choice experiment has been going on for many years involving millions of students. Side by side with public schools with assigned enrollments are private schools enrolling some six million children each year. These are "schools of choice" in the strictest sense: they enroll children irrespective of where they live, and every child is in a school deliberately chosen by his or her parents. By comparing the organization and outcomes of public and private schools, we can discern some of the consequences of privatization.

Pioneering research on public and private school comparisons was conducted by James S. Coleman and Thomas Hoffer (1987), and by Andrew Greeley (1981). Coleman and his colleagues helped assemble and analyze data from the High School and Beyond study that tracked sophomores from 1980 to their senior year in 1,015 public and private high schools. They found that sophomore students attending Catholic high schools had achievement levels 2.4 grade equivalents above those of public school students. After controlling for socioeconomic background, they found a difference in achievement of about one grade level, still a considerable difference. (Coleman and other researchers generally exclude private high schools other than Catholic schools from their analysis due to the small number of such schools and problems in interpreting their test scores.)

Critics of Coleman pointed out that Catholic school students tended to start at higher levels of achievement than public school students. Coleman responded by measuring the growth in student skills instead of the *level* of achievement. Once again, significant differences between Catholic and public schools were documented, this time with Catholic schools achieving a full-year's extra achievement in a two-year period.

Critics came back by contending that unmeasured differences—perhaps discipline in the home or religious conviction—that did not affect sophomore achievement nevertheless were affecting the growth of achievement during the following two years of schooling. Coleman responded to this latest hypothesis by comparing the achievement of Catholic students attending public schools near a Catholic private school to the achievement of Catholic students attending public schools that are not near Catholic schools. Coleman found that the achievement of the two groups of Catholic students is virtually the same, suggesting that the Catholic school is not "creaming" the best Catholic students away from the public schools (Coleman, 1990).

The unexplained difference in student achievement between

public and Catholic schools, while statistically significant, would be too small to justify changing the organization of schools were it not for the fact that Catholic schools are attaining this level of performance at half the cost of their public school counterparts. Catholic schools spent, on average, $1,902 per pupil in 1990, less than half as much as public schools (Genetski, 1992). Even if the performance of Catholic school students, after being controlled for socioeconomic background and other factors discussed above, only equals rather than exceeds the performance of public school students, then Catholic schools are still *twice as cost-effective* as public schools. This, certainly, is a finding with public policy implications.

Coleman has a plausible explanation for why Catholic schools outperform public schools. According to Coleman, while the youth revolution of the 1960s and 1970s led many public schools to water down their curricula and offer growing lists of easy-to-pass elective courses, private schools generally did not lower their academic standards. Catholic school students with comparable socioeconomic backgrounds are 7 percent more likely to have taken biology, chemistry, or physics, and 13 percent more likely to have taken specified mathematics courses, than their public school counterparts (Coleman, 1990).

The ability of Catholic schools to retain their strong curriculum derives, according to Coleman, from the fact that they are private, community-based institutions. Such institutions create "social capital"—the complex patterns of communication and association that parents can put to use in supporting their children during the difficult years of growing up. This sociological explanation is reinforced by political scientists John E. Chubb and Terry M. Moe (1990). Working with an expanded version of the High School and Beyond database, Chubb and Moe found that private schools are more likely than public schools to be effectively organized. They reason that public schools are encumbered by hierarchical and bureaucratic structures that necessarily accompany political oversight, whereas private schools are able to vest most authority directly in schools, parents, and students.

Additional evidence that private schools outperform public schools can be found in other countries where the differences have been studied. A recent survey published by the World Bank looked at studies of public and private school performance in Colombia, the Dominican Republican, the Philippines, Tanzania, and Thailand (Jimenez, Lockheed, and Paquuo, 1992). Each study controlled for students' socioeconomic background, and two (the Dominican Republic and Thailand) used panel data similar to the High School and Beyond study. With just one exception— mathematics instruction in the Philippines, where public and private schools tied—private schools outperformed public schools on student achievement. When the researchers incorporated per-pupil spending to estimate cost effectiveness, they found that private schools were more cost-effective in every case.

Comparing public and private schools sheds some light on the question of whether comprehensive educational choice would bring about more successful schools. The number of students attending both kinds of schools and the long duration of this "experiment" provide a sufficient database to allow us to control for extraneous effects, effects that make smaller voucher experiments so difficult to interpret. It may be provisionally concluded that

- Students attending Catholic schools learn more than students attending public schools, even after socioeconomic backgrounds are taken into account. How much more they learn, though, is debatable. The difference may not be enough to justify changing the organization of schools.
- Catholic schools are more cost-effective than public schools; in other words, they achieve equal or superior results while spending less than half as much as public schools. That they are able to at least match the performance of public schools while spending so much less indicates that they are more efficiently organized, a characteristic it is reasonable to attribute to their need to compete with other schools for students.
- Private schools are more likely to adopt governance structures that encourage parental involvement, retention of strong curricula, and development of the "social capital" that families need to pursue educational excellence. These structures arise when students voluntarily choose a school and parents make a commitment to support that school.
- The greater efficiency of private schools—schools of choice— over public schools is confirmed by research in at least five other countries.

## Research on Effective Schools

Research on the qualities of effective schools provides another opportunity to measure the effects of educational choice. There is an emerging consensus on the qualities of an effective school: strong educational leadership by the principal, high expectations, parental involvement, and a sense of teamwork shared by teachers and administrators (Fraser et al., 1987; U.S. Department of Education, 1986). Effective schools often exist side by side with schools that, though equally or better funded, exhibit few of the traits known to accelerate learning (Schultz, 1983; Lanier, 1982).

Is allowing educational choice more or less likely to create schools that have such characteristics of effective schools? The record is clear: Catholic school teachers are more likely than public school teachers to report satisfaction with their principals' leadership (59.1 percent versus 49.8 percent), staff cooperation (67.9 versus 52.4), teacher control over school and classroom policy (81.1 versus 65.9), and overall teacher morale (84.4 versus 74.1) (U.S. Department of Education, 1987).

The role of parental involvement in schools has been especially well studied and found to exert a major influence on student achievement. Deliberate cooperative efforts by parents and educators to modify academic conditions in the home have an outstanding record of success in promoting achievement. In twenty-nine controlled studies of the past decade, 91 percent of the comparisons favored children in such programs over nonparticipating children (U.S. Department of Education, 1986, p. 19; National Conference of State Legislatures, 1991, p. 21). The average measurable effect of these parental involvement programs was twice that of socioeconomic status, and some programs had effects that were ten times as large. Since few of the programs lasted more than a semester, the potential for programs providing sustained parental involvement is great.

Private schools also have higher expectations for their students than do public schools, as indicated by the number of years of coursework required for high school graduation. Private high schools in 1985–86, for example, required an average 2.8 years of mathematics versus 1.9 years required by public schools. In science, private schools required 2.5 years versus 1.8 for public schools; in English, 3.9 years versus 3.8 years; and in social sciences, 3.1 years versus 2.8 years (U.S. Department of Education, 1987, p. 85).

Research by Coleman and the recent experiences with the Milwaukee Parental Choice Program suggest that private schools also do a significantly better job encouraging parental involvement. Mary Anne Raywid (1989) also has reported that educational choice promotes parental involvement and the other characteristics of effective schooling. She writes:

> There is abundant evidence that public school parents want choice; that they are more satisfied with and have more confidence in schools that provide it; that parent choice increases the commitment and cohesion within schools extending it; and that these attributes combine to improve school quality and make schools more effective. [P. 18]

In their 1986 report on education, the U.S. governors recognized how compulsory attendance at assigned schools discouraged parental involvement:

> [T]oo often, parents of students in the public school system recognize that they have no choice, and they reason that they have no responsibility. They assume that a societal institution called public school in their neighborhood has a monopoly on the education of their children. Our model of compulsory, packaged education, as it now exists, is an enemy of parental involvement and responsibility simply because it allows no choice. [National Governors' Association, 1986, p. 67]

The strong tendency of private schools to better reflect the characteristics of effective schools than do public schools, combined with a strong theory linking choice to the adoption of these characteristics, is evidence of the benefits of allowing parents to choose. That such evidence should emerge even though market forces are very weak in the education field, and even though the average public school outspends the average private school two to one, is a strong confirmation of the benefits of educational choice.

## SUPPORT FOR PRIVATIZATION

In one sense, proposing that education be privatized is not radical at all. Most people already believe that some kind of privatization is needed to improve our nation's schools. Gallup Polls conducted in 1981, 1983, 1985, and 1986 asked if respondents supported a voucher system that would allow parents to choose nongovernment schools. In each year, more replied "yes" than "no" (Kirkpatrick, 1990, p. 150). Seventy percent of respondents to a Gallup Poll in 1992 supported comprehensive educational choice (Lawton, 1992). Support among blacks and Hispanics, who often have the least opportunity to enroll their children in good schools, was a remarkable 86 percent (*Wall Street Journal,* 1992b).

Many public school teachers agree that privatization is needed even though their powerful unions are spending millions of dollars a year trying to forestall such an eventuality. Proof can be found in the number of teachers who enroll their own children in private schools: 46 percent in Chicago, 50 percent in Milwaukee, 36 percent in Memphis, 29 percent in Los Angeles (Boaz, 1991, p. 8). After declaring his opposition to private school choice, newly elected President Bill Clinton sent his daughter to a private school.

Still more evidence that privatization is hardly a radical idea is that millions of parents pay tuition each year at private schools for some six million children whose attendance at public schools would be "free." Though it is only a small step in the direction of comprehensive educational choice, interdistrict public-school-only choice programs are now operating in eight states. (U.S. Department of Education, 1992, pp. 6–8). Many states and cities allow intradistrict public school choice, and it appears inevitable that more states will adopt interdistrict choice in the next few years.

Opponents of choice have suffered high-profile defections from their ranks. Wisconsin State Representative Annette "Polly" Williams, a black liberal democrat, coauthored and helped pass Milwaukee's landmark private school choice program and now travels the country speaking in favor of educational choice. The usually liberal Brookings Institution in 1990 published a volume by Chubb and Moe (1990), in which the authors suggested that their colleagues "would do well to entertain the notion that choice *is* a panacea" (p. 217).

It is likely that, over time, the battle will continue to go badly for opponents of choice. As mentioned earlier, support for privatization is almost universal among municipal government officials, and privatization is sweeping the world following the collapse of socialism abroad. Calls for privatization of education in the United States are getting louder and coming from ever more respected people: Chris Whittle, president of Whittle Communications and the originator of Channel One and the Edison Project; Benno Schmidt, former president of Yale University and now president of the Edison Project; former Secretary of Education William Bennett; John Taylor Gatto, 1991 New York State Teacher of the Year and three-time recipient of New York City Teacher of the Year awards; and Nobel Laureate economists Milton Friedman and Gary Becker.

## CONCLUSION

Allowing students to attend sectarian or independent private schools with the help of public funds is no longer such a radical idea in the United States; the general public favors the idea by nearly a three to one margin. Overseas, the consumers of educational services are already sovereign: Japan, for example, has a large private sector for upper-secondary and tutoring schools. Western Europe has long publicly funded religious and nonsectarian private schools. Consumer empowerment is a major reason why their educational systems, while less well funded than our own, nevertheless routinely and easily outperform our own (Glenn, 1989).

The definitive test of educational choice has not been conducted and may never be. Choice experiments are haunted by questions of selection, out-of-school influences, and differences that are difficult to quantify such as differences in teaching styles, student aptitudes, and the influences of peer groups. For these reasons, it is probably necessary, as well as wise, that we base our evaluation of educational choice on broader evidence.

The limited choice experiments taking place in Milwaukee and Vermont give us some assurance that a comprehensive choice program would not be disruptive, expensive, or a source of social inequality. That extending choice to include the selection of private schools is already working in two vastly different environments—a largely minority inner city, and a largely rural and nonminority state—is significant.

That private schools, both in the United States and abroad, are more cost-effective than public schools has been convincingly demonstrated by many researchers. This finding is consistent with research on a wide range of other services that have been contracted out to private companies or otherwise privatized. If choice could enable us to raise the efficiency of existing public schools to the level of existing private schools, we might achieve current student achievement levels at half the cost, or perhaps twice the current levels of achievement at current levels of investment.

Schools that must compete for the loyalty of students and parents seem to find ways to organize themselves for success. Research on the characteristics of effective schools, and empirical investigations of the schools that have these characteristics, tell us that schools of choice are more likely to succeed than today's public schools based on forced assignment. This, too, is a reassuring finding.

For over one hundred years, Americans have attempted to deliver high-quality education through taxation, elected school boards, government management of schools, and geographic assignment of students to schools. Much of the rest of the world tends to pursue a different method of organizing schools, one that allows schools to compete for parents and students armed with the power to choose. Schools in other countries, and even the small and underfunded private schools in the United States, frankly work better than do our public schools.

We rely on private businesses operating in a competitive marketplace to provide the food we eat, the clothes we wear, and the houses that shelter us. It is time the education researchers rose up from their study cubicles and took a long look at the markets that so reliably and efficiently deliver these essential goods. Why not organize our schools along the lines of this more successful model? Why continue to tinker with lesser reforms in the context of a model that, at its root and in its foundation, is flawed?

## REFERENCES

Adie, Douglas K. *Monopoly Mail.* New Brunswick, N.J. Transaction Publishers, 1989.

Bast, Joseph L., and Bast, Diane C., eds. *Coming Out of the Ice: A Plan to Make the 1990s Illinois' Decade.* Chicago: The Heartland Institute, 1990.

Bast, Joseph L., and Bast, Diane C., eds. *Rebuilding America's Schools: Vouchers Credits, and Privatization.* Chicago: The Heartland Institute, 1991.

Beito, David T. "Voluntary Association and the Life of the City." *Humane Studies Review* (Fall 1988): 1ff.

Blum, Virgil C. *Freedom of Choice in Education.* New York: Macmillan, 1958.

Blum, Virgil C. *Education: Freedom and Competition.* Chicago: Argus Communications, 1967.

Boaz, David, ed. *Liberating Schools: Education in the Inner City.* Washington, D.C.: Cato Institute, 1991.

Bryan, F., and McClaughry, John. *The Vermont Papers: Recreating Democracy on a Human Scale.* Chelsea, Vt.: Chelsea Green Publishing Co., 1989.

Chubb, John E., and Moe, Terry M. *Politics, Markets, and America's Schools.* Washington, D.C.: Brookings Institution, 1990.

Coleman, James S. "Do Students Learn More in Private Schools Than in Public Schools?" Madison Paper no. 4. Tallahassee, Fla.: James Madison Institute, 1990.

Coleman, James S., and Hoffer, Thomas. *Public and Private High Schools: The Impact of Communities.* New York: Basic Books, 1987.

Collins, Marva, and Tamarkin, Civia. *Marva Collins' Way.* New York: Jeremy P. Tarcher, 1982.

Coons, John E., and Sugarman, Stephen D. *Education by Choice: The Case for Family Control.* Berkeley: University of California Press, 1978a.

Coons, John E., and Sugarman, Stephen D., eds. *Parents, Teachers, and Children: A Case for Choice.* Berkeley: University of California Press, 1978b.

Coons, John E., and Sugarman, Stephen D. *Scholarships for Children.* Berkeley: University of California Press, 1992.

Cox, Wendell, and Love, Jean. "Competitive Contracting: Taking Control of Government Spending." Heartland Policy Study no. 46. Chicago: Heartland Institute, 1991.

Drucker, Peter. *The Age of Discontinuity.* New York: Harper and Row, 1968.

Ferrara, Peter J., ed. *Free the Mail: Ending the Postal Monopoly.* Washington, D.C.: Cato Institute, 1990.

Fitzgerald, Randall R. *When Government Goes Private: Successful Alternatives to Public Services.* New York: Universe Books, 1988.

Fraser, Barry J.; Walberg, Herbert J.; Welch, Wayne W.; and Hattie, John A. "Syntheses of Educational Productivity Research," *International Journal of Educational Research* 11, no. 2 (1987): 73–145.

Friedman, Milton. *Capitalism and Freedom.* Chicago: University of Chicago Press, 1962.

Genetski, Robert J. "Private Schools, Public Savings," *Wall Street Journal,* 8 July 1992.

Gilbert, Gorman, and Samuels, Robert E. *The Taxicab: An Urban Transportation Survivor.* Chapel Hill: University of North Carolina Press, 1982.

Glenn, Charles L. *Choice of Schools in Six Nations.* Washington, D.C.: U.S. Department of Education, 1989.

Greeley, Andrew M. "Catholic High Schools and Minority Students." In *Private Schools and the Public Good,* edited by Edward M. Gaffney, Jr. Notre Dame, Ind.: Notre Dame University Press, 1981.

High, Jack, and Ellig, Jerome. "The Private Supply of Education: Some Historical Evidence." In *The Theory of Market Failure: A Critical Examination,* edited by Tyler Cowen. Fairfax, Va.: George Mason University Press, 1988.

Ignas, Edward E., and Corsini, Raymond J. *Comparative Educational Systems.* Itasca, Ill.: F. E. Peacock, 1981.

James, Estelle. "Benefits and Costs of Privatized Public Services: Lessons from the Dutch Educational System," *Comparative Education Review* 28, no. 4 (1984): 605–624.

Jimenez, Eduardo; Lockheed, Marlaine E.; and Paquuo, V. "Public Schools and Private: Which Are More Efficient?" *World Bank Policy Research Bulletin* 3, no. 1 (1992): 2–4.

Kirkpatrick, David W. *Choice in Schooling: A Case for Tuition Vouchers.* Chicago: Loyola University Press, 1990.

Kolderie, Ted, and Hauer, Jody. "Contracting as an Approach to Public

Management." In *Privatization: The Provision of Public Services by the Private Sector*, edited by R. L. Kemp. Jefferson, N.C.: McFarland and Co., 1991.

Lanier, Alfredo S. "Let Us Now Praise Catholic Schools," *Chicago Magazine* (October 1982): 147–153.

Lave, Charles A., ed. *Urban Transit: The Private Challenge to Public Transportation*. San Francisco, Calif.: Pacific Institute for Public Policy Research, 1985.

Lawton, Millicent, "Gallup Poll Finds Wide Support for Tuition Vouchers," *Education Week*, 12, no. 2 (1992).

Lieberman, Myron. *Privatization and Educational Choice*. New York: St. Martin's Press, 1989.

Logan, Charles. *Private Prisons: Cons and Pros*. New York: Oxford University Press, 1990.

McClaughry, John. *Educational Choice in Vermont*. Concord, Vt.: Institute for Liberty and Community, 1987.

Mises, Ludwig von. *Human Action*, 3rd rev. ed. Chicago: Contemporary Books, 1947.

Naisbitt, John, and Aburdene, Patricia. *Megatrends 2000*. New York: Avon Books, 1991.

National Center for Education Statistics. *Digest of Education Statistics 1990*. Washington, D.C.: National Center for Education Statistics, 1991.

National Conference of State Legislatures. *Parent Enabling Policies for States*. Denver, Colo.: National Conference of State Legislatures, 1991.

National Governors' Association. *Time for Results: The Governors' 1991 Report on Education*. Washington, D.C.: National Governors' Association, 1986.

Olson, Mancur. *The Logic of Collective Action*. Cambridge, Mass.: Harvard University Press, 1971.

Poole, Robert W. *Cutting Back City Hall*. New York: Universe Books, 1980.

Raywid, Mary Anne. "The Mounting Case for Schools of Choice." In *Public Schools by Choice: Expanding Opportunities for Parents, Students, and Teachers*. St. Paul, Minn.: Institute for Learning and Teaching, 1989.

Reason. *Fourth Annual Report on Privatization*. Santa Monica, Calif.: Reason Foundation, 1990.

Savas, E. S. "Municipal Monopoly," *Harper's Magazine* (December 1971): 55–60.

Savas, E. S. *Privatization: The Key to Better Government*. Chatham, N.J.: Chatham House, 1987.

Schultz, Danielle. "Lessons from America's Best Run Schools," *Washington Monthly* (November 1983): 52–53.

Smith, George H. "Nineteenth-Century Opponents of State Education: Prophets of Modern Revisionism." In *The Public School Monopoly*, edited by Robert B. Everhart. San Francisco, Calif.: Pacific Institute for Public Policy Research, 1982.

Spring, Joel. *The American School: 1642–1985*. New York: Longman, 1986.

Stevens, Barbara. *Delivering Municipal Services Efficiently: A Comparison of Municipal and Private Service Delivery*. New York: Ecodata, 1984.

Touche Ross. *Privatization in America*. Chicago: Touche Ross & Co., 1987.

U. S. Department of Education. *What Works*. Washington, D.C.: U. S. Department of Education, 1986.

U. S. Department of Education. *The Condition of Education: A Statistical Report*. Washington, D.C.: Office of Educational Research and Improvement, 1987.

U. S. Department of Education. *Wallchart.* Washington, D.C.: Office of Planning, Budget, and Evaluation, U. S. Department of Education, 1990.

U. S. Department of Education. *Issue Brief Update: State Choice Legislation: 1992 Year-end Wrap-up.* Washington, D.C.: Office of Intergovernmental and Interagency Affairs, Center for Choice in Education, U. S. Department of Education, September–December 1992.

*Wall Street Journal,* "Poland's Liberated Schools," 7 January 1992a.

*Wall Street Journal.* "Choice Landslide," 21 September 1992b.

Witte, John F. *First Year Report: Milwaukee Parental Choice Program.* Madison: University of Wisconsin, Madison, 1991. ERIC ED 348429.

World Bank. "Escaping the Heavy Hand of the State," *Economist* 323, no. 7763 (1992): 73.

# 10

# New School Choice Plans

## *Michael Heise*

School choice programs vary considerably. In this chapter, I deal with only the major school choice programs that incorporate education vouchers and include private schools. These programs are either privately funded or publicly funded. Most privately funded programs are designed to increase the opportunity for a limited number of low-income students to attend private schools. Many school choice programs that use public funds to pay for students to attend private schools typically involve a limited number of at-risk students whom public school systems are either unable or unwilling to serve or low-income students who want to attend private schools but lack sufficient financial resources.

Both of these forms of school choice increase access to private schools, but only marginally. By increasing access to the private education market, these programs attempt to illustrate how radical education reform can be achieved by focusing on a few of the most salient characteristics of the American public school systems.

The delivery of public elementary and secondary education services in the United States is largely shaped by two fundamental characteristics. One is that most education services are supplied by the local government. The other is the general (though loosening) prohibition against using public funds for the support of private schools, particularly private religious schools. These new school choice programs can fairly be described as radical because they address both of these fundamental characteristics.

These new programs marginally affect the role of local government as the dominant supplier of education services. They do so by increasing the demand for (and theoretically and potentially, the supply of) education services supplied by private individuals, organizations, and institutions. Education voucher programs also help illustrate an alternative role for all levels of government in education—that of a purchaser, not just a supplier, of education services.

Some of these new school choice programs also address the general ban on the use of public funds for private schools. The programs do so by helping to provide data regarding the relationship between the use of education vouchers and the laws, rules, and regulations that shape education policy and reform today. For example, one important question is whether private schools that participate in a publicly funded voucher program can comply with the legal requirements imposed on them by the government while retaining the characteristics that distinguish private schools from public ones. These new school choice programs are too small and limited to provide complete answers to such questions. The study of these programs, however, will eventually provide insights into and information on these and other issues.

In the following discussion I first place education vouchers in the context of the broader education reform movement that began in earnest during the early 1980s. I then describe the major new school choice programs that use education vouchers, and in the last section I discuss the education voucher strategy in a broader context by addressing six important points relating to the use of private and public funds for private education.

## EDUCATION VOUCHERS AND SCHOOL REFORM

In 1983, the National Commission on Excellence in Education (1983) warned that the nation was "at risk." Since then, education reformers, public policymakers, and academics have refocused attention on the nation's elementary and secondary schools. The report and the subsequent attention also helped trigger a substantial education reform movement that continues today. As Chester Finn (1987) notes, this education reform movement is characterized by efforts to raise education standards and expectations for students and teachers and to inject into all the nation's public schools many of the attributes commonly associated with more successful schools (both public and private). After almost ten years, and largely as a result of this reform effort, the focus of the education reform debate has shifted somewhat from a preoccupation with education inputs to a consideration of outcomes—that is, from what is spent on education to what students learn and know.

While the focus of the education reform debate was shifting from inputs to outcomes, school choice policies were gaining support. John Coons and Stephen Sugarman (1978) note that the idea of a government purchasing education services as well as providing them directly is not new. The idea is popularly attributed to Milton Friedman (1962), who applied economic theory to John Stuart Mill's (1859) brief analysis of education policy.

In response to the growing perception that public schools are overly encumbered with complex bureaucratic structures that impede organizational responsiveness, proponents of school choice suggest that such policies might give more parents an increased measure of control over their children's education and thereby force schools to become more responsive to their students' education needs (Chubb and Moe, 1990). John Chubb and Terry Moe also argue that private schools, because they are controlled by market forces rather than by bureaucratic institutions, place a premium on responding to family needs and produce superior education results. James Coleman (1991) and others suggest that school choice policies might help form nongeographic communities that would establish and enforce desirable norms of behavior. Scholars have also asserted that public funding and support of private schools lead to increased pluralism (Sugarman, 1991). Still others suggest that traditional economic cost-benefit analyses support school choice. For example, Paul Peterson (forthcoming) notes that the ability of private schools to provide the same or better education than public schools for less cost would be important evidence supporting school choice policies. Finally, in disagreement with many school choice critics, Chubb and Moe (1992) argue that private schools promote educational equality better than public schools do.

Critics of school choice policies fear that choice will increase education inequality. Jonathan Kozol (Hayes, 1992), for example, questions whether all people will receive adequate information regarding their education choices. He also asserts that school choice will probably increase school segregation by race and class. Other critics of school choice argue that public schools would be placed at a competitive disadvantage if forced to compete with private schools for scarce education funds, partly because private schools have wider flexibility in selecting students and a greater ability to expel problem students (Shanker, 1991). Others suggest that the administrative burdens and associated costs incidental to establishing and maintaining school choice programs (Carnegie Foundation for the Advancement of Teaching, 1992; Levin, 1988) and to providing the oversight needed to protect against fraud and waste (Sugarman, 1991) are considerable and might overcome any benefits attributable to school choice.

While the academic and public debate surrounding school choice increases in tone and tenor, state legislatures—the governmental units primarily charged with the constitutional duty to educate Americans—continue to explore and implement various school choice policies. Already, twenty states have implemented programs described as school choice. Thirteen of those states have done so in the past five years, and two more (Michigan and Ohio) were scheduled to implement school choice programs in 1993 (Carnegie Foundation for the Advancement of Teaching, 1992). In addition to these state-led efforts, scores of individual school districts have introduced choice plans.

Most school choice programs, however, restrict the choices students and parents can make to schools within or among public school districts. Until quite recently, most of these programs excluded private schools and thus did not address the government's role as the dominant supplier of education services. By including private schools, however, the new school choice plans described in this chapter begin to challenge some fundamental precepts about how education services can be delivered to schoolchildren in the United States.

## NEW SCHOOL CHOICE PLANS

New school choice programs generally fall into two broad groups. The first includes the major privately funded voucher programs. The second group involves the use of public funds to purchase education services from private schools.

## Privately Funded Voucher Programs

Among the major privately funded school voucher programs is the Indianapolis Educational Choice Charitable Trust. The Trust was created in 1991 to provide education vouchers to low-income families in the Indianapolis Public Schools (IPS) district. Eligible families may select any private school located within the IPS district, including religious schools. The Trust was initially funded by the Golden Rule Insurance Company. Grants covering half of a private school's annual tuition, up to a maximum of $800, are available to eligible families and are awarded on a first-come, first-served basis. To be eligible for funds, a family must reside within the corporate boundaries of IPS and qualify for free or reduced-price lunch programs. Half the money available from the Trust is reserved for families whose children were enrolled in IPS schools before the creation of the Trust program. No other criteria, such as students' grades or behavior, are considered in the selection process. Admission to a chosen private school is determined by that school. However, none of the students who received grants was turned down by private schools during the Trust's first year of operation. The Trust began aiding families in September 1991, and in its first year 744 participating students attended 58 different private schools. Among the 744 students who participated during the Trust's first year were more than 350 students who transferred from Indianapolis public schools.

In Milwaukee, a privately funded voucher program is sponsored by the Partners Advancing Values in Education (PAVE). Like the Indianapolis Trust program, PAVE provides funds on a first-come, first-served basis to low-income families so that more families can afford to send their children to private schools, including religious schools. More than 1,925 students now participate in the PAVE program, which went into effect in September 1992.

The Atlanta-based Children's Education Foundation also uses the Indianapolis Choice Trust program as a model. The Foundation is restricted to low-income families and designed to increase access to Atlanta-area private schools. The Foundation began aiding more than 200 students on a first-come, first-served basis in September 1992. Two aspects distinguish this program from other privately financed school voucher programs. One is that members of the Foundation's Board of Trustees are required to meet the same qualifications as the participants in the program. As a result, the Foundation is governed by low-income individuals from the Atlanta area. This requirement illustrates the Foundation's desire to better ensure that it serves the needs of the people the Foundation is designed to serve. The other unusual element is that the Foundation provides students with one-half of the tuition cost of a private school, up to $3,000. The Foundation's $3,000 limit is significantly higher than those of other new choice programs.

A fourth major privately funded new choice program is the Children's Educational Opportunity (CEO) Foundation of San Antonio, Texas. The CEO Foundation committed $1,500,000 over a three-year period to provide education vouchers for low-income students to attend private schools. The CEO Foundation began funding 929 students in 1992, contributing up to one-half of a child's annual tuition, although the total per-student contribution may not exceed $750. A unique aspect of the CEO Foundation program is that it does not renew support for a participant unless the parent matches the grant and the student continues to succeed academically.

These privately funded voucher programs share many characteristics. One is that these programs allow funds to go to private religious schools. Moreover, the PAVE program allows a donor to direct a donation to a specific religious school. Because these funds are not public, First Amendment and other legal and regulatory issues are not raised.

Another characteristic these programs share is that they do not provide eligible students with full tuition vouchers. Undoubtedly this decision partly reflects the limited resources of the programs. The grant limits also reflect the programs' intention to induce participating families to buy into the voucher programs and, in particular, the selected schools. However, it is not yet clear whether the families actually pay the tuition balance or whether the participating private schools in effect discount tuition for participating students.

In addition, all these programs were created in response to a growing perception that the needs of students from low-income families are not being met by public school systems—particularly in inner-city public schools. Many of the individuals who provided initial funding for the education voucher programs wanted to offer low-income parents an opportunity to send their children to a school of their choice.

Also, the privately funded voucher programs are limited in size and potentially in duration. The size limitations are largely due to the limited financial resources of the programs. As a result, the number of students presently served by the privately funded programs ranges from 200 (Atlanta) to 1,925 (Milwaukee's PAVE program). Moreover, these privately funded programs may not last beyond their original charters. For example, the Indianapolis Trust was established as a three-year program. Plans for operation beyond the 1993–94 school year are tentative. San Antonio's CEO Foundation was likewise created for a three-year period. The duration of all these programs will likely be determined by available funding.

Finally, one of the implicit purposes (and explicit in the case of Milwaukee's PAVE program) of these privately funded programs is to bring pressure to bear on public policy. These limited programs may raise hopes and expectations to such an extent that the programs will be expanded with public support.

### Publicly Funded Voucher Programs

In addition to the privately funded voucher programs is a group of publicly financed school choice programs. These programs use public funds to purchase education services from private schools.

The Milwaukee Parental Choice Program (MPCP) has received most of the national attention given to this education reform strategy. The MPCP began in September 1990 and receives its funding from the state of Wisconsin. The origins of this program date back to 1988, when Wisconsin Governor Tommy Thompson proposed a scholarship plan that would permit 1,000 children from low-income families in Milwaukee to attend private schools of their choice, including private religious schools (Coons and Sugarman, 1992, p. 61). Although Governor Thompson's original plan was defeated, the Wisconsin Legislature passed the MPCP in 1989 with support from Governor Thompson and Democratic State Representative Annette "Polly" Williams. The MPCP legislation allocates approximately $2,500 to selected students to attend secular private schools.

Although the MPCP directs public funds to private schools, the program includes important limitations on the eligibility of students and private schools. John Witte (1992a) notes that the total number of students in the MPCP in any year is limited to 1 percent of the total number of students in Milwaukee's public schools. Approximately 1,000 students were eligible to participate in the MPCP's first year, 1990–91. Also, participating students must come from families with incomes of no more than 1.75 times the poverty level. In Milwaukee, this is approximately $22,000 for a typical three-person family. In addition, the Wisconsin statute sets each child's financial support at 53 percent of the average per-pupil expenditure for the Milwaukee Public Schools (MPS), which amounts to approximately $2,000 to $3,000 per student. Finally, eligible students cannot have attended private schools or public schools outside the MPS district during the year before their admission into the MPCP.

Besides restricting the number of students that can participate, the program limits the types of private schools eligible to receive funding. First, and most important, parochial schools are excluded because private schools participating in the MPCP may neither offer religious training nor be affiliated with a religious order. Second, participating schools are prohibited from discriminating on the basis of race, religion, gender, prior achievement, or prior behavioral records. Third, the number of participating students cannot exceed 49 percent of the students at any particular school. Fourth, participating private schools must meet at least one of four standards. The four standards relate to (1) attendance, (2) parental involvement, (3) student achievement on standardized tests, and (4) grade progress. Finally, if the demand for a particular private school exceeds the supply of space available, the school must randomly select MPCP students.

Since 1869, Vermont has had a publicly funded school choice program in which until 1961 private religious schools could accept students whose tuition was paid by public funds. (This practice was disallowed by a court decision [*Swart v. South Burlington*, 1961]). Because Vermont's population is sparse, not all the state's school districts can justify operating schools to serve the number of students available. John McClaughry (1987) notes that 95 of Vermont's 246 towns have no public high school and do not belong to union high school districts. Consequently, the state has allowed sparsely populated districts to send their students to other school districts. Vermont law requires that the school boards of these towns permit students to attend any approved high school or academy, public or private, in any district. School approval depends on typical criteria such as course offerings, availability of guidance and counseling services, extracurricular activities, performance assessment, school leadership, and record keeping (McClaughry, 1987). Moreover, if an eligible student chooses to attend an approved private school, the student's local school board is required to pay the full tuition cost (up to the average tuition for Vermont's union high schools).

A more recent school choice plan in Minnesota illustrates how public funds can be used to support private schools that educate at-risk students. In this program, eligibility is restricted to students who are either alcohol- or drug-dependent; two grade levels behind in academic achievement; one year behind in credits; pregnant or already a parent; or referred for other reasons by a public school district (Coons and Sugarman, 1992). Although the legislation applies statewide, the program is functioning primarily in Minneapolis, where approximately six hundred children attended private schools under this program (Sugarman, 1991).

Although components of these three examples of publicly funded school choice programs vary considerably, a few common themes emerge. First, to begin to demonstrate the possible benefits of school choice policies, these programs are taking on some of education's more difficult challenges. The consequences of these choice programs and whether they succeed in serving low-income or at-risk students are to a large degree empirical questions that require careful and sustained study. However, to the extent that these programs are successful with less-advantaged students, arguments for their extension to other students will likely follow.

The eligibility restrictions also serve an important political function by helping to insulate these plans from substantial legal or regulatory challenges. (The extended litigation surrounding the Milwaukee Parental Choice Program, discussed later in this section, is an important exception.) For example, many legal scholars agree that the First Amendment establishment clause would appear to permit the government to give parents public funds to spend on their children's education at private schools (see, e.g., Sugarman, 1974). Moreover, the private schools that already receive public funds to serve severely handicapped students, though regulated, have generally escaped the critical attention of government bureaucrats and attorneys. That these programs serve disadvantaged students provides some degree of insulation from legal and regulatory challenges.

A second theme that two of the publicly funded voucher programs share is that they were shaped (or altered) by legal decisions concerning the constitutional separation of church and state. In Vermont, for example, after the choice program had been operational for nearly a century, the *Swart* case signaled the end of participation for religious schools.

The MPCP's legal experiences are more recent and illustrative. The MPCP excluded private religious schools from the start and thus avoided a First Amendment test. However, the MPCP raised other subtle but important questions regarding whether private schools are subject to federal education regulations due to the schools' participation in a publicly funded voucher program.

Shortly after the MPCP legislation was enacted, State Superintendent of Public Instruction Herbert Grover went to court to have the MPCP statute declared unconstitutional under the Wisconsin constitution. Although the trial court did not agree with Grover, the Wisconsin appeals court found the program unconstitutional due to the unusual legislative procedure that enacted the program. (The Wisconsin Senate included the MPCP legislation as part of a multisubject budget bill, which Grover and others argued violated a procedural requirement imposed by Wisconsin's constitution.) However, in 1992, the Wisconsin Supreme Court, in a 5–4 decision, reversed the appeals court and ruled the MPCP program constitutional. Coons and Sugarman (1992) note that the uncertainty created by the protracted litigation surrounding the MPCP during its first year harmed the program.

Along with the MPCP's compatibility with the Wisconsin constitution, another disagreement focused on whether participating private schools were subject to federal laws concerning handicapped students. Governor Thompson requested a letter of opinion from the then U.S. Education Secretary, Lauro Cavazos, addressing whether specific federal statutes concerning handicapped students applied to private schools participating in the MPCP. Assistant Secretaries Robert Davila and Michael Williams responded on behalf of Secretary Cavazos in a letter (Davila and Williams, 1990) to Governor Thompson. The assistant secretaries concluded that if the funds used for the program were state and not federal and a free and appropriate public education was available to handicapped students in Wisconsin, private schools participating in the MPCP were not subject to certain provisions of the federal Education for All Handicapped Children Act (PL 94–142).

# NEW SCHOOL CHOICE PROGRAMS IN CONTEXT

As the complexity of the litigation and legal issues surrounding some of the publicly financed education voucher programs illustrates, policymakers still await answers to several important questions concerning the use of education vouchers. Nevertheless, a discussion of six points relating to privately and publicly funded school choice programs can clarify the context in which these strategies operate.

## Existing Precedent

Although the choice programs described in this chapter are characterized as new, precedent exists for the use of public funds for private schools. The most common example involves higher education. For decades, private American postsecondary education institutions have received public funds directly. Moreover, the public subsidization of private colleges and universities remained fairly constant during the 1980s and represented a significant source of revenue for private colleges and universities. Although governmental regulation has accompanied public funding, colleges and universities have managed to accommodate the need for public accountability while retaining their particular identities.

Precedent for public funding of private elementary and secondary schools also exists. Specifically, private schools quietly continue to receive public funds for specific needs. Examples of this support are the education services provided to handicapped students. As early as 1963, the federal government helped fund up to 75 percent of the total costs associated with the construction of private facilities designed to serve handicapped students and others with specific education needs that are not met in the public schools. After sustained and strategic litigation, the Education for All Handicapped Children Act of 1975 greatly expanded the federal role and permitted private schools to become eligible for federal funds (Encarnation, 1983). Under the Act, states and local education agencies are required to meet the particular needs of all handicapped children in their jurisdiction. A state or local education agency may choose, however, to contract with private schools for services not provided in the public sector. In addition, parents of handicapped students or students needing specific services can petition school boards and try to compel the placement of a child in these private facilities. Although reliable estimates of the value of this program to private schools are not available, Dennis Encarnation (1983) notes that "its importance is undoubtedly great, especially when combined with more extensive state programs" (p. 183).

## Public Opinion

Public opinion data suggest that support for school choice policies is increasing. In Gallup polls, the percentage of respondents supporting school choice increased from 43 percent in 1973 to 70 percent in 1992. A 1992 Associated Press survey found that 63 percent of the respondents supported former President Bush's G.I. Bill for Children, which would have provided $1,000 scholarships for low-income families to use at any school—public, private, or religious. Similarly, a 1992 Lou Harris Poll found that 69 percent of those surveyed favored school choice policies that included providing public funds to religious schools. Moreover, a 1992 survey of black Americans by the Joint Center for Political and Economic Studies found that 83 percent agreed that school choice policies would help poor children.

In contrast to these data are (1) results from a recent poll conducted for the Carnegie Corporation and (2) the failure of school choice legislative initiatives. The Carnegie Foundation for the Advancement of Teaching (1992) reports that 70 percent of parents of children in public schools oppose the use of public dollars to allow children to attend private schools.

A closer examination of the Carnegie survey sample and the wording of the question might help explain the conflicting results in survey data. The appendix to the Carnegie report does not fully describe how the respondents were selected, though the appendix does indicate that random digit dialing was used to obtain a sample restricted to approximately 1,000 parents of public school students. Also, the questions Carnegie asked were narrower than most questions asked in comparable surveys. The Carnegie survey asked questions about using "public dollars to attend private schools," while other surveys typically ask about using tax dollars to attend any school—public, private, or parochial.

Other evidence that raises questions about the depth of popular support for school choice involves the failure of school choice ballot and legislative initiatives. Colorado voters recently (1992) rejected a ballot initiative that would have created a statewide school voucher program and made private schools eligible for approximately $2,500 per student. Similar measures were previously rejected in Oregon (1990), Michigan (1978), and the District of Columbia (1981). Also, state legislatures such as those in Pennsylvania and Florida were unable to enact school choice programs.

The failure of school choice legislative initiatives can certainly be attributed to a variety of factors including the considerable political influence of teachers' unions. In view of this institutional opposition that school choice legislation attracted, that some legislative initiatives made it to a vote might encourage many proponents of school choice.

## Lack of Empirical Research

There are many important questions regarding the effects of school choice policies on students, parents, and public and private schools. These questions have evoked sustained public and academic debate. The debate over what is likely to result under school choice policies is hampered, however, by a lack of relevant data and a reliance on inferential evidence drawn from studies of differences between existing public and private schools. As Witte (1992b) correctly notes, little is actually known about the effects of school choice.

What data do exist are preliminary and generally involve the MPCP in Milwaukee, which began funding students in 1990, and the Indianapolis Trust program, which began one year later. Although Witte's first- and second-year reports on the MPCP (Witte, 1991, p. iv; 1992c, p. v) characterized the preliminary findings as "mixed," both reports recommended continuing the program for at least several more years.

Witte's first-year report attracted important and critical attention. Peterson (forthcoming) criticizes Witte's report for biases in design and interpretation. Of particular note is Peterson's argument that Witte's statistical comparisons between participating and public school students were not corrected for selection bias. Specifically, Peterson notes that Witte's evaluation was originally expected to compare participating students with those students who applied but were rejected because of a lack of space and were placed on a waiting list while remaining in the Milwaukee Public School (MPS) system. Peterson contends that although such a control group would not be a perfectly drawn random sample, it would be a reasonably close approximation.

Witte's reports, by contrast, compare participating choice

students with two MPS populations: all MPS students and all low-income MPS students. To the extent that the demand for places in the MPCP fell short of the supply (during the 1990–91 school year, only 458 students applied even though close to 1,000 students were eligible to participate under the statute), it is likely that the expected waiting list was not needed.

A research team from Hudson Institute and Butler University is currently conducting a three-year longitudinal study similar to those being conducted by Witte in Milwaukee and researchers from the University of North Texas in San Antonio. The Hudson Institute (1992) report on the Indianapolis Trust program shows that its baseline data are generally consistent with the MPCP baseline data found by Witte in Milwaukee. Although the Hudson Institute study intentionally shares many elements with Witte's study, there are important distinctions between the two.

One such distinction addresses one of Peterson's criticisms of Witte's research design. Unlike the MPCP, demand for the Trust program in Indianapolis exceeds the supply of existing resources, resulting in student waiting lists. Individuals on these waiting lists will provide Hudson Institute researchers with the opportunity to control more carefully for selection bias. Another distinction is that the Hudson Institute study includes a survey of teachers in participating schools. This survey, in addition to the parent and administrator surveys, should provide helpful classroom-level information on school climate and other related issues.

### Research and Evaluation Criteria

Analysis of school choice programs would benefit not only from more empirical data but also from a greater level of consensus on the appropriate research design and evaluation criteria.

An important element of any research design is the identification of the dependent variables. As with most school reform strategies, an essential consideration in the evaluation of choice programs is their effect on student achievement. Therefore, outcome-based indicators of student achievement—such as data from standardized achievement tests and grades—would be important variables in this regard.

Other dependent variables are suggested by the possible effects of school choice policies on students, parents, and schools. For example, student participation in school and nonschool activities, attendance, and attitudinal and behavior measures might warrant particular attention. Potentially interesting parent-level dependent variables, in addition to attitudinal measures, include participation rates in children's education at home and in activities and policy matters at school. The effect of school choice policies on private and public schools is important because the schools' responses to a more competitive market environment have significant consequences for supply and demand. Many of these variables, such as parental participation and student attendance, while interesting in their own right are also predictors of student achievement. (See, e.g., Coleman, Hoffer, and Kilgore, 1982).

Also important to the analysis of school choice programs is the determination of whether these programs are desirable from a public policy perspective. To do so, one must set standards by which to evaluate these programs.

Some argue, for example, that school choice is desirable as a matter of natural right. They contend that whatever policies increase an individual's ability to make choices that have important short- and long-term consequences constitute a net social gain. (See, e.g., Blum, 1963.) If one assumes that school choice is always good and uses that criterion in evaluating school choice programs, virtually all such programs will appear successful. Others argue that school choice is needed to better serve children from low-income families. (See, e.g., Coons and Sugarman, 1992.) Under this approach, the success of school choice programs might be determined by the performance of students from low-income families. Still others such as Peterson (forthcoming) suggest that traditional cost-benefit analysis might support school choice. This rationale would consider the cost-effectiveness of participating schools when evaluating a school choice program.

## International Examples

Placing school choice policy in an international context reveals an important point. Many of the issues surrounding the school choice debate in the United States—administration, school finance, government regulation of private schools, and government entanglement with religion—have to varying degrees also been confronted by other countries.

Unlike the United States, most industrialized nations have some form of school choice and allow public support for private schools. A brief list of such nations includes France, Ireland, Japan, Netherlands, Sweden, Belgium, Britain, Holland, Canada,

Germany, Australia, Spain, Denmark, Russia, and Israel (Glenn, 1989, 1992; Doyle, 1989). The pervasiveness of private education in many foreign nations is also interesting. For example, approximately 70 percent of Dutch elementary school students attend private (or nongovernmental) schools that receive public funds. The education reform experiences of former communist countries also warrant attention. Charles Glenn (1992) notes that in Russia nongovernment schools with approved charters are eligible to receive public funding pursuant to a comprehensive new education law that went into effect in August 1992. These schools can be organized by religious organizations, private firms (domestic or foreign), or individuals.

Denis Doyle (1989) notes that these international examples suggest that administrative obstacles to school choice policies can be overcome. Also, in many countries public accountability of private schools is ensured by a mechanism not widely used in the United States—examinations designed to reveal how much students know about different academic subjects. Although the degree to which one can generalize and perhaps benefit from other countries' experiences varies greatly, it is important to note that data exist on other industrialized nations' experiences with school choice policies.

## Private School Regulation Incident to Public Funding

Although most legal scholars agree that a well-crafted publicly financed school voucher program that includes private religious schools would probably survive constitutional challenge (see, e.g., Sugarman, 1974), the answers to other equally important legal issues are less certain. One such issue is the extent to which private schools that receive publicly funded vouchers are subject to the same laws, rules, and regulations—particularly those imposed by the federal government—that govern public schools.

The source of a school's funds plays an important role in determining the nature and extent of governmental regulation. Regarding state-funded programs, Milwaukee's MPCP suggests that participating private schools may not necessarily be subject to federal laws. It is likely that state law would control state-financed programs. However, these and other legal issues have yet to be litigated, and the U.S. Department of Education's letter of opinion (Davila and Williams, 1990) to Wisconsin Governor Thompson was notably narrow in scope.

For federally funded education voucher programs, a plain reading of the relevant statutes suggests that participating schools would be subject to federal law. Schools typically become subject to federal regulations when they receive federal funds (see, e.g., Code of Federal Regulations). The legal definition of "recipient" has traditionally been construed broadly, although the child-benefit theory might insulate private schools from extensive federal regulation.

Courts have held that the child-benefit theory protects private schools that receive federal funds for busing and lunch programs from some federal regulation. (See, e.g., *Everson v. Bd. of Education*, 1987.) Moreover, a school choice program designed so that education vouchers go directly to parents who redeem the vouchers at private schools may well avoid First Amendment issues altogether. Indeed, former President Bush and former Education Secretary Lamar Alexander relied on such a theory in their unsuccessful attempt to push the G.I. Bill for Children through Congress.

The resolution of these and other legal issues will have enormous consequences for any education reform strategy that includes publicly funded education vouchers for private religious schools. For example, if private schools that participate in a publicly financed voucher program are found to be subject to federal laws, the attractiveness of such a voucher program will diminish dramatically for private schools. It might become economically unfeasible for many private schools to participate. The cost of coming into compliance (where compliance is possible) and the ongoing administrative burdens incident to many bureaucratic regulations may be prohibitive for many private religious schools, particularly many inner-city parochial schools. Paradoxically, parochial schools are the only viable alternatives to public schools in many cities where dramatic education reform is needed most.

## CONCLUSION

The implications of the new school choice programs for education reform in the United States, particularly the privately funded programs, are significant. If successful, these programs could serve as a model for future government-financed programs. By allowing the private sector to experiment with radical education reform strategies, the government can simultaneously save money and reduce its risk of funding unsuccessful projects. At the same time, by doing so, the government risks ceding one of its traditional functions.

However, it is also possible that the implementation of these programs may slow down rather than increase experimentation with school choice. Private individuals and institutions have traditionally supported a wide variety of education scholarship programs. As a result, these new school choice programs may simply institutionalize an existing practice. In addition, school reformers may now direct their attention to other education reform strategies. And now that school choice is becoming a reality for a limited number of students, pressure to expand school choice policies may lessen while researchers evaluate the existing programs.

Whatever the future holds for these new school choice programs, the need for dramatic education reform in the United States is clear. This country faces many education problems. American children's level of academic achievement is "appallingly mediocre" (Chubb and Moe, 1992, p. 1). The achievement figures are particularly discouraging when compared with those of our foreign economic competitors. More Americans are beginning to comprehend the threat to our economic competitiveness posed by an inadequate education system and the need to invest more effectively in human capital. A sense of urgency to address these problems, particularly in our nation's major urban areas, is beginning to form. Curiously, though, most education reform efforts to date have avoided addressing structural or fundamental policy issues and have failed to deliver the promised improvements.

One strategy for radical education reform—the use of publicly and privately funded education vouchers for private schools—can begin to address important and fundamental components of the education system that currently serves most American children. Though limited, these new school choice programs should provide important information for future education policy.

## REFERENCES

Blum, Virgil C. *Freedom of Choice in Education*, rev. ed. New York: Macmillan, 1963.

Carnegie Foundation for the Advancement of Teaching. *School Choice: A Special Report*. Princeton, N.J.: Carnegie Foundation for the Advancement of Teaching, 1992.

Chubb, John E., and Moe, Terry M. *Politics, Markets, and America's Schools.* Washington, D.C.: Brookings Institution, 1990.

Chubb, John E., and Moe, Terry M. "Politics, Markets, and Equality in Schools." Paper presented at the Annual Meeting of the American Political Science Association, Chicago, 1992.

*Code of Federal Regulations (CFR).* 34 CFR § 104.3 (f).

Coleman, James S. "Changes in the Family and Implications for the Common Schools." In *University of Chicago Legal Forum 1991*, pp. 153–170. Chicago: University of Chicago Law School, 1991.

Coleman, James S.; Hoffer, Thomas; and Kilgore, Sally. *High School Achievement: Public, Catholic, and Private Schools Compared.* New York: Basic Books, 1982.

Coons, John E., and Sugarman, Stephen D. *Education by Choice.* Berkeley: University of California Press, 1978.

Coons, John E., and Sugarman, Stephen D. *Scholarships for Children.* Berkeley: Institute of Governmental Studies Press, University of California, 1992.

Davila, Robert R., and Williams, Michael. Letter to the Honorable Tommy G. Thompson, 21 September 1990.

Doyle, Denis P. "Family Choice in Education: The Case of Denmark, Holland, and Australia." In *Private Schools and Public Policy: International Perspectives,* edited by William L. Boyd and James G. Cibulka. New York: Falmer Press, 1989.

Encarnation, Dennis J. "Public Finance and Regulation of Nonpublic Education." In *Public Dollars for Private Schools,* edited by Thomas James and Henry M. Levin. Philadelphia: Temple University Press, 1983.

*Everson v. Bd. of Education,* 330 U.S. 1, 67 S.Ct. 304, 91 L.Ed. 711 (1987).

Finn, Chester E., Jr. "Education That Works: Make the Schools Compete." *Harvard Business Review* 87, no. 5 (1987): 63–68.

Friedman, Milton. *Capitalism and Freedom.* Chicago: University of Chicago Press, 1962.

Glenn, Charles L. *Choice of Schools in Six Nations.* Washington, D.C.: U.S. Government Printing Office, 1989.

Glenn, Charles L. "Organizing the Russian Educational System for Freedom and Accountability," *News & Views* 11, no. 11 (1992): 85–88.

Hayes, Larry. "A Simple Matter of Humanity: An Interview with Jonathan Kozol," *Phi Delta Kappan* 74, no. 4 (1992): 334–337.

Hudson Institute. *First Year Report: Educational Choice Charitable Trust,* no. HI-4199. Indianapolis: Hudson Institute, 1992.

Levin, Henry M. "Education as a Public and Private Good," *Journal of Policy Analysis and Management* 6 (1988): 628–641.

McClaughry, John. *Educational Choice in Vermont.* Concord, Vt.: Institute for Liberty and Community, 1987.

Mill, John S. *On Liberty.* London: Parker Press, 1859.

National Commission on Excellence in Education. *A Nation at Risk.* Washington, D.C.: U.S. Department of Education, 1983.

Peterson, Paul E. "Are the Big City Schools Holding Their Own?" In *The Seeds of Crisis,* edited by John Rury. Madison: University of Wisconsin Press, forthcoming.

Shanker, Albert. "In Defense of Public Schools," *Wall Street Journal,* 15 March 1991.

Sugarman, Stephen D. "Family Choice: The Next Step in the Quest for Equal Educational Opportunity?" *Law and Contemporary Problems* 38 (1974): 513–565.

Sugarman, Stephen D. "Using Private Schools to Promote Public Values." In *University of Chicago Legal Forum 1991*, pp. 171–210. Chicago: University of Chicago Law School, 1991.

*Swart v. South Burlington*, 122 VT 177, 167 A2d 514, 1961.

Witte, John F. *First Year Report: Milwaukee Parental Choice Program.* Madison: University of Wisconsin, Madison, 1991.

Witte, John F. *The Milwaukee Private School Parental Choice Program.* Madison: University of Wisconsin, Madison, 1992a.

Witte, John F. "Public Subsidies for Private Schools: What We Know and How to Proceed," *Educational Policy* 6, no. 2 (1992b): 206–227.

Witte, John F. *Second Year Report: Milwaukee Parental Choice Program.* Madison: University of Wisconsin, Madison, 1992c.

# 11

# Technology in School Improvement

## Dustin H. Heuston

The Waterford Institute is a nonprofit organization that has been doing research in the use of computers for instruction since it was founded in New York City in 1976. The Institute now has offices in Utah in Salt Lake City and Provo and in New York City. It owns a research school with approximately six hundred students (preschool through grade twelve) in a suburb of Salt Lake City. The school is used to test new concepts in the usage of hardware and to develop and test new courseware materials for instruction.

The school's earliest research efforts looked into some fundamental questions about how computers might best be introduced in the elementary school to help support the instructional program. We found that children could comfortably interact with a computer as early as three plus years of age. We also found that a kindergarten child could work comfortably with a computer for twenty minutes and a first-grade child for forty minutes. Sixty minutes a day was found to be optimal for interaction with the computer. These times, of course, vary significantly with individual children and with teachers' preferences, but they give us a sense of general parameters.

In our experiments with the placement of terminals, we discovered that placing laboratories with enough terminals to handle an entire elementary school class was the best way to begin the use of computer technology. There are a number of advantages to beginning with laboratories, among which are high use of equipment (80 to 90 percent) as compared with 5 to 20 percent use when terminals are distributed to classrooms; security of equipment; easier training in a community atmosphere; and the availability of paraprofessionals in the laboratory to help provide continuity of activity as well as support for teachers who stay with their children during the instructional period.

The teachers also learned to distribute smaller clusters of materials in the classrooms where a different type of usage took place. The laboratories provided students with a great deal of serious instruction in basic skills, whereas children used terminals in the classrooms to explore, as word processors, and to do more individual creative activities. Thus we concluded that ideally a school should have both laboratories and terminals distributed to classrooms, but if it was necessary to start with just one of these arrangements, then laboratories were probably more efficient.

The Institute, through its school, has developed a school improvement model called the Waterford Model, which is currently being implemented in public schools in New York City. The Waterford Model is a structured approach defining how to use the new computer technology to support instructional goals in reading and mathematics in the early elementary school years. The Waterford Institute believes that effective use of technology has an inherent advantage over other approaches to school improvement.

In this chapter, I draw heavily on research conducted at the Waterford Institute as well as on the experience of the Institute in its work in New York City schools and elsewhere in suggesting how computer technology can assist in the improvement of schools.


## THE HISTORY OF COMPUTERS IN EDUCATION

In order to understand the potential of technology and to plan for its effective use, school leaders should view technology in its historical perspective. For about twenty years, schools have been attempting to use computers to improve their educational offerings. During the first decade of this effort, the schools tended to concentrate on teaching students about computers rather than using the computer as an integral part of the instructional process. Under pressure from concerned parents and teachers, the schools began to acquire computer technology so that their students would have the opportunity to work with computers and learn about their potential. Many publishers offered textual materials to teach computer "literacy," and others introduced computer programming courses in which students learned a computer language such as BASIC or PASCAL.

As microcomputers became more prevalent and affordable, students gradually began to use them for word processing and desktop publishing. Then, depending on the bias and interests of the local users, some simple drill-and-practice programs were offered and simulation programs were used, particularly in science and history. The more ambitious users began to link their schools with other schools researching the capabilities of telecommunications, while others began to teach students about database programs. Usually the only aggressive use of computers during these years occurred when districts used larger mainframes for processing data.

During the mid-1980s, a number of vendors began to produce integrated learning system (ILS) software that purported to have serious instructional capabilities, particularly in reading and mathematics. These pioneering vendors were entrepreneurs whose businesses were later purchased by larger corporations. For example, Jostens, a traditional educational service corporation, acquired three separate corporations: Prescription Learning, ESC, and Wicat Systems. At the same time, Simon and Schuster purchased Computer Curriculum Corporation (CCC), and IBM spun off a separate software corporation called Eduquest.

In the past decade, in addition to the increased emphasis on producing serious educational software, a separate movement has begun to emphasize the use of computers as tools that offer unique new capabilities for teachers and students. The proponents of the "tool use" approach for schools tend to want students to engage in discovery learning instead of drill and practice, which they call "drill and kill." They are interested in encouraging the students to work in an unstructured way by using the computer for a variety of purposes such as retrieving materials from databases (e.g., encyclopedias), communicating with distant users, writing and editing their own materials, and accessing exciting new programs with multimedia capability stored on CD-ROMs or videodiscs. On the other hand, some educators have preferred the new structured approach represented by integrated learning systems (ILS), arguing that the computer can be used very successfully in helping students to acquire basic skills.

In addition to the debates between those favoring "tool use" and those who prefer a more structured approach, there is also a debate as to whether terminals should be placed in laboratories or in classrooms. To further confuse decision makers, there is a protracted war going on between proponents of IBM-compatible hardware and the Apple products, particularly the Macintosh series.

In order to make sense of the differing approaches, and to establish a sensible position for the school district, school leaders should begin their deliberations by considering the events in the development of microchip technology, for these events will determine what will be happening in the next decades with regard to education and computer technology. Important to understanding these trends is the "law" developed by Gordon Moore in the early 1970s. Moore is a distinguished scientist and cofounder of Intel Corporation, a leader in the development of microcomputer chips for industry.

According to Moore's law, beginning in the mid-1970s the number of transistors on a $\frac{1}{4}$-square-inch chip would double every year until 1990, after which the number was expected to double every other year (see Figure 11-1). When produced in large quantities, these chips usually sell for approximately four dollars each. The transistors can be used as memory cells, resistors, capacitors, and the like. They can be arranged on the chips to construct powerful computers.

Moore's law is having a profound impact on society, especially on the business community. For some of the more successful and larger computer companies, such as Digital Equipment Corporation (DEC) or IBM, Moore's law has been very destructive because it shows that the inexpensive single-chip computers are achieving the power of the large expensive mainframes. The companies that have sold large expensive machines are discovering that newer companies, with low overhead, are taking away their business by selling very powerful computers based on the inexpensive new chips. These companies avoid expensive overhead by selling their products through mail or telephone orders. Three of the faster-growing computer hardware companies with extremely satisfied customer bases have names that most people have never heard: Dell, Gateway, and Zeos.

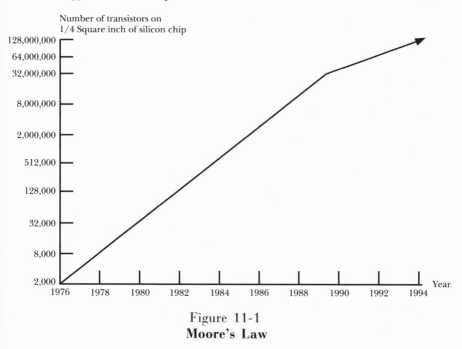

Figure 11-1
**Moore's Law**

Every time there is a quadrupling of the number of transistors on a chip, new processors are developed that are much more powerful. We are now within one or two generations of chips that will allow us to avoid typing in word processing because the computer will translate the sound of the human voice into textual materials on the screen.

Education has also been influenced by Moore's law, as suggested in Figure 11-2. The graph demonstrates how developments in computer technology used in education advanced as the number of transistors on a silicon chip increased. In 1993, the Intel Premium chip became available, as shown to the left of the line at the upper part of the graph. This chip has over three million transistors running at over 100 million instructions per second. The successor to the Intel Premium chip, the P6, is expected to become available in 1995–96. It will have approximately 10 million transistors and should run at over 250 million instructions per second. This new power will increase the potential for educational use. For example, some time in the next decade, as children practice reading with a computer, it will display what they say on the screen and begin to interact with them much as a private tutor would.

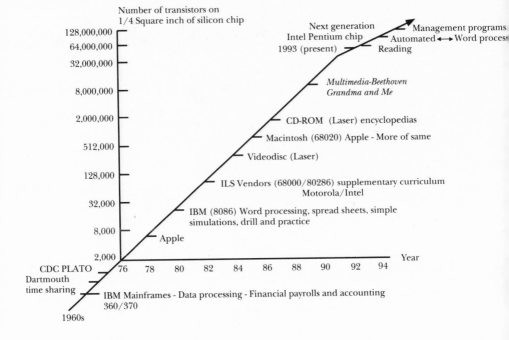

Figure 11-2
**Moore's Law and Education**

A number of lessons can be learned from studying the effects of Moore's law:

1. There will be a new generation of computers coming that will allow significantly greater educational support for students and teachers.
2. Schools should plan to update their hardware constantly to allow for new educational capabilities.
3. The schools should not hesitate to explore new methods of purchasing where computers can be purchased from reputable corporations.

## COMPUTERS AND EDUCATION

Beyond issues of hardware, a number of educational matters relating to the use of computers will need to be addressed.

## Using Computers as Supplements to Core Instruction

Although computers have become important enough in society so that schools will have to continue to teach students about them and about the commercial programs they will be using in their homes and at work (such as word processing and spread sheets), for the most part the potential of computers has not been harnessed to help the schools in their core educational mission. At best, computers have been supplemental to mainline instructional practices and thus far have not been seen as essential. As a group, the vendors of software for integrated learning systems have probably come closer to offering real support to schools in their central educational mission than other vendors, but the hardware and software capabilities have been too limited to allow schools the type of instructional support that will be emerging over the next decade.

High schools can use currently available materials for successful supplemental programs for word processing, teaching spread sheets, using CD-ROMs for retrieval from databases, using computers in the library, communicating with distant sites, using videodiscs for exploration and learning, and learning programming. Some high school teachers are excellent at using the technology to demonstrate concepts on computer monitors, at times using overheads directly from the computer screens. They can also run simulations and videodisc programs that give them quick access to stimulating specialty programs. Despite all these possibilities, however, these programs at best offer some supplemental support for teachers who appreciate the potential of technology, but the current state of the art will not offer support to help a weak teacher, particularly one who is afraid of the machines.

## Use of Computers for One Period Each Day

Because of the general pattern of school organization, it seems likely that new instructional capabilities provided by computers will be concentrated first in elementary schools. In those schools, students are generally under the care of a homeroom teacher for most of the day, whereas high school students usually have each of their teachers for only one period a day. Thus the daily schedule has a profound impact on the extent to which computers are used to give serious support to instruction. For example, if a school desires that students work with computers for a period each day, the elementary school schedule encourages this usage while the high school schedule discourages it. In elementary schools, the teacher will indeed welcome a period of computer instruction for her children, while the high school teacher, who has her students for only one period a day, is frequently unwilling to turn this time over to a machine.

The scheduling problem in high schools has been circumvented in some instances by using computers in laboratories for special programs, such as to prevent students from dropping out by providing remediation in basic skills for a number of periods a day on the terminals. These programs can be successful because the academic performance of the students is so poor that the school is willing to abandon the traditional schedule for them and assign them as a group to the remedial programs for a period or two a day on the computer.

From its research in its own school and from its experience in the public schools, the Waterford Institute has concluded that students must use the computer at least one period a day if computer technology is to offer serious instructional support for the achievement of educational goals. Because the elementary school schedule allows this readily, and the high school schedule does not, school districts interested in using the computer to support their core instructional goals should plan to make their preliminary investment in technology in the elementary schools. Political realities may dictate that computers be purchased for students in other age ranges, but the scheduling issue places the elementary school in a clearly favorable position to use the technology more effectively than it can be used in secondary schools.

## Use of Computers in the Early Grades

In the elementary school, the youngest children will benefit most from the use of computers. The Waterford Institute has been engaged in a multiyear research project in New York City working with over a dozen elementary schools. Now in its fourth year, the project will be operating in over thirty schools by the fall of 1993. The results from this work thus far suggest that the schools should start with the younger elementary school students if they desire that the technology should support the teaching of reading, writing, and mathematics.

The Waterford model has a school construct two laboratories, each with thirty-two terminals, where children from grades two through five work on reading and mathematics for a period a day. A paraprofessional is assigned to the laboratory and the classroom teacher works with her class in the computer room. Extensive reports are generated to track each student's achievement. After helping the school design the laboratories, Waterford then trains the staff for two days a week during the first year and for a day a week each year thereafter. Research data are also collected at a database in Utah, where the scores on the city tests are examined and then presented to the teachers in ways that help clarify the students' performance.

Some unexpected results from the project have convinced the Waterford Institute that wherever computer intervention is scheduled, priority should be given to having it available for the youngest students. After providing two years of training, the research staff noted that there were significant problems surfacing among children who had begun to fall behind. Initially we had been confident that if we produced substantial gains in test scores we would help to solve reading problems in the city's schools. But our experience taught us that even substantial gains by students whose achievement is below grade level do not assure that they will ever catch up with their peers. A series of graphs helps to illustrate this problem.

One line in Figure 11-3 depicts the average student achievement in reading over five years, assuming that, on average, students advance one grade level for each year in school. Unfortunately, however, many students have trouble learning to read, particularly those who are at-risk. These at-risk children, many of whom live in an inner city or are immigrants, typically tend to learn only half as fast as their "average" counterparts. The second line in Figure 11-3 depicts their achievement if one assumes that, on average, at-risk students learn at only half the rate of the average student. Thus it appears that at-risk students fall half a grade level behind for every year they are in school.

If this problem were to be addressed by introducing a computer-assisted instructional program in grade 4, it might be possible to increase the learning rate of at-risk students to equal that of the "average" students. If such an intervention were successful, the achievement in reading for these students might progress as shown in Figure 11-4. (This is not a literal depiction of our experience with the use of computers in New York City schools; rather it is a hypothetical representation of the problem we discovered as we attempted to improve the learning rate of the students.) Figure 11-4 illustrates that, even if one could

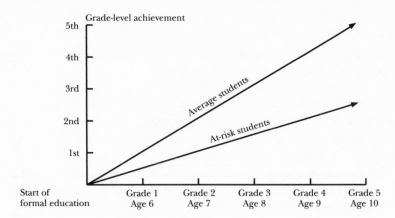

Figure 11-3
**Achievement in Reading for Average Students and for
At-Risk Students**

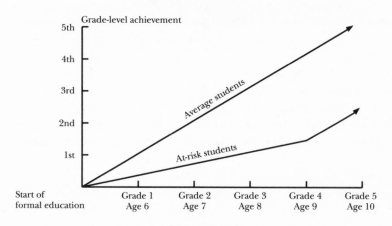

Figure 11-4
**Achievement in Reading (a) for Average Students and (b) for
At-Risk Students Receiving Computer-Assisted Instruction One
Period a Day in Grade Four**

successfully double the learning rate of at-risk students by such
an intervention at grade four, the problem would not be solved.
Even though the at-risk students will have learned much faster
than previously, the intervention will have only arrested the tendency for them to fall behind. They would still be two years
behind those who, on average, have been able to stay on grade
level. If they were to catch up, they would have to learn even
more rapidly than their peers, conceivably by again doubling
their learning speed. How realistic is it to assume that these learners

would be able to learn up to four times more rapidly than they had learned in earlier grades?

This problem illustrates vividly the importance of intervening as early as possible to help children learn to read, a matter that is often overlooked. One possibility for dealing with this very difficult problem is to use a computer intervention in the early grades along with tutorial programs such as those suggested by Marie Clay (1979) or by Robert Slavin and colleagues (1990). The ideal would be to use a great many resources to help all children in grades one and two, especially those who are at risk, stay on grade level. Figure 11-5 suggests the hypothetical effect of such a strategy.

In her research on reading, Marie Clay has suggested that if a child learns to read well in the first grade, every future reading trial will strengthen the child's ability to read. If Clay is right, and if the children are properly taught in the earliest grades, then the likelihood that these children would be able to maintain average growth rates in subsequent years is enhanced.

Computer software for use in grades two through five seems to improve the performance of the students who have learned to read reasonably well. Thus the long-term strategy would be to hold the students on grade level until the second grade and then gradually make additional improvement through the use of currently available materials. This thesis is as yet untested,

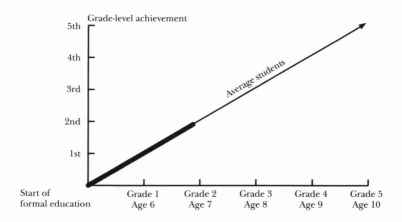

Figure 11-5
**Hypothetical Effect of Using Many Resources to Help All Children in Grades One and Two Stay on Grade Level in Reading Achievement**

but it appears to be very promising. We shall not be able to complete our tests of this idea until we finish developing reading materials for kindergarten and the first grade. The Institute is about half way through this development cycle, which we expect will cost $15 million to complete.

Another problem in executing a strategy to help children in the early grades stay on grade level is that there is a marked difference in the amount of preliteracy training parents provide for their children from birth until they enter first grade. Marilyn Jager Adams (1990) suggests that some parents may spend a total of 3,000 hours providing preliteracy experiences for their preschool children, while others may spend as little as 20 to 200 hours providing such training. Such a difference would presumably be reflected in the reading achievement of these students in the early grades, with those whose preschool years included a significant amount of preliteracy training being greatly advantaged over those whose preliteracy experiences were minimal. This suggests that schools might consider taking on a new role in which they would help parents understand the importance of providing a variety of preliteracy activities for their preschool children. At present, schools are not equipped to offer parents instruction in how to do this effectively.

As the Institute staff worked in the New York City schools, they became aware of the necessity of working with kindergarten and first-grade children in the Waterford laboratories. Here they discovered another problem: the computer materials presently available for teaching reading in kindergarten and first grade are of extremely poor quality in the opinion of the teachers in the schools that have tried to use them. The primary defect is that the materials had apparently been developed with the assumption that the children had had extensive preliteracy experiences. Certain key instructional components were omitted, omissions that became apparent only when the materials were used with children who had not had the advantage of preliteracy training. For example, Marie Clay has pointed out that it takes up to a year for a child to stabilize the habit of reading from left to right and down on a page. A child who has been read to for hundreds of hours learns this concept automatically. When children have not had preliteracy experiences, there is a serious risk that they will attempt to read from right to left or up the page instead of down. None of the currently available materials teaches a child to read from left to right.

A second difficulty with these materials is that they offer only one explanation of each learning task. If the children do not understand the task, they are then recycled back for the same treatment over and over again. This experience antagonizes both the children and the teachers. Materials should have multiple presentations of each concept involving different approaches so that if children do not learn the concept from one presentation there is a chance that one of the other presentations will provide them with additional help. In short, the materials are too thin and leave out too many important steps for the at-risk learner.

The difficulty that vendors face is that developing materials that work requires an investment of a considerable amount of money. What used to be an investment of $1 to $1.5 million in development costs now requires between $10 and $15 million. After discovering the shortcomings of current vendors' materials, the Institute has launched a large effort to develop software reading materials for kindergarten and first grade. The Institute has been working on this problem for about three years and expects to have products available for vendors to sell by the fall of 1994.

The Institute will also be experimenting with a nontechnological program to help parents learn how to provide valuable preliteracy experiences for their children during the preschool years. This will entail developing inexpensive reading materials, videotapes, and radio and television programs to emphasize the importance of the prereading activities and teaching parents how to use them with their children.

## SCHOOL MANAGEMENT PRACTICES FOR THE EFFECTIVE USE OF TECHNOLOGY

In our experience with implementing the Waterford laboratories in the New York City schools, we have learned a number of lessons relating to school management that should be noted before computers are introduced. These lessons should not be ignored, since they can have a strong impact on the effectiveness of the computer program. In fact, in order to introduce an effective computer program, these matters should be addressed as part of any successful implementation strategy.

## A Policy on Substitute Teachers

Some of the schools in which we worked did not have an adequate policy for providing substitute teachers when regular teachers did not show up. Very often as many as four teachers were absent, and the school would either put children in those teachers' classes together in the auditorium where they would watch cartoons, or add children from these classes to other classes where the teachers were present. Obviously, no instruction would take place in the auditorium. When pupils were assigned to the classes of other teachers, we noted that not only was the instruction not appropriate for the children in the classes without a teacher (some of which were increased in size from thirty to forty-five pupils) but that their presence disrupted the normal flow of instruction in the class that they had joined. Under these circumstances, the classes whose teachers were absent would not come to the computer laboratories.

Without question, the lack of a policy on substitutes is devastating to the effectiveness of a school. No program can produce successful results under such conditions. We were surprised by the rationalizations for the lack of an adequate substitute policy, which generally had to do with the problem of getting substitutes in some of the difficult inner-city schools. While acknowledging the difficulty, we felt that the establishment of an adequate procedure for obtaining substitute teachers was absolutely essential if children were to have daily instruction in an orderly atmosphere.

## Strong Kindergarten Teachers

In schools where students were not learning effectively, we found that the least effective teachers were assigned to kindergarten because the administration believed that the best teachers should be reserved for the third grade, at which point citywide tests are given for the first time. The problem with this approach is that if the kindergarten year is wasted and treated as a babysitting year, and given the lack of suitable preliteracy experiences at home for at-risk children, there is very little chance that the first-grade students will be successful in learning to read. And as our research has indicated, if the students are having reading problems in the second grade, in most cases it is too late to salvage this skill. Thus the Waterford staff concluded that the strongest teachers should be assigned to kindergarten, and they should have a strong interest in providing the children with preliteracy training.

## A Consistent Schedule

We have assumed that successful learning will occur if there is enough time spent in a reasonable learning environment and if an acceptable rate of learning can be achieved. We found, however, that the time for learning was often interrupted by the scheduling of alternative activities. As already indicated, the students missed many days of instruction because substitute teachers were not regularly available. We also found that computer laboratories were closed and regular classroom instruction canceled when special activities, such as celebrations of cultural traditions, were being planned. For example, many classes and computer laboratories were canceled for a period of up to two weeks for the preparation of a particular assembly. In addition, students would often leave school to go on field trips to visit activities throughout the city. Clearly it is difficult to deny students and faculty the opportunity to explore the city and to participate in meaningful school activities  that bond the culture. But when loss of instructional time because of such activities is combined with the loss of time because substitute teachers are not available, the students are not receiving enough instruction to acquire needed skills.

## The Use of Homework

In the schools with large concentrations of economically disadvantaged students, we found either formal or informal policies that worked against the use of homework because homework for students would cause extra work for the teachers. Such policies again cut into the number of hours the child will spend in mastering important skills.

## Rapidly Changing Programs

Schools that are not working well tend to become victims of the latest academic fads. For example, in the second year of our work in one school the faculty became enamored with the new "whole language" approach. In their excitement, they threw out all skills-based training and locked out of the computer any instructional interaction that had to do with helping children master basic skills. When the tests came in the following spring, reading scores for students in that school had fallen to among the lowest in the city.

### Quality Control

The Waterford personnel were surprised to discover that there was no attempt to perform daily quality control of programs. While energy would be expended by the administration in finding new programs and trying to get them established in the school, there was no attempt to see that the implementation was successful. In the case of the computer laboratories, after the initial enthusiasm no one would monitor the paraprofessionals to see if they opened the laboratories in time for the first period of the day, worked with the homeroom teacher during each period, and refrained from conducting personal business on the computer or the telephone. Without reasonable quality control, the laboratory hours get shorter, the interactions with teachers become fewer, and attention to the children's needs begins to fade.

## ADVANTAGES OF THE COMPUTER

While excellent tutorial programs can help keep first-grade students on grade level, such programs are costly if implemented properly. Experienced and well-trained reading teachers are needed, and each such teacher will probably be able to tutor between only eight and ten children a year at a cost of between $5,000 and $8,000 per child per year. Because of this cost, some school districts have attempted to introduce a watered-down version of a tutorial program by supplying only a few teachers for a great many students. Thus they can say they have the program, although it has little chance of succeeding because of too few teachers. In contrast, a well-run technology program using computers can provide students with a kind of individualized instruction for a period a day at a cost of $250 to $300 per student per year. Using computers to help first-grade students stay on grade level thus has a significant cost advantage over tutorial programs that also have that capability.

A second advantage that the computer has is its ability to replicate educational programs accurately and rapidly once the materials are developed and the network put in place. A tutorial program may not be fully and accurately implemented as each tutoring teacher adds his or her own interpretation of the program.

The computer also has an advantage over other technologies in that it is the only technology that involves students actively as they learn. All other technologies (the book, television, video, radio, cassettes, movies) do not provide comparable opportunities for the active involvement of the learner.

## SUMMARY

Based on its experiences in its own research school and in the New York City project over the past few years, the Waterford Institute recommends the following strategies for schools interested in using technology for school improvement:

1. Concentrate initially on elementary schools by placing two or more computer laboratories in each school so that students in grades two through five can have a period a day of computerized instruction in reading and mathematics.
2. For planning purposes, schools should assume that new programs will require a separate investment for kindergarten and first-grade children. Laboratories being used for children in grades two through five cannot be modified to serve the younger children adequately.
3. There should be at least one day a week of ongoing staff training.
4. Teachers should be required to be with their children in the laboratories so that they can concentrate on the integration of classroom goals with the potential of the computer to serve those goals.
5. A paraprofessional should work full time in each laboratory.
6. Appropriate policies with regard to scheduling and providing substitutes should be followed if the effectiveness of instruction with computers is to be maximized.
7. The best teachers should be assigned to kindergarten and first grade, where every effort should be made to provide preliteracy activities.
8. In recognition of the extremely limited preliteracy experiences of at-risk children as compared with "average" students, schools should consider building relationships with local community-based organizations such as Headstart

to encourage parents to provide preliteracy experiences for their children of preschool age. Schools should also consider the possibility of opening preschools to enhance preliteracy training of very young children.

9. Schools might investigate some of the excellent tutorial programs to be used until such time as the technology is ready for use.

10. When using tutorial programs, schools should also provide a schedule that allows each child to have daily activity on the computer.

11. Schools should follow the market to prepare for new products that have the potential to improve reading performance dramatically.

## REFERENCES

Adams, Marilyn Jager. *Beginning to Read: Thinking and Learning about Print.* Cambridge, Mass.: MIT Press, 1990.

Clay, Marie. *The Early Detection of Reading Difficulties: A Diagnostic Survey with Recovery Procedures.* Exeter, N.H.: Heinemann Educational Books, 1979.

Slavin, Robert E.; Madden, Nancy A.; Karweit, Nancy L.; Livermon, Barbara J.; and Dolan, Lawrence. "Success for All: First-Year Outcomes of a Comprehensive Plan for Reforming Urban Education," *American Educational Research Journal* 27, no. 2 (1990): 255–278.

# 12

# Technology in the Edison Schools

## *Nancy Hechinger*

Technology is not an isolated subject; it pervades all aspects of school life. What and how we teach depends on the technologies we teach with. Here is a passage about a once-new technology: Theuth, the inventor of writing, exhibited his invention to Thamus, King of Egypt:

> [W]hen it came to writing, Theuth declared: "Here is an accomplishment, my lord the king, which will improve both the wisdom and the memory of the Egyptians. I have discovered a sure recipe for memory and wisdom."
>
> "Theuth, my paragon of inventors," replied the king, "the discoverer of an art is not the best judge of the good or harm which will accrue to those who practice it. So it is in this case; you, who are the father of writing, have out of fondness for your offspring attributed to it quite the opposite of its real function. Those who acquire it will cease to exercise their memory and become forgetful; they will rely on writing to bring things to their remembrance by external signs instead of on their own internal resources. What you have discovered is a recipe for recollection, not for memory. And as for wisdom, your pupils will have the reputation for it without the reality: They will receive a quantity of information without proper instruction, and in consequence be thought very knowledgeable when they

are for the most part quite ignorant. And because they are filled
with the conceit of wisdom instead of real wisdom they will be a
burden to society." [From Plato's *Phaedrus*]

Thamus was resistant to the technology of writing in education because he felt it would change the world as he knew it. He
was right. Today we do not live in an oral society because the
technology of writing, despite its opponents, succeeded in changing
society and its concepts of intelligence and wisdom. With the
written word came a new way of record keeping, a print industry, a legal system, a revolution in education. The ability to express oneself in writing is a prime benchmark for how well
educated a person is. Imagine if students were not allowed to
use writing in their learning process—they would be ill prepared
for a society that used this technology and was shaped by it.
Education, as Theuth argued, had a need and a use for the technology of writing. Education can drive the selection of new technologies and in turn be influenced by those technologies.

Most of the adults reading this essay would say we still live in
a society dominated by the written word. And we would resist,
when thinking about education and intelligence, any suggestion
to the contrary. Yet we may be on the brink of another profound change in the acquisition and transmission of knowledge.
Children come to school (and, sadly, too many leave it) illiter-
ate and "innumerate." But they are very *media* literate when they
enter. They watch television: by the time they are six, they have
seen more dramas than Plato did in a lifetime. We ignore that
in school. They play electronic video games that demand far more
in skill and coordination and strategy than the board games I
played in my youth. This, too, we ignore in school.

Technology is often defined as those things invented after
you were born. Telephones and television are not "technology"
to me, but computers still are. My daughter, however, played
with computers before she ever saw a typewriter. Before we set
about to design a school system, and especially the technology
for a school system of the twenty-first century, we have to ask:
Who is this new child in this new world? What is the difference
between reading and writing and video media?

Computers and other electronic technologies will be used in
ways that we can scarcely imagine now. And the reason we can
scarcely imagine their uses is that we, who are of the inventing
generation and "the discoverers of the art," still have one foot

in the generation that came before. We hold on to the things that were important to us. That is right, up to a point. Of course, we should retain what is important—our ideas, values, passions. But not necessarily the artifacts or containers of those things. For example, in the early years of film, people just set up a camera in front of a stage play. The new technology was defined and referenced in terms of its antecedent. A movie was conceived of as a "play on film that you can see over and over." The point of view was always the best seat in the orchestra. It was not until D. W. Griffith came along that a new vocabulary, the medium's own, was developed. Jump cuts, swipes, blackouts, fades, establishing shots—all these were innovations that did not disorient people, make them lose the thread of a story, or become confused.

Similarly, computers are still using an old idiom. They have not added a new dimension or been integrated into the classroom. Computers in schools have been used mostly to teach about computers and to do the same things we do without computers—more effectively, often; sexier and more expensively, surely. Computer-aided instruction (CAI) puts a child through paces that are essentially the same as a drill-and-response workbook. True, they can be tailored to the child and analyses can be done; the computer is patient and nonjudgmental; test scores improve. These are important and nontrivial benefits. But no matter how good CAI is, it is still using computers as a souped-up workbook. It still follows a model of instruction that derives from the factory model. It assumes right and wrong answers. It measures routines. What if I gave you a pencil and told you, "Here is a great and powerful tool. You must become pencil literate to be successful in the future. Now, here's what you do. First, you go to the Pencil Lab. Then, you fill in the blanks on multiple-choice exercises. You cannot use it to write poetry or music or a letter to your mother, and you can't draw, design, or doodle."

Now that technology is easier to use and less expensive, the time has come to get it out of labs and into laps, out of dull routines and into creative expression, research, and productivity. The big question is: What will teachers and students do with this powerful tool when they begin to tell it what to do and use it, instead of just responding to a prompt? The answer is: They will use it in ways we have not dreamed of.

Our job is to put in place a system that facilitates discovery and invention, flexibility, and serendipity. Beginning in 1995 or thereabouts, the Edison Project will bring electronic technologies into all parts of its multischool system and thus profoundly change every aspect of school life: how children learn, how teachers teach, how schools communicate with parents and the outside world, and how student and teacher performance is assessed. It will also have a remarkable impact on how the system itself is organized and managed.

The Edison Project was founded in 1992 by Knoxville entrepreneur Christopher Whittle. His ambitious goal was—and remains— to create the best school system in America with an educational program that will work for all children, and to do so for approximately the same cost per pupil as the average public school.

We are completing the design of, and will soon begin to create, a national Edison school system made up of two kinds of schools, different in their organizational arrangements and aegis but virtually identical in educational program: a small number of private, tuition-charging schools, and a larger number of schools run in partnership with public school systems. The first group of such schools is expected to open in 1995.

The Edison Project seeks to promote innovation, excellence, and a passion for learning. As a service organization, it will provide families with safe, caring places for their children, and with a rich and varied program that challenges and nurtures mind, body, and spirit. Its goal is to be on the cutting edge of innovation in every aspect of the education industry. The Edison Project's mission is both to do good and to do well: to make a significant contribution to the nation's future while also running a profitable business.

The use of technology is one of the major ways in which the Edison Schools will differ from their academic ancestors. And it will also be the primary engine for change in our system as it evolves and grows. The design of the technology is driven, as is everything else, by our educational purposes that are encapsulated in the core values and beliefs of the Edison Project.

1. *We are a student-centered school.* Any technology we use in a classroom will be at the service of educational goals. Edison Schools will be learning communities in which technologies are designed to support the pedagogical purposes rather than drive them. Technologies are tools that should support tasks appropriately, easily, and as transparently as possible.
2. *Children are active participants in their own education.* They learn through constant interactions and explorations with their environments and with the abstract world of knowl-

edge. We will not plug children into an electronic version of "jugs-to-mugs" teaching. We do expect our students to be plugged into the world, the life of the school, the life of the mind. Our job is to provide them with resources for exploration.

3. *The student-teacher relationship is of primary importance.* Our technologies will support teachers; enhance what they do; provide them with resources, services, connection to other professionals, and ongoing professional development; and relieve them of as much administrative work as possible.

4. *The central system should serve the schools and provide services and resources, not be a bottleneck.* We want as flat an organization as possible, a streamlined and responsive bureaucracy. We want a system that seeks improvement and enhancement, not one that stifles innovation, initiative, and creativity. We must design flexibility and the potential for change into everything—our networks, curriculum delivery, professional development. Technology will help achieve these goals.

As complex as any electronic technology may be, as exotic as its descriptions may sound, we began with a very simple premise that guides the design. We start with the student, build to the school community, and then extend to the outside world. The Edison Plan for technology is simple, profound, and revolutionary. It revolves around a commitment to ensuring that every person in the system will have equal access to the tools, both hardware and software, that they need to learn about and to operate in the twentieth and twenty-first centuries, and every person will also have access to resources for research and exploration, questioning, communication, and creative expression.

This commitment has five main elements:

1. Everyone will have a personal computing device.
2. Everyone will be linked on a systemwide network at school and at home.
3. We will provide open-ended tools that encourage and facilitate exploration, research, and creative expression.
4. We will build and provide a rich landscape to explore with video and electronic libraries that will bring the world into the classroom and extend our community's reach into the world.

5. All these elements will be integrated into a powerful, transparent, friendly system.

This system will grow as technology grows and as people become more comfortable with it. When we first open schools, everyone may be communicating with simple e-mail and bulletin boards. In ten years, there would be extensively distributed multimedia projects going on the network among children and teachers in different schools.

Certain changes we can predict. This open-ended integrated system could:

- eliminate mediators of information.
- reinvent publishing and distribution.
- help change schoolchildren from passive receivers to active explorers.
- help change teachers from functionaries to professionals.
- streamline administration and management.

Nothing on this list is pie in the sky. We do not have to invent technologies—you can find most of them in any office in America. The innovation is in the integration. All technologies will be integrated into our educational program, will connect the different constituents of our system, and will provide a seamless flow among different media.

People talk about the information age. The papers report the arrival of information superhighways and five hundred channels of television. What are people going to do with so much information? How will they use it, find it, handle it, interact with it—after they watch videos, pay their bills, and buy zircons on a homeshopping channel? The answers to some of these questions will be discovered in school. Schools are institutions whose business *is* information. At Edison we hope to define a knowledge-building and knowledge-using community. We will be a model—a demonstration, always emerging—of a community of the future.

How, specifically, will this approach to technology alter the life of a school? We envision five major changes made possible by technology: flexibility, access, ongoing accountability and assessment, communication, and a profound change in the nature of relationships within the school community.

- *Flexibility.* Today, teachers are bound by the pages of a textbook. But if your curriculum materials are delivered electronically, they can be updated as needed. Teachers can select the units they want to teach and that are appropriate to their class and to individual students.

Teachers will talk to one another on a network, research other lesson plans, find better ways to teach a particular lesson. Imagine just-in-time curriculum delivery.

- *Access.* Through electronic libraries that bring great resources from the outside world, teachers and students will have access to archives and information previously available at only major universities. Teachers will have access to ongoing professional development and research on learning and teaching. Students can study original sources of material, and have on-line conversations with experts in the field. In some networked schools today, fourth graders have conversations with scientists, even some Nobel Laureates. Exploration will become the dominant activity, not recitation and passive seatwork.
- *Accountability.* We are committed to an accountable system that maintains very high standards. Teachers are as accountable as professionals in any field. And we are committed to the success of each child. We can monitor each child's progress, see where he or she is having problems, and adjust the curriculum to fit the child. Assessment is not a test given to place or judge a child. It is an ongoing way to evaluate performance and remediate the teaching before you have to remediate the child.
- *Communication.* All the constituents of our schools—students, teachers, administrators, parents, experts in the outside world—are linked through the network. That makes possible a free-flowing communication system. The network is an open channel of communication. Students are linked to one another within a school and throughout the system. Timely feedback is the key to maintaining the high standards we expect—and ease of communication is the key to timely feedback.

Communication between school and home will be facilitated by simple technologies—such as voice mail, electronic mail, and fax that will change the relationship of the school to the home and of the teacher to the parent. The membrane that separated the two will become increasingly permeable as parents see that the school intends a serious partnership with them in the education of their children.

- *Relationships.* If information is power, then networks often redistribute power as they redistribute knowledge. For instance, a network might make information accessible to administrators and parents (on, say, student achievement) that would otherwise be the sole possession of a teacher. When children gain direct access to information, the power relationship of the classroom will change. The teacher will be a guide and a resource, as well as a deliverer of information. Students will become more active in their pursuit of knowledge. They will change from receivers to doers.

  Participants in electronic networks establish relationships that otherwise would not exist. Students, for example, meet and work with people in different parts of the country, from different cultures. Gender, disabilities, and race become invisible.

  Teachers who are given more responsibility, resources, and freedom in their work will become more professional. In our system, they will be treated with great respect, and will have high expectations—not as a result of technology but as part of our belief and mission. Yet technology will help them achieve these goals.

These are not the dreams of the Edison Project alone. This is the direction in which most technology-savvy educators have been headed for years. Perhaps, though, we can make it happen because of the scale of our effort and its relative freedom from customary constraint. The important question, and the one to which we can only predict the answer, is: How will these technologies make a difference in our children's education and in their lives?

It is well and good to say that no one can foresee all that students and teachers will create when this system is installed and becomes part of the school culture. But we do have some idea of the direction in which we are heading. As part of an education system with great expectations for its constituents, we also hold great expectations for the technology.

The Edison Project's vision is to make a profound and systemic change in the place where youngsters learn, grow, and spend quite a bit of their childhood. Social institutions change slowly, and we know that unless we can demonstrate improvements in expected and desired areas (e.g., better reading and mathematics scores) we will not get to make the dramatic changes in the unexpected areas. We will be judged by familiar external standards and we must help our students meet them. The teachers and curriculum, supported by technology, will help accomplish that. But our long-term vision is much larger than percentage gains on test scores.

Electronic technologies—computers, video, interactive multi-media—hold out the possibility for development of important skills that our children will need as adults. Earlier I posed the question: What is the difference between reading and writing and electronic media? One big difference is linearity. Things happen in sequence in language; things happen all at once in film and video—words, music, pictures. In a computer, things are always interactive, navigable, interconnected. Time is experienced in a different way. This new technology is really a new approach to teaching and learning, and its strengths lie in precisely the areas where linear media are weakest. Let me give two examples: intuition and multiple representation of information.

While it may take pages of text and awkward diagrams to explain the concept and formula of angular momentum, it can be perceived straightaway in an interactive video, in which you not only can see the movement, but can also overlay data and manipulate the film. In other words, a dynamic illustration does more than explain; it engages the user in observation and analysis. A person looking at children going faster and slower on a merry-go-round or an ice skater spinning will develop a very different understanding of the concept—one that is gut level and intuitive.

Intuition is something you can develop, and these new technologies are good at it. Children develop concepts of the world at a very young age based on their perceptions and initial intuitions about how the world works. Sometimes these intuitions are wrong, but initial perceptions are not easily supplanted by learned information. How can you get a sense of the size of the universe, that the world is round, that it spins constantly and revolves around the sun? You cannot get this from your own observation, but you can if you see drawings and data, manipulate them, and see time-lapse movies.

Marvin Minsky has said that you do not really know something unless you can represent it to yourself in more than one way. That is a way of restating the most fundamental thing about learning, which dates back to Locke and before—that is, the more associations you have with something, the more likely you are to remember it. Electronic technologies allow for multiple representations of ideas—text, pictures, and sound.

Imagine a report on U.S. immigration from a student that comes on the computer and includes writing with citations from original source material, pictures, excerpts from oral histories, a homemade video of the child's great-grandparents, images from her family's photo album, and an interactive family tree. Technologically, this can be done now. It's a question of content accessibility, teacher ability and enthusiasm, and time for students to develop some profound work.

Besides all the wonderful cognitive benefits of the new technologies, there are also some striking effects in the social and community life of a school. We have noticed an interesting and counterintuitive phenomenon in classrooms that use computers. Although people always worry that computers will be alienating, the reverse is the case. Children collaborate naturally on the computer; they teach each other how to use programs. Children who normally have nothing to do with each other start to communicate and learn to live and work together. In a school where I worked a few years ago, students learning English as a second language (ESL students), Chapter I students, and gifted children were in the same class that was experimenting with interactive multimedia. Several of the ESL students and the Chapter I children became the champions of the paint programs and Hyper-Card, a profoundly nonlinear software application. The gifted students found themselves asking for help in animations and appreciating the differences and talents of their new friends (who they might never even have met in the normal course of attending a large middle school). Paul Reese, an innovative teacher in a New York City public school, asked a group of his students how they would redesign a school. This question grew out of a meeting we had with him and other educators. A passionate and interesting dialogue sprang up on the school's electronic bulletin board between two girls who would never have anything to do with each other before. On the bulletin board they gave full expression to their ideas, disagreed, argued, and communicated with respect.

At the beginning of this chapter, I asked the question: Who is this new child in this new world? In some ways, it seems that we have come full circle to a new place. Our children's culture is dominated by oral tradition. Its stories are passed down by storytellers on television and in the movies, dramas, sitcoms, talk shows, even the nightly news. Teachers tell; learners listen. The children have been passive observers. Computers insert interactivity, and that changes everything. With computers, the viewer becomes part of the action.

The rich resources of information we will provide to teachers and students are worth nothing if students are not engaged. This is not technology for the passive. To have students who are explorers, we need teachers who encourage exploration. To make sure that students are not overwhelmed by information, we need teachers who can teach them how to manage information well, how to research, how to select, and how to edit. Furniture and classrooms must also change because of new technologies. And technology alone does not make a good school. It is the curriculum and the human interactions among teachers, parents, and students that make a good  school.

Margaret Mead coined the phrase "immigrants in time" to describe the fact that in a technological world, our children will grow up in a society and culture very different from the one we grew up in, even if in the same town. As educators, we need to start where the children are. We need to understand that place. Just as important, we need a vision of where we want them to be, who we want them to be—an idea of an educated person. And we have to acknowledge that we cannot know specifically what they will need to know in their future. What we can do is given them powerful tools to build that future with. Some of these tools are electronic and very new; other more important ones like integrity, compassion, responsibility, curiosity, and delight are as old as civilization.